OUR
MUTUAL
ROOM

Published by
PEACHTREE PUBLISHERS, LTD.
494 Armour Circle, N.E.
Atlanta, Georgia 30324

Manufactured in the United States of America

10 9 8 7 6 5 4 3 2 1

Library of Congress Catalog Card Number 87-80977

ISBN 0-934601-32-1

Cover design by Paulette L. Lambert

Cover art: Moses Soyer, *Artists on WPA*, 1935
oil on canvas
36 1/8 x 42 1/8 in. (91.7 x 107.0 CM)
1968.61
National Museum of American Art, Smithsonian Institution;
Gift of Mr. and Mrs. Moses Soyer

OUR MUTUAL ROOM.

Modern Literary Portraits of the Opposite Sex

EDITED BY EMILY ELLISON AND JANE B. HILL

PEACHTREE PUBLISHERS, LTD.

ACKNOWLEDGMENTS

From *Falling in Place* by Ann Beattie. Copyright © 1980 by Ann Beattie. Reprinted by permission of Random House, Inc.

From *Cathedral* by Raymond Carver. Copyright © 1981, 1982, 1983 by Raymond Carver. Reprinted by permission of Alfred A. Knopf, Inc.

"Housekeeping" from *Dale Loves Sophie to Death* by Robb Forman Dew. Copyright © 1979, 1981 by Robb Forman Dew. Reprinted by permission of Farrar, Straus, and Giroux, Inc.

From *A Yellow Raft in Blue Water* by Michael Dorris. Copyright © 1987 by Michael Dorris. Reprinted by permission of Henry Holt and Company, Inc.

Raney by Clyde Edgerton, copyright © 1985, Algonquin Books of Chapel Hill, Chapel Hill, NC. Reprinted by permission of the author.

From *Love Medicine* by Louise Erdrich. Copyright © 1984 by Louise Erdrich. Reprinted by permission of Henry Holt and Company, Inc.

Mexico from *Singing on the Titanic* by Perry Glasser. Copyright © 1987 by Perry Glasser. Reprinted by permission of the University of Illinois Press.

From *Glass People* by Gail Godwin. Copyright © 1972 by Gail Godwin. Reprinted by permission of Alfred A. Knopf, Inc.

From *Ordinary People* by Judith Guest. Copyright © 1976 by Judith Guest. Reprinted by permission of Viking Penguin Inc.

From *Dreams of Sleep* by Josephine Humphreys. Copyright © 1984 by Josephine Humphreys. Reprinted by permission of Viking Penguin Inc.

From *The World According to Garp* by John Irving. Copyright © 1976, 1977, 1978 by John Irving. Reprinted by permission of the publisher, E. P. Dutton, a division of NAL Penguin Inc.

From *Family Dancing* by David Leavitt. Copyright © 1983, 1984 by David Leavitt. Reprinted by permission of Alfred A. Knopf, Inc.

From *The War Between the Tates* by Alison Lurie. Copyright © 1974 by Alison Lurie. Reprinted by permission of Random House, Inc.

From *Linden Hills* by Gloria Naylor. Copyright © 1985 by Gloria Naylor. Reprinted by permission of Viking Penguin Inc.

Reynolds Price, excerpted from *Kate Vaiden*. Copyright © 1986 by Reynolds Price. Reprinted with the permission of Atheneum Publishers, a division of Macmillan, Inc.

From *Celestial Navigation* by Anne Tyler. Copyright © 1974 by Anne Tyler Modarressi. Reprinted by permission of Alfred A. Knopf, Inc.

From *Marry Me* by John Updike. Copyright © 1971, 1973, 1976 by John Updike. Reprinted by permission of Alfred A. Knopf, Inc.

CONTENTS

It's a great gift to imagine. It helps you see.

— Bernard Chaet

Introduction

Men and women working in an atmosphere of common respect and productivity, their work not limited by the boundaries of their gender but, rather, strengthened and broadened because of their ability to transcend gender — that is the theme this volume is most concerned with. When writers, male or female, broaden the scope of their work by crossing the gender barrier and imagining the interior life of characters of the opposite sex, how does that imaginative act enrich the experience of fiction? The surest answer to that important question is to be found in the best examples of such writing, labeled cross-gender writing by Reynolds Price, and the seventeen selections assembled in this anthology are just that — examples of the best cross-gender writing in American fiction of the seventies and eighties.

Moses Soyer's painting *Artists on the WPA 1935* makes tangible the atmosphere of the symbolic mutual room created by the writers we have chosen. The artists Soyer portrays are workers; they pursue their art as a craft, an occupation. These are not nineteenth-century aesthetes, dabbling to pass their time till the next high tea or formal ball. They are women and men working to support themselves during troubled times.

Soyer places his artists in one spacious room filled with the tools of their trade. The room itself is a picture of creative activity, the artists set against a background of their own works-in-progress. The females

i

and the males work alongside each other, all of them different and distinct characters within a shared, common room. Yet the group strongly suggests that its members are as similar as they are different. The work they do is likewise a study in contrasts and a lesson in connections. Though each featured artist has his or her personal style, the paintings they create will be assembled as a single mural that Soyer called *Children at Play*.

One woman is dressed casually and comfortably in loose trousers and a baggy workshirt. But just as prominent are a woman in the form-fitting sweater and skirt ensemble typical of the era and a third woman who is perhaps a little defiantly smoking a cigarette.

Other men and women are positioned around the room, each working, each engrossed by the work. Their paintings share certain elements of design and composition; they each also strike some individual chord. What Soyer is saying has much to do with a community of artists, a group of people of both sexes engaged in an activity that absorbs and stirs them.

It is, in part, their creative spirit in the face of baffling times, one presumes, that Soyer celebrates. In much the same way that the thirties were economically troubled times, the seventies and eighties — the two decades from which the work in this anthology comes — have been a sexually confusing time. With the rise of the women's movement and the advent of the sexual revolution, sexual roles became fluid when for centuries they had been rigidly defined. In much the way that men and women of the Depression era struggled to find constructive work after being accustomed to great prosperity, the women and men of the past two decades have searched for constructive sexual identities after lifetimes of presumed and assumed roles.

Visual artists and writers, film-makers and singers have explored what it means to be male and what it means to be female in the last half of the twentieth century — a world that often seems to have crashed as resoundingly as the economic world of the thirties, and part of the fruit of their exploration has been the effort to portray their opposites with honesty and sensitivity, reality and hope. Soyer's painting is an emblem for contemporary fiction, the best of it, from the seventies and eighties, in that authors of both genders have made remarkable efforts to enter into a mutual room with their peers of the opposite sex.

Of course, such cross-gender portraits are not new. In his essay "Men, Creating Women" (*New York Times Book Review,* 9 November 1986), Reynolds Price briefly examines the historical context of such efforts. He presents a roll call of authors who have attempted such writing from the Elizabethan and Jacobean theater with its male actors in female roles to the earliest days of the novel as practiced by Daniel Defoe, Samuel Richardson, John Cleland, and, later, by America's foremost practitioner of the art, Henry James. Women, too, are part of this history: Emily Bronte, Mary Shelley, and Willa Cather.

However, Price sees the contemporary scene in all the arts as much bleaker in regard to bridging the gender gap. He blames this bleakness on enormous parental and social pressure on children to retreat from their inherent broad and sympathetic sexuality into a strictly defined and limited sexuality. This limited gender sense, when juxtaposed with the role confusion created by the women's movement and the sexual revolution, results in a fear of reconnecting with our truest, fullest selves. Thus, writers, according to Price, create what is safest, instead of venturing the imaginative act that would allow them to rediscover what they share with the opposite gender. He sees female writers as even less likely than male writers to take this aesthetic risk.

Regardless of these conclusions, Price is not entirely hopeless. He calls for a return to cross-gender writing (not androgynous writing, or what some critics have termed "the androgyne of the imagination" when referring to Henry James), to entering the interior life of the opposite sex because that entry leads to a better, purer, more aesthetic writing — one that tries to encompass the total human experience.

Spurred by his observations, we set out to see if Price was correct, if contemporary artists are, in fact, not creating successful central characters of the opposite sex as often as in the past and if men were actually doing so with greater frequency than women. Without any initial thesis of our own, we wanted only to look at the best contemporary writing in America in the last two decades, the writing of the post-sexual revolution. In order to eliminate the probably easier task of entering into the childhood experience of the opposite sex, we chose to consider only those characters who were adults. For similar reasons, we also decided not to examine the aged opposite sex characters created by contemporary writers. In most cases, such elderly characters no longer actively question their sexuality and their gender identification; at the very least, such questions are a secondary rather than a primary concern.

Within these admittedly arbitrary boundaries, we discovered that there is a rich body of work, written by both women and men, that accomplishes sympathetic and convincing portraits of the opposite sex. Indeed, it seems there is a common room, like the room of Soyer's painting, where our best contemporary fiction writers can practice their art.

In October, 1986, at the Eighth Institute of Southern Affairs in Savannah, Georgia, Smith Kirkpatrick, novelist, professor, and director of the University of Florida's Creative Writing Program and founder and director of the Florida Writers Conference, said that, in his experience in teaching fiction writing, "almost never do the boys write from the point of view of girls, almost never. I bet I haven't had fifteen stories in thirty years written by a male from the point of view of a female. The females, they write these marvelous stories. They get inside the male's head . . . [and] it becomes totally believeable."

As we read and made selections, we began to agree with Kirkpatrick. These days, women do seem more inclined than men to enter into the experiences of their opposites. Just as women have become freer in expressing themselves in all areas since the sexual revolution, they are the ones attempting cross-gender writing with the greatest frequency and often with the greatest success. But, perhaps most importantly, we also found that Price's essential argument is correct: cross-gender writing does often create fiction that is fuller and more imaginative than it would have been had the author not risked the shift in point of view.

The selections that we present here are not intended to be a comprehensive or definitive sampling of opposite gender portraits. Nor do the authors collected here always attempt to sustain these portraits throughout entire novels; neither are these selections necessarily typical of the writers' other work. What these seventeen stories and excerpts from novels *do* provide is a thorough sense of the vitality of cross-gender writing in contemporary American fiction. They also demonstrate that those who do this writing are among the best and most acclaimed writers at work today. In addition, we made a serious effort to make selections that presented characters from a broad spectrum of American society — different classes, races, and economic and educational backgrounds — in order to demonstrate that the interior lives of all people are rewarding material for both writer and reader.

Of the women writers in contemporary American fiction, no one has been more successful at writing from the opposite gender point of view than Anne Tyler. It's probably no coincidence that Tyler was one of Price's students at Duke University in the early 1960s. Like Price, she attempted a central character of the opposite sex in her first book-length work of fiction. Throughout that novel, *If Morning Ever Comes*, published in 1964 when she was twenty-two years old, she stays in the mind of southerner Ben Joe Hawkes, a young law student living in New York who is preoccupied with the daily lives of his sisters, mother, and grandmother back home in Sandhill, North Carolina.

Since that impressive debut, Tyler has gradually created her own definitive brand of fiction (in ten novels and numerous short stories), moving rapidly from the southern gothic tone of *If Morning Ever Comes* to a broad, complex family of characters, most of whom reside in cramped, overcrowded homes in Baltimore, Maryland. In these homes we find at least one male descendant (either protagonist or supporting character) of Ben Joe Hawkes: the three Emerson brothers in *The Clock Winder*, who suffer life in varying degrees of insecurity and inertness; ninety-year-old Caleb Peck in *Searching for Caleb*; eccentric, long-limbed, make-shift spouse and substitute obstetrician Morgan Gower in *Morgan's Passing*; cheerful, gentle, recorder-playing Ezra Tull and his jealous, domineering brother Cody in *Dinner at the Homesick Restaurant*; and the cautious and routine-loving Macon Leary in *The Accidental Tourist*. Many critics have described this cast of Tyler men as ineffective and weak and claim that she is unable to create strong, supportive males who are not dominated or at least steered by one or more stronger women. In a *New York Times* review of *The Accidental Tourist* (8 September 1985), Larry McMurtry wrote that Tyler's men "frequently are accidental tourists in their own lives."

"Their characters, like their professions," McMurtry writes, "seem accidental even though they come equipped with genealogies of Balzacian thoroughness. All of them have to be propelled through life by (at the very least) a brace of sharp, purposeful women — it usually takes not only a wife and girlfriend but an indignant mother and one or more devoted sisters to keep these sluggish fellows moving. They poke around haphazardly, ever mild and perennially puzzled, in the foreign country called Life. If they see anything worth seeing, it is usually because a determined woman on the order of Muriel Pritchett thrusts it under their noses and demands that they pay some attention."

All this is true, and it indeed looks as if Tyler's men are weak, or at least meek, by the standards often applied in our culture. The meekest of all is perhaps Jeremy Pauling in *Celestial Navigation*. A character not unlike the late artist Joseph Cornell, Jeremy is an artist who spends his life removed from the world, never stepping far from home, creating his collage "pieces" in isolation and at a safe distance from all he dreads. Jeremy is *unable* to move, his fears are so great; and he is afraid of nearly everything: answering the phone or the mail or the front door, "wearing new clothes, standing in open spaces, meeting the eyes of a stranger, eating in the presence of others, turning on electrical appliances."

Yet, Jeremy Pauling turns out to be one of the most heroic male characters in contemporary American fiction. If he were a less fearful man, his actions certainly would not seem heroic. But because Jeremy Pauling is simply scared to death, the moves he makes are profoundly brave. "For Mary Tell's sake he was slaying dragons," Tyler writes, "and yet to keep her respect it was necessary that she never even guess it." This one sentence is the key to Tyler's men: they're terrified, yet, unlike society, Tyler is giving them the right to be so. Rather than condemning them for their fears and vulnerability, she understands this side of the male psyche and realizes the demands of the role they are expected to play. We're all scared at some time or another, she seems to be saying over and over again with her characters — from Ben Joe Hawkes to Macon Leary — and men should be able to admit it as freely as women instead of having to hide it until it comes out in neurotic, self-defeating ways.

If Anne Tyler is the female writer currently most sympathetic to the pressures on and expectations of the opposite sex, close examination reveals a similar empathy — in varying forms — in the other female writers gathered in this collection.

In *Dreams of Sleep,* Josephine Humphreys writes beautifully of Will Reese, a man surrounded by sad women — his wife, his girlfriend, his two young daughters, the patients in his gynecological practice — all of whom place "a burden on him." One afternoon when he decides he must get away from all these sad females by cancelling that day's remaining appointments, "He steps out into the waiting room, courageous as a gladiator." The valor of such an act is not as great as Jeremy Pauling's, but Will has to keep his fears every bit as well concealed.

"[I have] the whole responsibility of her," he thinks of his lover Claire. "And she wants a future. Maybe that is what they all want, love that does not rot but lasts into the future. Unfading, unshrinking love, good as Sea Island cotton." The catch is that Will has begun to believe that such love does not exist, that the kind of love most people want carries with it a promise that can't be kept; Humphreys shows through Will Reese that this failure of love is as great a tragedy for men as it is for women. Not only is she sympathetic about the burdens her male character carries, but she also understands his needs, which are not so dissimilar from those of the women in his life. When Humphreys reveals the one thing that Will believes a man must have, his thought is as valid for a woman as it is for him: "A man has to have a treasure in his heart," she writes, "whether it is a god or an art or a love, something he can turn his inward eye on as consolation for the rest."

Typical of many of the central male characters created by women writers, Will Reese is heavily burdened by the women in his life, actually seeks that burden, needs it as an anchor, as weight to a life that might otherwise float away, as that treasure in his heart that serves as "consolation for the rest." This paradoxical yet essential element of the male figure that dominates the portraits by female writers comes into focus for Will Reese and for Humphreys's readers in the following passage:

> He had wanted a family. Unmarried and childless he was loose in time, fatherless, mother-threatened. After he got his family, his sense of orientation and stability improved, but at times now, and increasingly often, a new, dizzying suspicion grabs him and spins him: the suspicion that the stability is false; that he will round his corner one day and there will be no house; and worse, that he will be glad to see it gone.

In another passage Humphreys writes that Will had wanted a large family, one that would be "big enough to boom through life, absorb its difficulties and spring back from trouble robustly."

But, despite Will's self-knowledge, his recognition of his paradoxical desires, the most telling image of Will Reese — and the figure that dominates his sense of himself — is that of "a stickman at a crossroads — a tatterdemalion who can neither find his way nor ask for help." Humphreys's and Tyler's men, as well as many of the other characters created by women, become, in part, an assurance that asking for help is all right, that it is an acceptable male behavior.

Anne Beattie's panicky male protagonist in *Falling in Place*, John Knapp, is a man going through life almost as accidentally, as much by celestial navigation, as Tyler's Jeremy Pauling or Macon Leary, and he is every bit as much at a crossroads as Humphreys's Will Reese. Like Jeremy, who even as an adult never moves from his mother's home, middle-aged John has returned to his mother's home to live; here he's trying to be son, husband, father, and lover, and he is confused, overwhelmed, almost defeated by each of these roles. Like Will, who fears the stability of his family is a false one and that he might be glad to see his own house gone, John has lost all faith in the importance of his family and at times wishes they would "all disappear in a puff of smoke."

In a line similar to something Tyler might have written about Jeremy or Macon, Beattie says that when John Knapp appears outside his girlfriend Nina's apartment after a shooting accident involving his son and daughter, "He had just stuffed wadded bills into the cab driver's hand because he couldn't think — he might as well have been a man in a foreign country where he didn't understand the currency." And as he climbs the stairs in her building he wonders, "What if Nina opened the door and said something, said some important thing, and he didn't know what she was saying?" His dominant emotion is a feeling of being incapable of comprehending, much less acting upon, the events that have transpired. In all areas he thinks of himself as "reacting instead of acting," and later in the novel, when a psychiatrist asks if he feels out of control, he replies that he is moving by means of "cruise control."

With Nina, John is looking for a core, an anchor, a security out of which to act, to keep himself from floating — once he even calls his movement a "dead-man's float." When Nina relates a dream to him, one in which he sits in a boat while she is in the water, Beattie describes his thoughts: "The truth was that he did not think of her as someone who needed saving. He thought that she could save *him*, that her light grip on his arm . . . was anchoring his body to earth."

John and Nina's connection is tenuous, though, and their most frequent means of connecting — the telephone — is an artificial link. He constantly phones her in the middle of the night, waking her up, just to make sure she exists, is still connected to him in some way. The calls are so frequent that, as a joke, Nina gives him a toy telephone for Christmas, one that has a small voice saying, "I am five, how old are you?" This image of the younger Nina as parent and the older John as child is repeated in various ways throughout the book, particularly in his thinking of her tiny apartment as a "womb" and his hiding there as "playing peek-a-boo."

Like Tyler and Humphreys, Beattie is not critical of this man who feels as if he's a foreigner in his own life. She too is respectful of and emphatic toward the limitations and vulnerabilities of the opposite sex.

In *Dale Loves Sophie to Death*, Robb Forman Dew shows still another man baffled by the women around him — wife, lover, friend

— and swamped by the fear that he can never anticipate what these women might do or want. When Martin Howells's friend Ellen beckons him from her kitchen and gestures at a windowsill full of ruined loaves of bread, Dew writes: "Martin was at a loss. He stared and stared at them and then back at her, only to see her face turned to him with that widened look of expectation, so that the tension had left her features, and her expression had gone blank in anticipation of his sympathetic reaction." Martin feels alone, inadequate, even though he is in surroundings that are familiar and sometimes comforting to him. And later, when Martin realizes how much he misses his wife and children, who are away for the summer, Dew says of him, "He had a heartsick need for that quiet and continual celebration of the spirit when it is bound fast by the expectations and wants and demands of other people whom one desires above all else to please and cherish and be nurtured by in turn."

Unlike John Knapp, Martin Howells does not abandon the known and orderly (his family) for randomness (lover Claire); and instead of sedating his sexuality, as Beattie does with John, Dew deflates his by turning collapsing birthday party balloons — once symbols of joy and bouyancy — into memories of water-filled condoms he once saw thrown to the street at Mardi Gras. Here, sex is turned into a joke, but it also serves Dew's sympathetic revelation of her male character's ineffectual anticipation of the turns of his life and his great desire is to be "bound" by the expectations of others.

In Nector Kashpaw's first-person narrative in Louise Erdrich's *Love Medicine*, we find a male character who shares much with John Knapp, despite the substantial differences in their place, time, and class. These men find themselves afraid of stillness, of time's arrest, because they are forced to evaluate what they have done with their lives. Nector says:

So much time went by in that flash it surprises me yet. What they call a lot of water under the bridge. . . . Seventeen years of married life and come-and-go children. And then it was like the river pooled. Maybe I took my eyes off the current too quick. Maybe the fast movement of time had made me dizzy. I was shocked. . . . I was sitting on the steps . . . when everything went still. . . . In that stillness, I lifted my head and looked around.

What I saw was time passing, each minute collecting behind me before I had squeezed from it any life. It went so fast, is what I'm saying, that I myself sat still in the center of it.

Finally spurred to take some decisive action, Nector begins a life that closely resembles John Knapp's, living in several places at once. He makes a connection between love and his official role as head of his tribe; both finally come to involve a sense of duty without great personal reward. He serves in both, yet in neither is there free will or choice: "I could not fight this, either," he says. "I had to speed where I was took. I only trusted that I would be tossed up on land when everyone who wanted something from Nector Kashpaw had wrung him dry." His position as tribal chairman forces him to take Lulu's land, but his basic feeling is of being out of control — again, a feeling of being inadequate to the task he has set himself.

Nector's goal in his initial approach to his former lover Lulu has to do with the memory of their youthful playfulness and intimacy. The contrast between the memory of sweetness with Lulu and his wife Marie's bitterness is crucial. When Lulu becomes like Marie — requiring punctuality, dependability, the rigors of marriage — Nector feels pressed, hemmed in, drawn too tight. With Lulu he had wanted to feel young again, and instead he feels old, similar to the exhausted response of John Knapp, as he falls asleep on Nina's bed.

In her Cameron Bolt in *Glass People*, Gail Godwin presents yet another man overwhelmed by the supposed demands in his life and anxious about anticipating the expectations of women. Here the male character, afraid of losing his wife, Francesca, lives behind a calm mask that all is well, never letting on how much he knows or how shaky the ground is upon which their relationship stands. "He always liked to sample Francesca's pleasures first," Godwin writes, "to make sure she wouldn't be disappointed." Cameron is so concerned with guessing his wife's pleasures and trying to prevent disappointments that he's always working ahead, living in the future, rather than enjoying the present: "This way of living in time he had practiced ever since he could remember. It cut down discomfort and increased efficiency. If he was quicker at tasks than others, it was because he had mentally rehearsed them many times, had seen himself doing them hours, days, before he had to do them, anticipated all eventualities. In the act of doing them, he was somewhere else already, rehearsing new tasks." Cameron's ability "not to be here" makes him seem as impervious and as lost in many ways as Jeremy Pauling or John Knapp. Once again, though, Godwin does not scorn her character's lack of confidence, but shows the greatest empathy for it.

Calvin Jarrett, the husband and father in Judith Guest's *Ordinary People*, is almost as self-conscious about his life and his relationships as Cameron Bolt. But his facade of control and cool efficiency is more dangerously threatened than Cameron's, and he is forced by events into a more honest and deeper exploration of his fears and inadequacies. Like Cameron, he is a self-made man and a devoted husband, but Calvin also must deal with the role of father to a disturbed adolescent son. In fact, Guest's emphasis here is on the father-son relationship and Calvin's feelings of inadequacy at being a parent. "Responsibility," Guest writes. "That is fatherhood. You cannot afford to miss any signs. . . . The responsibilities seem enormous. Staggering. His job alone, nobody else's. Motherhood is different, somehow. And what about fathering girls? . . . Is there more, or less responsibility? He couldn't take more."

Calvin Jarrett shares many of the same feelings as Will Reese and especially John Knapp, who shows total befuddlement when his children are in trouble. Calvin is more aggressive in his efforts to right the situation than John, but he is no less overwhelmed by his role as father. And although Calvin's relationship with his wife, Beth, is active and loving, he finds himself waiting to be guided by her in the sexual encounter in the excerpted passage — as if he believes there, too, he is inadequate.

Similar understanding for a man's vulnerability surfaces in Gloria Naylor's *Linden Hills*. "Xavier Donnell was falling in love with a black woman," Naylor writes. "It was one of the most terrifying experiences of his life." But in *Linden Hills* Naylor takes the terrors and pressures a step farther and shows a black man trying to operate in a white man's world: "While his rise had been meteoric and his cashmere suits managed to withstand the change of altitude, that tenth-floor office with its shag carpet and oak panels housed a fragile god. Because Xavier was forced to see his exploits as much more than those of a superman, he had to join the rest of General Motors and worship the rise of a Super Nigger. So he found himself as only a high priest perched in a temple and burdened with the care of this image. And like all fragile gods, it demanded constant attention and surveillance for any telltale cracks in the clay feet, a softening around the knees, a dulling of the luster." Because of his race, Xavier finds the overbearing pressure of expectations of males compounded by additional expectations associated with his blackness. His ability to act is doubly threatened; his self-knowledge must be doubly accurate.

In Alison Lurie's *The War Between the Tates*, we have an interesting and sometimes humorous look at a man who perceives his failures as directly related to the size of his body. Forty-six-year-old Brian Tate presumably has it all — beautiful wife; two bright, healthy children; an endowed chair at a prestigious university; well-received scholarly publications — yet the world does not realize that "internally, secretly, he is a dissatisfied and disappointed man." Brian, who is "five feet five, weighing a mere one hundred and thirty-five pounds," believes that all his "defeats and his size are connected: that his appearance is the objective correlative of a lack of real stature. . . . It was felt everywhere that he was in every sense a small man, not suited to authority over anything beyond a small department." Like Tyler's Jeremy Pauling and Godwin's Cameron Bolt, Brian keeps these feelings to himself. He "never spoke of this to anyone, but he thought about it — not every day, but frequently."

Brian also shares Nector Kashpaw's and, in some ways, Calvin Jarrett's belief that his physical, sexual, romantic side is tied to his professional (or academic) standing. A roommate at Harvard had said once, when Brian decided not to go out on a date before an important exam, that "Brian thinks it all comes out of the same faucet." And the roommate, who did go out, "received a grade of only B-plus . . . while Brian was rewarded for his abstinence with a straight A." It is imperative that Brian be a "big" man, and if he can't do it in physical stature, he must do everything within his power to make sure he does it with his work. Unfortunately, as is the case with

Humphreys's Will Reese, never does Brian's work give him the satisfaction, the success he is looking for; never does it become "consolation for the rest." And neither does his affair with student Wendy Gahaghan; here, too, he feels inadequate, even in breaking off the illicit relationship: "Just thinking and worrying about it has begun to exhaust his energy to the point where he is functioning only in second gear."

Again and again, words such as "burdens," "responsibilities," "expectations," "anticipations," "demands," and "failures" are used to describe the feelings of the men whose minds each of these women writers tries to enter. Rather than displaying envy of men's powers or anger at their use of such powers, the female writers are more interested in expressing their sympathies for the pressures inherent in the exhausting roles they believe these men are forced to play. And rather than saying that these men are heartless, the writers say that they are anything but: the masks and armor men wear are to prevent anyone's penetrating the inner workings of those hearts. Thus, the female writer striving to create a whole male character comes up against precisely what the male psyche frequently resists.

Juxtaposed against the pressures are the repeated feelings of "floating," of being "lost," of needing an "anchor." Once again these descriptions are not so much criticism as a willingness to demonstrate the male's more vulnerable side. These particular patterns in male characters do raise an interesting question, however: are these women projecting onto their male characters stereotypical female feelings of inadequacy and vulnerability, or are they *allowing* men to participate openly, by way of the fiction, in emotional states natural to either sex?

These men also believe their fears and failures are easily detected by the women around them and therefore must be concealed at all costs. On the other hand, the men frequently seem baffled by their wives, lovers, and mothers. They spend their energy and their time trying to anticipate the women's actions and to intuit their thoughts. Even when they are given all the right cues, they remain afraid, still feel ignorant about women's wishes. Like John Knapp, they're afraid the women will speak and they won't understand the words. The women's relationships with other people, particularly with women friends (such as those between Dinah and Ellen in *Dale Loves Sophie to Death*, Francesca and Kate in *Glass People*, and Louise and Tiffy in *Falling in Place*) are also puzzling to the men; the men have friendships too, but they're never as intimate or as exotic as the friendships of their wives and lovers. Men never walk "step for step" as women do in *Falling in Place*; such closeness is mysterious, incomprehensible, one more thing to feel insecure about.

In 1962 Reynolds Price began his literary career with the publication of *A Long and Happy Life*. In that novel he creates Rosacoke Mustian, a young woman of the Piedmont South who, Price has written in the preface to *Mustian*, "was the fictional equivalent of any one of a dozen girls who had treated me kindly eleven years before when we moved to my parents' home, a small county-seat in eastern North Carolina." Like Anne Tyler after him, Price grew up in North Carolina, graduated from Duke University (having studied writing with William Blackburn), and constructed his first novel around a central character of the opposite sex. Though Tyler continued to bring Ben Joe Hawkes back to the page through his descendants, Price returned with the same protagonist, Rosacoke Mustian (along with Milo, Rato, and Wesley), in *A Generous Man* and in a play called *Early Dark*. Throughout his career, more than any other male writer in recent fiction, with the possible exception of John Updike, Price has continued to move through the minds and sensibilities of female characters — from the pregnant young Rosacoke to the wizened old black woman Aunt Zimby (in his short story "The Warrior Princess Ozimba") to his most recent, *Kate Vaiden*.

It is in *Kate Vaiden* that he makes the greatest leap into the female consciousness, writing in the first person and taking the reader through the length of Kate's life, from the time she is a young girl being raised by her great-aunt after the deaths of her parents, to the time she is old, living alone and acutely aware of her mortality.

Although Kate Vaiden is not formally educated, she is sharp, intelligent, articulate, and full of purpose. Yet, despite these qualities, Price has placed her in a time when women have few options; through the first half of her life, she is in the care of others — first her parents, then her Aunt Caroline, and later a adoring taxi driver named Tim Slaughter and her much older cousin Walter. In each of these positions, she is placed in a passive role — a role where she sees few opportunities or alternatives. And, in every case, her form of action or aggression is to leave. In one way or another, Kate abandons every person she has ever loved and been loved by. Her leaving begins with Caroline, after the death of her childhood love, and continues until the end of the book when, having been told she has cancer, she decides to contact the grown son she left when he was an infant; the pattern continues, the reader knows, because when Kate dies, she will abandon her son, Lee, once again. Price is not critical of this pattern, but, like ·the women writers with their male characters, sympathetic to the causes that make Kate react the way she does.

"The miracle is," Price writes in *Kate Vaiden*, "you can last through time. You pray to die when you pass a calendar — all those separate days stacked before you, each one the same length and built from steel. But then you butt on through them somehow, or they through you." Life is something to get through for women, Price is saying, and barriers are everywhere, hard as steel.

After the birth of her baby, Kate feels "locked in," and as she nurses the sick infant back to health, she drifts "in a lazy dream of freedom." "I'd stay in Macon," she decides, "finish high school by mail; then Lee and I would live our lives somewhere down the highway with rooms and jobs and men who wouldn't give a damn about history. It seemed that easy. It seemed crazy too. But so did the whole weight of my short life (which felt about as short as U.S. 1 from Maine to Miami)."

In *Marry Me*, John Updike is also sympathetic about the burdens women carry and their dreams of freedom. Sally Mathias is Jerry Conant's lover; she is also a wife and mother. The first role is seen as a kind of escape and the other two as prisons. And much like Kate Vaiden, Sally has one form of aggression: to leave. When she makes an impetuous flight to Washington to meet Jerry, who doesn't know she's coming, she "carried a toothbrush in her pocketbook, and that was her luggage; she had inherited from her father a love for traveling light. Free, cool in her black linen, she felt like an elegant young widow returning from her husband's June funeral; he had been an old man, greedy and unkind." Here "traveling light" means without the weight of children; and here the role of "widow" is looked on with pleasure instead of grief. In real life her husband Richard is not "old" but because of what he takes from her and seems to need from her, she does indeed think of him as "greedy."

Raymond Carver uses the word "bridle" in the title of his short story about a married woman who watches another woman and her family move into the apartment complex she runs, and then watches them pack up and leave again. Both women — the observer and the observed — are "bridled"; both are restrained by their positions and roles, and both are resentful of it. For neither one, outside death, is there permanent escape. The closest they come to leaving their situations is when Marge, the apartment manager, washes and styles the other woman's hair: "I'm wearing the rose-colored uniform that I put on when I do hair. I go on filing my nails and looking up at the window from time to time.

"She walks by the window and then pushes the doorbell. 'Come on in,' I call. 'It's unlocked.'

"She settles into the chair and draws a breath.

"I say, 'Put your head back. That's it. Close your eyes now, why don't you? Just relax.'"

Marge, in her rose-colored uniform, provides a temporary escape from reality by allowing Betty, her client, to close her eyes, to relax, while she gives almost equally temporary transformation to her hair and nails. For those who can't muster the money or the nerve to get on an airplane, narcissism and voyeurism must provide flight for women, Carver lets us know. And for some women, that seems almost as selfish or as bold a move as physical leaving.

The first-person narrator, Marge, shows her clearest act of rebellion, of trying to break out of her confined existence, by printing her name in all caps across the forehead of U. S. Grant on the fifty-dollar bills the Holits family pays her with when they move in. She sees the bills winding their way across the country to all sorts of exotic and freer places and imagines people wondering about her, about this Marge. This is an artificial connection, like the telephone in *Falling in Place*; but Marge's plight is worse than John Knapp's — she has far fewer options and means of escape. Betty Holits is even more bridled than Marge; she has learned the hard way that "Dreams . . . are what you wake up from." Betty is like Kate Vaiden in that both see life as something to get through, an endless series of days and events to endure.

Christine Taylor, one of three female first-person narrators who tell their stories in Michael Dorris's *A Yellow Raft in Blue Water*, cannot settle for the vicarious escape of a Marge, nor can she wake up from dreaming as Betty Holits does. She grows up without much sense of duty to her background and her family's values. But her persistent and unyielding rebellion against those values indicates that they have been as powerful a force in shaping her life as they are in the lives of women who follow their culture's values without question.

Christine doesn't want to be bound by the limitations of her heritage; she doesn't want to stay on the Indian reservation in Montana, where she grew up. She takes very self-conscious and decisive steps to escape those limitations: engaging in spontaneous and wide-ranging sexual experience at an early age, but always taking "precautions" to avoid being "trapped" with a child or children, as all the "grown women" she knows are; moving to Seattle and working at a series of tedious and unfulfilling jobs in order to sustain her "real" life, which appears to take place in bars and bedrooms; creating and directing a scenario that will propel her beloved brother toward fulfilling the highest expectations of the heritage she herself is rejecting; falling in love with a black man, getting pregnant with his child (a result of purposefully abandoning her precautions for the first time), and then marrying him.

The cruel irony of Christine's story lies in a whole new set of limitations that seem to spring full-blown from her decisions. The genuine joy and heady freedom that mark the afternoon of her child's conception are as fleeting as the sensual pleasure of Kate Vaiden's afternoon with Douglas Lee in Noony's cabin. The more restrained but richer, more mature happiness of the walk home on her wedding night also fades into a dull routine: days and nights spent alone in a cheap hotel room, unable to go out even for food because she has no raincoat large enough to cover her belly, waiting for her husband to return from his work as a substitute mail carrier.

Sometime during the months of waiting for her child's birth, Christine realizes that she has become just the thing she wanted to avoid. Although she suspects Elgin, her husband, of cheating on her, she remains silent, clinging to her belief that "Men cheated on wives who gave them no peace or understanding, never wanted to have fun, and probably fooled around themselves. In my mind those wives merged into a fat, mean, money-mad woman."

But, like a "ticking bomb," she comes to the inevitable explosion, accuses Elgin, and then sees herself through his eyes: "I was that fat, mean woman." Once she confronts this image of herself, all her efforts toward escape begin to collapse. She leaves Elgin and eventually finds herself back on the reservation, with her daughter living with her grandmother, and her brother dead in Vietnam, victim of her carefully constructed scenario. Later in her life, Christine takes to her bed, literally, becoming a regular patient in the hospital for a series of ill-defined ailments, apparently designed to elicit the attention of her husband and her daughter.

Many of the women in this collection have apparently acquiesced to the notion that real power resides in the male, even if he must be continually prodded and manipulated by females. But Christine's sense of male power is so extreme that it may be a partial explanation for her failure to create a satisfying life for herself. The key to understanding her sense of male power lies in her relationship with her brother. She always sees him as the special child, the favored being. Her role is to enhance and orchestrate his gifts and power. When she is pregnant, she is positive that the child will be a boy, choosing only the name Raymond, after the consummately powerful Perry Mason played by Raymond Burr. After the birth of her female child, she insists on modifying the name to Rayona, and she seems to give up any ideas for the child's having the bounteous and masterful life that would have been possible had she given birth to a boy.

Clyde Edgerton's Raney Bell is a woman bound by guilt and her sense of others' expectations of her, partly because she comes to adulthood without having questioned the values that a woman like Christine Taylor knows she must reject, even before she reaches womanhood. Raney is particularly hindered by the conflict between what she desires and what she presumes her husband, Charles, and her father want for and of her. But, unlike the women in Carver's story or in Dorris's novel, Raney is able to change and to cause her husband, her father, and others to accept the changes in her. She is even able to foster change in them.

The excerpt from Edgerton's novel conveys two strong messages: Raney wants to work, and she wants to be sexual. But these things — work and sex — are not dreams from which Raney must eventually awaken; they are concrete goals, attainable through her own efforts. They both require an adjustment in attitude. Because of her sheltered Free Will Baptist background, she has grown to womanhood without realizing that the world is made up of conflicting points of view. She has always believed that everyone, or at least everyone who is good, shares the same view that she has come to through her church and family life. As she grows, she learns to test out that view, which she comes to recognize as a narrow and limiting one in many ways, and through that testing of perceptions and values, she begins to think for herself for the first time.

The story of Raney's marriage is, in large measure, the story of the conflict between her point of view and her husband's, and perhaps the greatest measure of Raney's strength is that she does not feel that that conflict is destructive. Instead, she uses it as the motivation for her personal growth and eventually constructs a compromise, a productive merging of the two views, perhaps best embodied in the christening announcement that closes the novel. She learns, in essence, to exert the free will that her church and her environment have kept in check throughout her growing up.

It is not easy to escape social pressures and years of moral conditioning, and Raney sometimes finds that she needs help from outside stimuli. When she and Charles are in the feed room at the back of her daddy's store, she needs the wine and the Southern Comfort to support her passion. However, this need comes more from her personal history than from any lack of conviction on Raney's part.

Edgerton isn't making fun of Raney or criticizing her, but he is, instead, exploring the reasons for her thinking the way she does and for why she might consider herself to have fewer options than Charles believes she has. Again, the serious reader must question whether Edgerton allows Raney to evolve out of her *own* needs or out of what

Charles (who, even with the best intentions is still, after all, one more man) wants for her. The sort of lovingly imposed direction suggested by Charles's encouraging her to drink the wine at the Ramada Inn makes Charles much like Raney's father, who gives the newlyweds money each month so that they will never know hardship. But, finally, Edgerton suggests, through Raney's eyes, that Charles and the father move just as far toward Raney's view as she does toward theirs.

Doralee Jackson, in Perry Glasser's novella *Mexico*, is as young, restless, and desperate to get away from Des Moines, Iowa, as Christine Taylor is to leave her reservation. Doralee thinks of Des Moines as being close enough to the edge of the world to throw off rocks. Whereas Raney Bell's life has conditioned her to acceptance and continuity, Doralee's experience, like Christine's, has had just the opposite effect. The need for escape is so great, the need to have something better in life than what her mother has had, that she leaves with Kirk Dugan, someone she quickly realizes she is not in love with. But she gradually learns that you can't just take what comes along and get "better"; almost like Dorothy in *The Wizard of Oz*, she begins to long for home, stability, security, the things she had meant to escape:

> What *did* people do with money? Maybe settle someplace, buy a business, a little card shop or something, and she caught herself, right then, it was revelation, here she was thinking about not being on the move, just like the men she'd known back in Iowa that she'd thought were so damned lame with their heads and asses buried so deep in black Iowa dirt they'd never think to move. It was a revelation that she, Doralee Jackson, wanted a place that was hers and something to do there. Yes, it was Doralee that was changing, faster than Kirk Dugan might or probably ever could.

Like Kate Vaiden, Doralee runs away only to find that escape (even though it may be her only alternative) does not provide her with the things she thought she'd find by going someplace else. Still, Doralee's trip with Kirk does free her in the sense that she learns about herself. When she realizes that no man (not Kirk or the baseball player Bobby Kelly) can provide all the things she needs, she knows she must secure her needs herself, just as she always has. It is only then that she takes the first steps for herself — and toward any kind of real freedom.

Doralee is younger than most of the other women in these selections, but her social class and her economic circumstances are similar to those of Carver's Marge and Betty, Dorris's Christine, and Edgerton's Raney. All of these women have far fewer options than a woman such as Updike's Sally, who, though grounded in many ways, does have the money to provide her an occasional symbolic flight. Doralee's chances for escaping her background and her limitations are further hindered by her history of sexual abuse and her mother's history as battered wife. These added pressures are, in part, an explanation for her apparently unfeeling escape at the novella's end. More than any other female portrayed in this collection, Doralee must deal with emotional scars that may be ultimately inescapable. For her, normal life, settling down in a prosperous and peaceful routine, may be the only feasible escape from what has come before.

Doralee sees sex as a part of her escape, in many ways the easiest part to deal with. John Irving's Helen Holm Garp doesn't want to escape the family, the husband, the job that make up her life. In *The World According to Garp*, Helen enjoys a pseudo-freedom from familial and wifely duties by having an affair with one of her students, Michael Milton. Testing the boundaries of her life is almost entirely a matter of sex for Helen, and the test is designed to be a fleeting thing. Of all the women in this anthology, Helen Garp has the least frustration, finds her life the least confining, or, to put it in more positive terms, Helen enjoys the greatest freedom and contentment of these women.

That such a woman would still feel compelled to seek escape, however temporary and insignificant she designs it to be, speaks to the fundamental nature of that desire in females. And even though Helen Garp's escape is, in part, a reaction to her husband's infidelities and self-absorption, guilt accompanies her actions from the very outset and appears endemic to the territory in which rebellious women live.

The automobiles that Helen spends time in during her affair serve as a metaphor for the kind of freedom she is seizing and the guilt that it brings with it. Michael Milton buys a 1951 Buick Dynaflow in which "The front seat was so long and deep that Helen could lie across it, almost without having to bend her knees — or without having to put her head in Michael Milton's lap, though she did this anyway." The Buick embodies both the pleasure and the duplicity of the affair. In her own car Helen "developed a fondness for the bare sharp shaft of the Volvo's stick shift; its bite at the end of the day, driving home from her office, felt good against the heel of her hand, and she often pressed against it until she felt it was only a hair away from the pressure necessary to break her skin." Thus, the Volvo suggests both her guilt and her self-inflicted ritual of retribution.

Such identification with automobiles is usually considered masculine, thus raising again the question of whether the author, in this case a male author, Irving, is projecting this stereotypical male trait onto Helen or allowing her to participate in such a connection between person and machine and the sense of freedom and power that a speeding car or a gear shift in hand might bring. As with the women in Carver's story, her form of escape is ultimately seen by Helen as a selfish one. She begins to think about her husband, her children, that Walt should not be out in the cold. Control, power, guilt are all connected to and separate from Helen's sexual encounter with Michael Milton. And, in the end, her act of aggression (the affair) creates tragedy for them all — perhaps Irving's way of allowing (or forcing) her to experience the cost of freedom, its heavy burden, as well as its power. It is also important to note that Helen's husband, T. S. Garp, is put through the same cycle of freedom, power, reconsideration, and consequence as his wife, a similarity that suggests that Irving's portrayals are free of character manipulation based on gender.

In the story "Aliens," David Leavitt suggests that there is easier escape for almost anyone than for his unnamed female narrator. Her husband, Alden, makes a penultimate escape when he drives their car over a cliff. Alden now lives in the state hospital, having lost his sight in one eye "and the English language." Her daughter Nina has constructed a complex history for herself, claiming that she is an Alien "implanted" on Earth, waiting for her relatives from the small planet Dandril to "retrieve her." "She speaks like an oracle," her mother says, as Nina watches the skies patiently for her escape. But Nina's real escape is in her imagination. Her brother Charles's escape comes through his computers and through designing a machine that "will create for us a whole world into which we can be transported." Once people can live inside this machine, the individual imagination will be obsolete: "We'll live the adventures the machine creates for us," Charles says, in a world of "artificial imagination."

Each member of this family, in the year since Alden and his wife's car accident, has become an alien; they're all traversing foreign land; they all want escape. Only it is the female narrator — as mother and wife — who must remain in the real world, who must somehow keep her strange and disjointed family together as well as possible. But even she, in the early days after going home from the hospital, wanted escape. "For weeks after my release," she says, "I begged to be readmitted." Life in the hospital, with injured spleen and broken bones, seemed preferable to the real world she knew she had to face. But the narrator soon begins going through each day, visiting Alden at the hospital, trying to communicate with her distant children, trying to perform the duties of her role. Her only escape, in the last scene, is when she and her silent husband sneak into a supply room in the hospital and make love, where the things she is thankful for are gravity and the fact that "the planet has not yet broken loose from its tottering orbit. If nothing else, we hold each other down."

Leavitt's story is typical of the theme we see running through the selections by men in this collection. Torn between the need for freedom and their sense of the limitations inherent in being female, these women struggle and experiment and start over, again and again, but their essential emotion comes out of feeling trapped, of living in a world too small, too confining, and too unrewarding for their inner selves. This pervasive theme emerged from our selections in much the way the dominant theme in the selections by women emerged, without our having anticipated it. We did not make the selections based on the themes. They came as an additional connection after we chose those portraits and those writers that we felt best argued for cross-gender writing.

The women writers created male characters who are drifting, who seem dangerously lost; and the men writers created female characters whose danger comes from being so anchored. The men want stability; the women want escape.

Both genders hold up the fears and faults of the other not for ridicule, but for understanding. These writers have a far greater empathy for both fear and failure in those characters of the opposite sex whose interior lives they have entered than have writers who never move beyond simple observation of such shortcomings.

If Jeremy Pauling were a character merely observed, he could be seen by readers as a bumbling failure, a fool, a nerd wearing a pocket protector to seem authoritative and competent. But when Tyler enters his mind, the fiction transcends satire and black comedy to become a total portrait, one in which both artist and reader are forced to confront the whole man. The reward for that confrontation is truer understanding of what it means to be *this* human.

Kate Vaiden, too, would be a most unsympathetic character were she only observed. But as Price enters Kate's consciousness and lets her own voice tell her story, he automatically increases his reader's sympathy for a woman who abandons her child and walks away from situation after situation in which she has accepted love. Thus, even readers who disagree with Kate's actions will know what it is to be Kate Vaiden. And, once they have that understanding, there is the possibility for forgiveness.

Perhaps the greatest irony in writers' choosing not to attempt such fiction is that it cuts them off from an essential tool of their craft. Cross-gender writing does create deeper understanding; thus, it brings a writer closer to what fiction is all about: a journey to understand the workings of humankind.

When the writers here assembled are joined by such excellent peers as Mark Childress, Andre Dubus, Laurel Goldman, Mary Hood, Stephen King, Bobbie Ann Mason, Toni Morrison, Joyce Carol Oates, Lowry Pei, Walker Percy, Jayne Anne Phillips, Lee Smith, Robert Stone, and others who have attempted at least once to enter into the point of view of a character of the opposite sex, the importance of cross-gender writing to the state of contemporary fiction is obvious; its current use, inarguable. In addition, numerous young writers are attempting this imaginative act in their first works (Tyler, Price, Humphreys, Guest, Erdrich, Dorris, Dew, and Edgerton, along with Beattie's *Chilly Scenes of Winter*, Lowry Pei's *Family Resemblances*, Mark Childress's *A World Made of Fire*, Laurel Goldman's *Sounding the Territory* and others), which suggests not only that they are less intimidated by the task but also that the future of cross-gender writing is bright.

Rather than intending our conclusions as final answers, we mean for them to generate new questions and further discussion of the ability to imagine life beyond the boundaries of traditional sexual roles. These selections should also draw all of us closer to that harmonious space that Price evokes when he says, "It's in our power — writers and readers — to take the next step, back and forward, to a common gift: our mutual room."

Emily Ellison
Jane B. Hill
Atlanta, Georgia
June 1987

Ann Beattie

from
Falling
In Place

HE WALKED UP the stairs, trying to remember that he was in love. There was a fact, and an important one: He was in love. He was there because she said more in a glance than anyone else said in a touch, and a touch from her meant more than an embrace from anyone else. When you were in love, it was logical to go be with the person you loved. Only, he didn't know where to begin. What he had to talk about seemed to have nothing to do with the world of love and everything to do with the world of hate, and that world had never been real when he was with Nina. If she was getting away, it was because he was letting her get away. She was inside the apartment. He knew that she would not have left for work yet. She would be having her little-girl breakfast of cereal and fruit, and brushing her hair, listening to the news on the radio, tidying up the room. She wasn't mean in the morning. You could talk to her and she'd answer. The two times they had gone away together, he had been amazed at how cheerful she was in the morning. He tried to remember that it was morning now, that if he put his mind to it, he could stop his legs from shaking enough to climb the stairs, that at the top was Nina, that he could reach out and touch her and she would be there. He felt as crazy and foolish as an old drunk who finds his way home but can't remember to climb the stairs, so he's found in the morning and catches hell anyway. God —

if he was really comical. If she meant that, really, and didn't just say it to tease, because she was fond of him. If it was all explained in Passages: a simple answer. Nothing was simple. Not even loving Nina was simple. This was the only place he could imagine being, and already he felt that the place wasn't there, that he wasn't going to make it to the top of the stairs, and that if he did, he wouldn't know where to begin. He would have to invent some logical explanation for what he was going to tell her, or maybe it was just because he was in a panic that he thought that. He realized that he was in a panic, and that gave him enough energy, returned enough breath to him, that he was able to continue walking up the stairs. He couldn't believe what he had left behind, what he had just walked out on. He had thought at the time that he was doing the logical thing, that he was doing something out of self-preservation. There had been so much chaos: He had been afraid that he was losing his senses, going deaf. And only the summer before, the six of them, his mother, Brandt, John Joel, Louise, Mary and he, had been at the carnival. Brandt — as usual — hanging on to his arm and trying to bring him to the ground, dangling and swaying. They had been a family at a carnival. He had been awake all night, and he couldn't think straight. He knew that he would have to get to the point and not edge up toward it; that he couldn't talk to her about the summer before, the things they had done as a family; that there was no point in trying to explain to her that they were typical; that maybe even his love for her figured in a pattern; that they were typical and then suddenly they weren't. He was going to say to her: I want you to help me. He didn't know what help he needed. He had no memory of how he had gotten from Connecticut to New York. He did remember being in the city, and taking the car to the garage he usually went to, the keys left behind, the cab to Nina's. The cab driver had talked to him about the weather they were supposed to have over the weekend, and he had remembered, only then, what day it was. He had just stuffed wadded bills into the cab driver's hand because he couldn't think — he might as well have been a man in a foreign country where he didn't understand the currency. Better just to overpay and run, to be embarrassed that way rather than the other. He tried to breathe more softly. He wanted to at least be breathing normally when she saw him. More than anything he wanted to see her standing there. He wanted no harm to have come to her, at least. At the top of the stairs he made a fist and knocked. The reverberation that began in his hand shot through his arm and ended in his heart. And then she opened the door.

* * *

He was walking up the stairs. It was a simple accomplishment — the sort of thing they teach brain-damaged people to do. Later, when they master the mechanics of climbing, they teach them not to frown or squint. The trick is not to show that you're concentrating. There was a school for brain-damaged people — teenage children, mostly — somewhere near where he worked, and several times during his lunch hour he had seen them parading down the street. They had things to do: trash to throw away. Well — maybe that was the only thing. They had trash to throw away. He and Nick had been coming back from lunch the first time, and Nick had called his attention to them. As months went by he and Nick had watched their progress. It was horribly slow progress, and it might never have occurred to them to think of it as progress at all if Nick hadn't noticed the way they had stopped holding hands. At first, they held hands like small schoolchildren. Then they walked close together, almost shoulder to shoulder. Then, by the time spring came, when everybody else in the city was walking close together — men steering women along, their hands on their bare shoulders, people hip to hip on the grass in Central Park — the brain-damaged people had let go of each other and walked farther apart. Either they had been taught not to frown and look frightened or the spring had touched them in some way. One time, as they watched, a man carrying a blaring cassette player got into the middle of them, and they started to scatter like frightened ducks; then the two men at the front came and tried to round them

5

up. Eventually they did, and the parade huddled together again and turned the corner. Nick claimed he watched because it reminded him that there were worse problems than having to deal with Metcalf. He claimed he watched because Nick had gotten him hooked. He was not used to seeing slow, regular movement in the city. He had gotten used to watching people slap down change for the newspaper without missing a beat, to arms suddenly stretched out for cabs, to people walking down a street so that you couldn't tell whether or not they were together. Even when they spoke to each other, that didn't mean for sure that they were together.

Walking up the steps to Nina's apartment, he had thought for a second that something was missing — a leader was missing. And no one was behind him. He was there alone, doing this simple thing; and he thought that he was never going to be able to make it to the top, and that if he did, it was too much to expect that he would have a pleasant expression on his face when he got there. He would just have to get there and be there, and then — and then what? The stairs were buckling and shifting under him; they were delivering him to a room that would tilt crazily. He rubbed his face. He hadn't had any sleep, and he was exhausted, and the faint stinging-itch across his neck, below his ears, had started: the signal that he was about to have a pounding headache. He must have been on the stairs for a long time. He kept looking over his shoulder, as though there were better air below him, and if he turned his head he might be able to breathe. He kept turning his head, and the building was quiet — no one behind him. But every time he moved forward, there were just as many stairs, it seemed. His legs felt heavy. His head. Finally he had dashed up the stairs and gotten to the top, panting, feeling as crazy as one of the brain-damaged people would feel if he were capable of seeing himself in perspective. If the piece of paper drops on the sidewalk instead of into the trash container, so what? So what? he was saying out loud. So what? he whispered. No one heard the whisper, and he did not hear any noise: no breakfast dishes clattering, no radio music, no alarms going off. He put his hands over his ears and took them away, to see if there was more sound when he removed his hands. His hearing was fading. What if Nina opened the door and said something, said some important thing, and he didn't know what she was saying? His eyes hurt too much to concentrate on reading her lips. Her lips. Nina. He knocked on the door, and he smiled. He heard something. From inside, he heard water running. And then he knocked again, and then she was there: he could see her breasts almost down to the nipples. She had on the robe she had given him, and when she spoke, he heard what she said. He saw the man, standing to the side. For an awkward second, nobody said anything. He looked behind him and saw the stairs. When he blinked, they stopped slowly swaying.

* * *

He called Nina at Lord and Taylor's to tell her that Louise had called, and that he thought she was going to ask for a divorce. He changed his mind about telling her, though, and he was half glad when he was connected with the wrong person. He knew that Nina thought he was a coward. "A wise coward," she said, qualifying it. "I don't know that I'd walk out on a family." She had had dreams, when they first met, that she was bobbing in the water along with Louise and John Joel and Brandt and Mary, and that he was in a boat only large enough to take one of them on board. Sometimes he would reach for her, sometimes Louise, sometimes one of the children. She would tread water for what seemed like hours. And then she would dream the rest of it: No matter who he reached for, everything got blurry, and then she was somewhere looking down, puzzled because what was in the boat was a starfish, or a sea nettle, a sea anemone, a water lily, a conch shell. Some small, beautiful sea creature would be in the boat with him. She had told him the dream in early May, the second time they had gone away together, to Nick's sister's house in Provincetown. High up on one of the dunes, a bright day with still an edge of winter, she had suddenly remembered, looking out at the water, her peculiar dreams about the drifting boat, the outstretched arm. They had sat on top of one of the dunes, the beach deserted, and she had told him about it, shaking her head in embarrassment, because the dream obviously meant that she thought he could save her. He had made light of it. The truth was that he did not think of her as someone who needed saving. He thought that she could save *him*, that her light grip on his arm, as they sat on top of the dune, was anchoring his body to the earth. Who *would* he really save if they were all in the water? He thought that he would try to haul all of them into the boat, too ashamed to claim the one he really wanted. She was right: He was a coward. He kicked a little sand down the slope and watched it gather more with it and go like a trickle of water until it stopped. Now the shape of the dune was different, though no one else would notice. He looked at it. He couldn't look at her. He didn't know what to say when she was so honest. He didn't know how to say, simply, okay, if you think that having me will save you, you can have me. If he could really have believed that he would be leaving Louise and the children to save *her*, then he probably would have done it instantly, but he was sure that he was leaving to save himself. She thought she couldn't cope very well with things, but she could. She was more complicated than she knew. She dreamed questions while he dreamed answers: In the morning her questions were still good, but his answers were simple, facile. They didn't apply. Later that day he and Nina had gone back to the house, sure that everyone would know that they had made love, and Nick had been in the kitchen with Laurie, who was his girl then, scrubbing clean a bucket of mussels. They had had a stew made of mussels and shrimp, and they had all gotten a little drunk on ale. Nick's sister had a movie projector, and they had watched *Dial M for Murder* after dinner, and then gone for a walk along the beach. Nick's straw hat had blown off, and Laurie had chased it into the cold, black water. When she retrieved it, she shook it and put it on, holding the hat with one hand, and Nick's hand with her other. Back at the house, Nick had talked about living with people who mattered to you: having some huge, grand house somewhere by the sea, and all your good friends living in the house. There couldn't be any cats, because he hated cats; but there could be dogs, hundreds of collies, poking their long snouts into everything, miracle collies that would go to the beach to sniff out mussels and come up with truffles instead. Truffles would roll around the huge house like billiard balls. They would play indoor miniature golf with truffles. Nick's sister had sighed. She was just back from France, and had made the mistake of telling him about the white truffle she had brought back with her. The next afternoon they had eaten it, grated over pasta. When they left on Sunday night, they were high on nothing but the good time they had had. He and Nick had bought a present for Nick's sister at a greenhouse they walked to early Sunday morning: a plant with pink and silver leaves. He remembered driving a nail into the top of her window frame, and Nick standing below him, handing up the plant. Those wide, tall windows, the view of grapevines and poison ivy just starting to leaf out, clots of tangled green pouring over rocks and onto the sand behind the house. And then the way that scene had looked later, when it was almost dark: the way the vines turned and tangled had reminded him of some nightmare creature crawling toward him, all legs and arms and lumpy greenness. He had jumped when Nina touched him from behind. He hadn't known she was there. She had complained — jokingly, but she had also been serious — that he never let her out of his sight. That was Nina: She thought he was her salvation, and she didn't want him around all the time. What Nick had said earlier about a group of friends living together had really touched him; he talked to Nina about it, standing at the darkening window. It was so nice to see plants outside, instead of a parade of retards; it was so nice to be able to breathe clean air. "You'd never make it living this way," she had said. "You'd be like Thoreau, going home to get his wash done."

* * *

He hated to talk to her on the telephone and always had. That night he had made a fool of himself by blurting out: "Listen — do you want any donuts?" When he called her at work she could never reply to what he said, and what he said was never what he meant to say. Someone was always standing behind him waiting for the phone; or he'd call from the office and he'd hear her voice and realize how bleak his surroundings were, and overwhelmed by that, would be unable to talk. Or at phones along the highway: He'd know the road was out there and he could never put it out of his mind. There were always dark spaces, highways, impatient people — something to make what he was saying, or trying to say, not make sense. He would call and tell her he loved her as someone pushed change into a vending machine. Something they wanted would be falling through the machine — a soft drink or a candy bar — and his eye would wander, and it would seem that everything was so mundane, that his words couldn't carry any conviction. He woke her up more than he should. He would get obsessed with calling her. At night, in New York, he would tear himself away from her, and then he would stop to call three times before he got back to Rye and then call again from the dark hallway, whispering like a criminal who had broken into the house. He would talk to her about love, standing in the dark of his mother's house, feeling like a child who couldn't possibly know what he was saying. Then, sometimes, he would explain to her, when she was sleepy and perturbed, why he knew he wasn't getting through to her: Suddenly he would be telling her something that wasn't about the two of them at all, but about his mother and father, some memory, or he would describe the place he was calling from, his hand nervously touching the phone, putting his finger into the dial, touching inside the 1, the 2, the 3, his finger probing the phone as if one circle might be the right one, and somehow he would really connect with her. Again and again, standing in the same place, late at night, in the dark, Henri the poodle staring and panting as he whispered, he would hear her voice and his finger would start to move, as though the phone were a Ouija board. Or sometimes he would know that he had awakened her and say nothing about love, say only that he was sorry for having made her get up to answer the phone. Once he had called her from a phone outside the parking garage — he had left her apartment, so upset about leaving that he had walked for half an hour instead of taking a cab — and there was something wrong with the phone. He had had to put four dimes in before he made the connection, and when she answered, he had only been able to tell her that he had walked, that there was a phone out of order in New York. Then he had stared at a couple walking by; he had held the phone tightly in one hand, his claim check for his car in the other, and he remembered thinking that if he let the phone go, he was going to disappear. He had dropped endless nickels into the phone and kept her talking for an hour. She didn't understand about him and the phone. He tried to explain it to her in person, but even then he never really got through. At first when he would leave and call her half an hour later, an hour later, she got angry and accused him of being paranoid and checking on her. She had first said that to him on the phone, and he couldn't deal with criticism on the phone: He would just lose his words, and be silent, and then she would think that he had gone, and he would panic, thinking: Please don't hang up. Think I'm not here, but please don't hang up. It was only in the movies that you could jiggle the cradle of a telephone up and down saying three or four times "Hello? Hello?" and still be connected. He couldn't stand it, either, if she joked on the phone. Once, five minutes after he had left her, he had called and told her he loved her and she had said, sounding genuinely confused, "Who is this?" He would seek out phones because they connected him to her, knowing all the time that that was an illusion: a piece of black plastic, his hand on a piece of black plastic miles away from her hand. How could he think he was touching her? He would call her and imagine her standing there, holding the telephone. She was used to all of it by now. She said "That's okay" reflexively when he said he was sorry for waking her; she would tell him without protest whether she was sitting or standing, wearing clothes or pajamas: whatever he wanted to know. She had said to him, early on, that maybe it would be better if they didn't talk on the telephone, and he had been amazed that she hadn't understood: It was like admitting that they were defeated. They were already separated too much, and the phone was a false link, but still a link. "You wouldn't not answer your phone, would you?" he had said. "Maybe if you didn't look around you when you called," she said, "you could concentrate on what you wanted to say." So he had closed his eyes, holding the phone against his ear, everything black. She had given him a toy telephone for Christmas, her face glued in the center, smiling a big smile. When you dialed the phone, a childish voice would say: "I am five, how old are you?" Dial again, and the voice would say: "Will you be my friend?" He knew that it was funny, but it also wasn't funny: It was his nightmare telephone, the telephone on which you couldn't say what you wanted, on which words were just words and went nowhere. He had given the toy telephone to Nick to give his son. He would have given it to Brandt, but he didn't even want it around. The little circular picture was in his desk drawer. It reminded him of the telephone, and it was the one picture of Nina he didn't really like to look at. But he kept it. It was there. Until Nina had shown him, he had never thought about his favorite sleeping position: on his side, with one arm along his body, the other arm raised, fingers curled, just below the ear. In bed one night, she had faced him, imitating his position, and said, "Hello, John? Everything all right?"

He opened his eyes and saw that she was on the bed facing him now, and he wanted to rouse himself to console her. But his body felt heavy — the sudden heaviness you feel when you've been treading water and are about to sink, a signal from your body that it wasn't worth it to fight anymore. He was lying on his back, hot and heavy on the mattress, and she was on her side, supporting herself on one arm, her free hand resting on the sheet. If she were to put her hand on him, that little bit of added weight would push him under. He looked at her hand, and not at her face. It was such a small hand, the fingers long and thin — he had forgotten if he had ever held such a hand when he was young, when his own hand was smaller.

She had once said that he was a coward. Cowardly to leave his family and not totally cut the tie. Cowardly to go, and cowardly to return, and all the time he was in Connecticut feeling heavy — his heart heavy. He felt old, and more tired than he felt when he was physically tired, driving home late to his mother's house in Rye. The truth was that he didn't have much grace. He could have eased Louise into discussions, but he hadn't. Louise could still take him by surprise, and he was afraid of that. The only thing that had taken him by surprise that had been a good surprise, a surprise he could deal with, had been Nina. When she had opened the door and he had seen the man standing there, he had misunderstood, in a flash, what kind of scene he had walked in on; and he had only been able to stand there, as stunned as he was when somebody pulled a trick on him on the telephone, unable to think about what was happening but staring at her breast, the robe fallen away so that he saw the curve of her breast almost to the nipple. He had no idea what he would have done or said if she had not spoken. He could imagine standing there still.

At the hospital, it had seemed that he was watching the action from a great distance, as if he were standing outside a dance hall where strobe lights were flashing. The hospital had seemed garishly bright, and he had closed his eyes often, needing to rest them. When he opened them, he would get a flash of something new, something he would only see quickly: the blood-covered shirt, the notebook that was open and then closed, a needle going into Louise's arm. When he blinked the needle had been pulled out; Louise had been standing and then she was sitting. He saw people but not groups of people; a nurse's hand, but not the nurse's body. His son, in a white bed: For a second he had seen all of him, a little boy in a bed, but then he had seen only his eyes. John Joel had said that Mary was a bitch. His mouth had moved, but nothing else, and he had wanted to move toward him, but the nurse had stepped in. He blinked, and then the nurse was between him and his son, and he was staring at her hand, turning. The corridor stretched before him, long and narrow and bright; and from there, somehow, to the inside of the car, with Louise on the seat beside him. Then he managed to focus on the important things, one by one: key in ignition, hand on wheel, foot on accelerator. He had gotten to New York the same way. He had not seen the whole backyard, but only the tree under which it had happened; and then he had seen his car, gotten into the car, and from there to New York it was a series of simple, mechanical movements. They tell you when you are learning to drive not to stare straight ahead, but to take in what is happening around you. Next to him was an empty seat. He looked at his hands on the wheel, then through the windshield, and then at the speedometer: He watched the needle climb and climb until he was going the right speed. He knew that he was falling asleep, and that he shouldn't sleep. Her hand was on his chest, but he had been wrong — it was inadequate to hold him down. He wasn't heavy, as he had thought, but light, speeding.

"What's the matter?" she said, when he sprang up from the bed.

He stood in the room, shaking sleep out of his head. He had to go back, but he was afraid to move out of the room, afraid to move from the spot he stood in. Nina was standing beside him, pulling his arm the way Brandt did, but she had more power. She could lead him back to the bed. He blinked, and he was sitting on the bed, Nina's arm around his shoulder, Nina pressing up against him. She was crying. He talked to her, said words, said something, but she kept on crying. Talking to her was as futile as trying to get to the top of the stairs. Time had stopped. He was telling her that they were stopped, and she was shaking her head no. She didn't believe him? He decided to trust her. He smiled and pulled her down on the bed with him. If time hadn't stopped, then it was safe to sleep, and when he woke up things would go on. It was possible that things could go on. If he slept, it did not mean that he would sleep forever.

"What are you going to do?" she said.

He thought that she knew him so well that she had read his mind. He thought she was asking him whether or not he was going to stay awake.

On his side, next to her in the bright room, he slept.

Raymond Carver

The Bridle

THIS OLD STATION wagon with Minnesota plates pulls into a parking space in front of the window. There's a man and woman in the front seat, two boys in the back. It's July, temperature's one hundred plus. These people look whipped. There are clothes hanging inside; suitcases, boxes, and such piled in back. From what Harley and I put together later, that's all they had left after the bank in Minnesota took their house, their pickup, their tractor, the farm implements, and a few cows.

The people inside sit for a minute, as if collecting themselves. The air-conditioner in our apartment is going full blast. Harley's around in back cutting grass. There's some discussion in the front seat, and then she and him get out and start for the front door. I pat my hair to make sure that it's in place and wait till they push the doorbell for the second time. Then I go to let them in. "You're looking for an apartment?" I say. "Come on in here where it's cool." I show them into the living room. The living room is where I do business. It's where I collect the rents, write the receipts, and talk to interested parties. I also do hair. I call myself a *stylist*. That's what my cards say. I don't like the word *beautician*. It's an old-time word. I have the chair in a corner of the living room, and a dryer I can pull up to the back of the chair. And there's a sink that Harley put in a few years ago. Alongside the chair, I have a table with some magazines. The magazines are old. The covers are gone from some of them. But people will look at anything while they're under the dryer.

The man says his name.

"My name is Holits."

He tells me she's his wife. But she won't look at me. She looks at her nails instead. She and Holits won't sit down, either. He says they're interested in one of the furnished units.

"How many of you?" But I'm just saying what I always say. I know how many. I saw the two boys in the back seat. Two and two is four.

"Me and her and the boys. The boys are thirteen and fourteen, and they'll share a room, like always."

She has her arms crossed and is holding the sleeves of her blouse. She takes in the chair and the sink as if she's never seen their like before. Maybe she hasn't.

"I do hair," I say.

She nods. Then she gives my prayer plant the once-over. It has exactly five leaves to it.

"That needs watering," I say. I go over and touch one of its leaves. "Everything around here needs water. There's not enough water in the air. It rains three times a year if we're lucky. But you'll get used to it. We had to get used to it. But everything here is air-conditioned."

"How much is the place?" Holits wants to know.

I tell him and he turns to her to see what she thinks. But he may as well have been looking at the wall. She won't give him back his look. "I guess we'll have you show us," he says. So I move to get the key for 17, and we go outside.

I hear Harley before I see him.

Then he comes into sight between the buildings. He's moving along behind the power mower in his Bermudas and T-shirt, wearing the straw hat he bought in Nogales. He spends his time cutting grass and doing the small maintenance work. We work for a corporation, Fulton Terrace, Inc. They own the place. If anything major goes wrong, like air-conditioning trouble or something serious in the plumbing department, we have a list of phone numbers.

I wave. I have to. Harley takes a hand off the mower handle and signals. Then he pulls the hat down over his forehead and gives his attention back to what he's doing. He comes to the end of his cut, makes his turn, and starts back toward the street.

"That's Harley." I have to shout it. We go in at the side of the building and up some stairs. "What kind of work are you in, Mr. Holits?" I ask him.

"He's a farmer," she says.

"No more."

"Not much to farm around here." I say it without thinking.

"We had us a farm in Minnesota. Raised wheat. A few cattle. And Holits knows horses. He knows everything there is about horses."

"That's all right, Betty."

I get a piece of the picture then. Holits is unemployed. It's not my affair, and I feel sorry if that's the case — it is, it turns out — but as we stop in front of the unit, I have to say something. "If you decide, it's first month, last month, and one-fifty as security deposit." I look down at the pool as I say it. Some people are sitting in deck chairs, and there's somebody in the water.

Holits wipes his face with the back of his hand. Harley's mower is clacking away. Farther off, cars speed by on Calle Verde. The two boys have got out of the station wagon. One of them is standing at military attention, legs together, arms at his sides. But as I watch, I see him begin to flap his arms up and down and jump, like he intends to take off and fly. The other one is squatting down on the driver's side of the station wagon, doing knee bends.

I turn to Holits.

"Let's have a look," he says.

I turn the key and the door opens. It's just a little two-bedroom furnished apartment. Everybody has seen dozens. Holits stops in the bathroom long enough to flush the toilet. He watches till the tank fills. Later, he says, "This could be our room." He's talking about the bedroom that looks out over the pool. In the kitchen, the woman takes hold of the edge of the drainboard and stares out the window.

"That's the swimming pool," I say.

She nods. "We stayed in some motels that had swimming pools. But in one pool they had too much chlorine in the water."

I wait for her to go on. But that's all she says. I can't think of anything else, either.

"I guess we won't waste any more time. I guess we'll take it." Holits look at her as he says it. This time she meets his eyes. She nods. He lets out breath through his teeth. Then she does something. She begins snapping her fingers. One hand is still holding the edge of the drainboard, but with her other hand she begins snapping her fingers. Snap, snap, snap, like she was calling her dog, or else trying to get somebody's attention. Then she stops and runs her nails across the counter.

I don't know what to make of it. Holits doesn't either. He moves his feet.

"We'll walk back to the office and make things official," I say. "I'm glad."

I *was* glad. We had a lot of empty units for this time of year. And these people seemed like dependable people. Down on their luck, that's all. No disgrace can be attached to that.

Holits pays in cash — first, last, and the one-fifty deposit. He counts out bills of fifty-dollar denomination while I watch. U.S. Grants, Harley calls them, though he's never seen many. I write out the receipt and give him two keys. "You're all set."

He looks at the keys. He hands her one. "So, we're in Arizona. Never thought you'd see Arizona, did you?"

She shakes her head. She's touching one of the prayer-plant leaves.

"Needs water," I say.

She lets go of the leaf and turns to the window. I go over next to her. Harley is still cutting grass. But he's around in front now. There's been this talk of farming, so for a minute I think of Harley moving along behind a plow instead of behind his Black and Decker power mower.

I watch them unload their boxes, suitcases, and clothes. Holits carries in something that has straps hanging from it. It takes a minute, but then I figure out it's a bridle. I don't know what to do next. I don't feel like doing anything. So I take the Grants out of the cashbox. I just put them in there, but I take them out again. The bills have come from Minnesota. Who knows where they'll be this time next week? They could be in Las Vegas. All I know about Las Vegas is what I see on TV — about enough to put into a thimble. I can imagine one of the Grants finding its way out to Waikiki Beach, or else some other place. Miami or New York City. New Orleans. I think about one of those bills changing hands during Mardi Gras. They could go anyplace, and anything could happen because of them. I write my name in ink across Grant's broad old forehead: MARGE. I print it. I do it on every one. Right over his thick brows. People will stop in the midst of their spending and wonder. Who's this Marge? That's what they'll ask themselves, Who's this Marge?

Harley comes in from outside and washes his hands in my sink. He knows it's something I don't like him to do. But he goes ahead and does it anyway.

"Those people from Minnesota," he says. "The Swedes. They're a long way from home." He dries his hands on a paper towel. He wants me to tell him what I know. But I don't know anything. They don't look like Swedes and they don't talk like Swedes.

"They're not Swedes," I tell him. But he acts like he doesn't hear me.

"So what's he do?"

"He's a farmer."

"What do you know about that?"

Harley takes his hat off and puts it on my chair. He runs a hand through his hair. Then he looks at the hat and puts it on again. He may as well be glued to it. "There's not much to farm around here. Did you tell him that?" He gets a can of soda pop from the fridge and goes to sit in his recliner. He picks up the remote-control, pushes something, and the TV sizzles on. He pushes some more buttons until he finds what he's looking for. It's a hospital show. "What else does the Swede do? Besides farm?"

I don't know, so I don't say anything. But Harley's already taken up with his program. He's probably forgotten he asked me the question. A siren goes off. I hear the screech of tires. On the screen, an ambulance has come to a stop in front of an emergency-room entrance, its red lights flashing. A man jumps out and runs around to open up the back.

The next afternoon the boys borrow the hose and wash the station wagon. They clean the outside and the inside. A little later I notice her drive away. She's wearing high heels and a nice dress. Hunting up a job, I'd say. After a while, I see the boys messing around the pool in their bathing suits. One of them springs off the board and swims all the way to the other end underwater. He comes up blowing water and shaking his head. The other boy, the one who'd been doing knee bends the day before, lies on his stomach on a towel at the far side of the pool. But this one boy keeps swimming back and forth from one end of the pool to the other, touching the wall and turning back with a little kick.

There are two other people out there. They're in lounge chairs, one on either side of the pool. One of them is Irving Cobb, a cook at Denny's. He calls himself Spuds. People have taken to calling him that, Spuds, instead of Irv or some other nickname. Spuds is fifty-five and bald. He already looks like beef jerky, but he wants more sun. Right now, his new wife, Linda Cobb, is at work at the K Mart. Spuds works nights. But him and Linda Cobb have it arranged so they take their Saturdays and Sundays off. Connie Nova is in the other chair. She's sitting up and rubbing lotion on her legs. She's nearly naked — just this little two-piece suit covering her. Connie Nova is a cocktail waitress. She moved in here six months ago with her so-called fiance, an alcoholic lawyer. But she got rid of him. Now she lives with a long-haired student from the college whose name is Rick. I happen to know he's away right now, visiting his folks. Spuds and Connie are wearing dark glasses. Connie's portable radio is going.

Spuds was a recent widower when he moved in, a year or so back. But after a few months of being a bachelor again, he got married to Linda. She's a red-haired woman in her thirties. I don't know how they met. But one night a couple of months ago Spuds and the new Mrs. Cobb had Harley and me over to a nice dinner that Spuds fixed. After dinner, we sat in their living room drinking sweet drinks out of big glasses. Spuds asked if we wanted to see home movies. We said sure. So Spuds set up his screen and projector. Linda Cobb poured us more of that sweet drink. Where's the harm? I asked myself. Spuds began to show films of a trip he and his dead wife had made to Alaska. It began with her getting on the plane in Seattle. Spuds talked as he ran the projector. The deceased was in her fifties, good-looking, though maybe a little heavy. Her hair was nice.

"That's Spud's first wife," Linda Cobb said. "That's the first Mrs. Cobb."

"That's Evelyn," Spuds said.

The first wife stayed on the screen for a long time. It was funny seeing her and hearing them talk about her like that. Harley passed me a look, so I know he was thinking something, too. Linda Cobb asked if we wanted another drink or a macaroon. We didn't. Spuds was saying something about the first Mrs. Cobb again. She was still at the entrance to the plane, smiling and moving her mouth even if all you could hear was the film going through the projector. People had to go around her to get on the plane. She kept waving at the camera, waving at us there in Spuds's living room. She waved and waved. "There's Evelyn again," the new Mrs. Cobb would say each time the first Mrs. Cobb appeared on the screen.

Spuds would have shown films all night, but we said we had to go. Harley made the excuse.

I don't remember what he said.

Connie Nova is lying on her back in the chair, dark glasses covering half of her face. Her legs and stomach shine with oil. One night, not long after she moved in, she had a party. This was before she kicked the lawyer out and took up with the longhair. She called her party a housewarming. Harley and I were invited, along with a bunch of other people. We went, but we didn't care for the company. We found a place to sit close to the door, and that's where we stayed till we left. It wasn't all that long, either. Connie's boyfriend was giving a door prize. It was the offer of his legal services, without charge, for the handling of a divorce. Anybody's divorce. Anybody who wanted to could draw a card out of the bowl he was passing around. When the bowl came our way, everybody began to laugh. Harley and I swapped glances. I didn't draw. Harley didn't draw, either. But I saw him look in the bowl at the pile of cards. Then he shook his head and handed the bowl to the person next to him. Even Spuds and the new Mrs. Cobb drew cards. The winning card had something written across the back. "Entitles bearer to one free uncontested divorce," and the lawyer's signature and the date. The lawyer was a drunk, but I say this is no way to conduct your life. Everybody but us had put his hand into the bowl, like it was a fun thing to do. The woman who drew the winning card clapped. It was like one of those game shows. "Goddamn, this is the first time I ever won anything!" I was told she had a husband in the military. There's no way of knowing if she still has him, or if she got her divorce, because Connie Nova took up with a different set of friends after she and the lawyer went their separate ways.

We left the party right after the drawing. It made such an impression we couldn't say much, except one of us said, "I don't believe I saw what I think I saw."

Maybe I said it.

A week later Harley asks if the Swede — he means Holits — has found work yet. We've just had lunch, and Harley's in his chair with his can of pop. But he hasn't turned his TV on. I say I don't know. And I don't. I wait to see what else he has to say. But he doesn't say anything else. He shakes his head. He seems to think about something. Then he pushes a button and the TV comes to life.

She finds a job. She starts working as a waitress in an Italian restaurant a few blocks from here. She works a split shift, doing lunches and then going home, then back to work again in time for the dinner shift. She's meeting herself coming and going. The boys swim all day, while Holits stays inside the apartment. I don't know what he does in there. Once, I did her hair and she told me a few things. She told me she did waitressing when she was just out of high school and that's where she met Holits. She served him some pancakes in a place back in Minnesota.

She'd walked down that morning and asked me could I do her a favor. She wanted me to fix her hair after the lunch shift and have her out in time for her dinner shift. Could I do it? I told her I'd check the book. I asked her to step inside. It must have been a hundred degrees already.

"I know it's short notice," she said. "But when I came in from work last night, I looked in the mirror and saw my roots showing. I said to myself, 'I need a treatment.' I don't know where else to go."

I find Friday, August 14. There's nothing on the page.

"I could work you in at two-thirty, or else at three o'clock," I say.

"Three would be better," she says. "I have to run for it now before I'm late. I work for a real bastard. See you later."

At two-thirty, I tell Harley I have a customer, so he'll have to take his baseball game into the bedroom. He grumps, but he winds up the cord and wheels the set out back. He closes the door. I make sure everything I need is ready. I fix up the magazines so they're easy to get to. Then I sit next to the dryer and file my nails. I'm wearing the rose-colored uniform that I put on when I do hair. I go on filing my nails and looking up at the window from time to time.

She walks by the window and then pushes the doorbell. "Come on in," I call. "It's unlocked."

She's wearing the black-and-white uniform from her job. I can see how we're both wearing uniforms. "Sit down, honey, and we'll get started." She looks at the nail file. "I give manicures, too," I say.

She settles into the chair and draws a breath.

I say, "Put your head back. That's it. Close your eyes now, why don't you? Just relax. First I'll shampoo you and touch up these roots. Then we'll go from there. How much time do you have?"

"I have to be back there at five-thirty."

"We'll get you fixed up."

"I can eat at work. But I don't know what Holits and the boys will do for their supper."

"They'll get along fine without you."

I start the warm water and then notice Harley's left me some dirt and grass. I wipe up his mess and start over.

I say, "If they want, they can just walk down the street to the hamburger place. It won't hurt them."

"They won't do that. Anyway, I don't want them to have to go there."

It's none of my business, so I don't say any more. I make up a nice lather and go to work. After I've done the shampoo, rinse, and set, I put her under the dryer. Her eyes have closed. I think she could be asleep. So I take one of her hands and begin.

"No manicure." She opens her eyes and pulls away her hand.

"It's all right, honey. The first manicure is always no charge."

She gives me back her hand and picks up one of the magazines and rests it in her lap. "They're his boys," she says. "From his first marriage. He was divorced when we met. But I love them like they were my own. I couldn't love them any more if I tried. Not even if I was their natural mother."

I turn the dryer down a notch so that it's making a low, quiet sound. I keep on with her nails. Her hand starts to relax.

"She lit out on them, on Holits and the boys, on New Year's Day ten years ago. They never heard from her again." I can see she wants to tell me about it. And that's fine with me. They like to talk when they're in the chair. I go on using the file. "Holits got the divorce. Then he and I started going out. Then we got married. For a long time, we had us a life. It had its ups and downs. But we thought we were working toward something." She shakes her head. "But something happened. Something happened to Holits, I mean. One thing happened was he got interested in horses. This one particular race horse, he bought it, you know — something down, something each month. He took it around to the tracks. He was still up before daylight, like always, still doing the chores and such. I thought everything was all right. But I don't know anything. If you want the truth, I'm not so good at waiting tables. I think those wops would fire me at the drop of a hat, if I gave them a reason. Or for no reason. What if I got fired? Then what?"

I say, "Don't worry, honey. They're not going to fire you."

Pretty soon she picks up another magazine. But she doesn't open it. She just holds it and goes on talking. "Anyway, there's this horse of his. Fast Betty. The Betty part is a joke. But he says it can't help but be a winner if he names it after me. A big winner, all right. The fact is, wherever it ran, it lost. Every race. Betty Longshot — that's what it should have been called. In the beginning, I went to a few races. But the horse always ran ninety-nine to one. Odds like that. But Holits is stubborn if he's anything. He wouldn't give up. He'd bet on the horse and bet on the horse. Twenty dollars to win. Fifty dollars to win. Plus all the other things it costs for keeping a horse. I know it don't sound like a large amount. But it adds up. And when the odds were like that — ninety-nine to one, you know — sometimes he'd buy a combination ticket. He'd ask me if I realized how much money we'd make if the horse came in. But it didn't, and I quit going."

I keep on with what I'm doing. I concentrate on her nails. "You have nice cuticles," I say. "Look here at your cuticles. See these little half-moons? Means your blood's good."

She brings her hand up close and looks. "What do you know about that?" She shrugs. She lets me take her hand again. She's still got things to tell. "Once, when I was in high school, a counselor asked me to come to her office. She did it with all the girls, one of us at a time. 'What dreams do you have?' this woman asked me. 'What do you see yourself doing in ten years? Twenty years?' I was sixteen or seventeen. I was just a kid. I couldn't think what to answer. I just sat there like a lump. This counselor was about the age I am now. I thought she was *old*. She's old, I said to myself. I knew *her* life was half over. And I felt like I knew something she didn't. Something she'd never know. A secret. Something nobody's supposed to know, or ever talk about. So I stayed quiet. I just shook my head. She must've written me off as a dope. But I couldn't say anything. You know what I mean? I thought I knew things she couldn't guess at.

Now, if anybody asked me that question again, about my dreams and all, I'd tell them."

"What would you tell them, honey?" I have her other hand now. But I'm not doing her nails. I'm just holding it, waiting to hear.

She moves forward in the chair. She tries to take her hand back.

"What would you tell them?"

She sighs and leans back. She lets me keep the hand. "I'd say, 'Dreams, you know, are what you wake up from.' That's what I'd say." She smooths the lap of her skirt. "If anybody asked, that's what I'd say. But they won't ask." She lets out her breath again. "So how much longer?" she says.

"Not long," I say.

"You don't know what it's like."

"Yes, I do," I say. I pull the stool right up next to her legs. I'm starting to tell how it was before we moved here, and how it's still like that. But Harley picks right then to come out of the bedroom. He doesn't look at us. I hear the TV jabbering away in the bedroom. He goes to the sink and draws a glass of water. He tips his head back to drink. His Adam's apple moves up and down in his throat.

I move the dryer away and touch the hair at both sides of her head. I lift one of the curls just a little.

I say, "You look brand-new, honey."

"Don't I wish."

The boys keep on swimming all day, every day, till their school starts. Betty keeps on at her job. But for some reason she doesn't come back to get her hair done. I don't know why this is. Maybe she doesn't think I did a good job. Sometimes I lie awake, Harley sleeping like a grindstone beside me, and try to picture myself in Betty's shoes. I wonder what I'd do then.

Holits sends one of his sons with the rent on the first of September, and on the first of October, too. He still pays in cash. I take the money from the boy, count the bills right there in front of him, and then write out the receipt. Holits has found work of some sort. I think so, anyway. He drives off every day with the station wagon. I see him leave early in the morning and drive back late in the afternoon. She goes past the window at ten-thirty and comes back at three. If she sees me, she gives me a little wave. But she's not smiling. Then I see Betty again at five, walking back to the restaurant. Holits drives in a little later. This goes on till the middle of October.

Meanwhile, the Holits couple acquainted themselves with Connie Nova and her long-hair friend, Rick. And they also met up with Spuds and the new Mrs. Cobb. Sometimes, on a Sunday afternoon, I'd see all of them sitting around the pool, drinks in their hands, listening to Connie's portable radio. One time Harley said he saw them all behind the building, in the barbecue area. They were in their bathing suits then, too. Harley said the Swede had a chest like a bull. Harley said they were eating hot dogs and drinking whiskey. He said they were drunk.

It was Saturday, and it was after eleven at night. Harley was asleep in his chair. Pretty soon I'd have to get up and turn off the set. When I did that, I knew he'd wake up. "Why'd you turn it off? I was watching that show." That's what he'd say. That's what he always said. Anyway, the TV was going, I had the curlers in, and there's a magazine on my lap. Now and then I'd look up. But I couldn't get settled on the show. They were all out there in the pool area — Spuds and Linda Cobb, Connie Nova and the long-hair, Holits and Betty. We have a rule against anyone being out there after ten. But this night they didn't care about rules. If Harley woke up, he'd go out and say something. I felt it was all right for them to have their fun, but it was time for it to stop. I kept getting up and going over to the window. All of them except Betty had on bathing suits. She was still in her uniform. But she had her shoes off, a glass in her hand, and she was drinking right along with the rest of them. I kept putting off having to turn off the set. Then one of them shouted something, and another took it up and began to laugh. I looked and saw Holits finish off his drink. He put the glass down on the deck. Then he walked over to the cabana. He dragged up one of the tables and climbed onto that. Then — he seemed to do it without any effort at all — he lifted up onto the roof of the cabana. It's true, I thought; he's strong. The long-hair claps his hands, like he's all for this. The rest of them are hooting Holits on, too. I know I'm going to have to go out there and put a stop to it.

Harley's slumped in his chair. The TV's still going. I ease the door open, step out, and then push it shut behind me. Holits is up on the roof of the cabana. They're egging him on. They're saying, "Go on, you can do it." "Don't bellyflop, now." "I double-dare you." Things like that.

Then I hear Betty's voice. "Holits, think what you're doing." But Holits just stands there at the edge. He looks down at the water. He seems to be figuring how much of a run he's going to have to make to get out there. He backs up to the far side. He spits in his palm and rubs his hands together. Spuds calls out, "That's it, boy! You'll do it now."

I see him hit the deck. I hear him, too.

"Holits!" Betty cries.

They all hurry over to him. By the time I get there, he's sitting up. Rick is holding him by the shoulders and yelling into his face. "Holits! Hey, man!"

Holits has this gash on his forehead, and his eyes are glassy. Spuds and Rick help him into a chair. Somebody gives him a towel. But Holits holds the towel like he doesn't know what he's supposed to do with it. Somebody else hands him a drink. But Holits doesn't know what to do with that, either. People keep saying things to him. Holits brings the towel up to his face. Then he takes it away and looks at the blood. But he just looks at it. He can't seem to understand anything.

"Let me see him." I get around in front of him. It's bad. "Holits, are you all right?" But Holits just looks at me, and then his eyes drift off. "I think he'd best go to the emergency room." Betty looks at me when I say this and begins to shake her head. She looks back at Holits. She gives him another towel. I think she's sober. But the rest of them are drunk. Drunk is the best that can be said for them.

Spuds picks up what I said. "Let's take him to the emergency room."

Rick says, "I'll go, too."

"We'll all go," Connie Nova says.

"We better stick together," Linda Cobb says.

"Holits." I say his name again.

"I can't go it," Holits says.

"What'd he say?" Connie Nova asks me.

"He said he can't go it," I tell her.

"Go what? What's he talking about?" Rick wants to know.

"Say again?" Spuds says. "I didn't hear."

"He says he can't go it. I don't think he knows what he's talking about. You'd best take him to the hospital," I say. Then I remember Harley and the rules. "You shouldn't have been out here. Any of you. We have rules. Now go on and take him to the hospital."

"Let's take him to the hospital," Spuds says like it's something he's just thought of. He might be farther gone than any of them. For one thing, he can't stand still. He weaves. And he keeps picking up his feet and putting them down again. The hair on his chest is snow white under the overhead pool lights.

"I'll get the car." That's what the long-hair says. "Connie, let me have the keys."

"I can't go it," Holits says. The towel has moved down to his chin. But the cut is on his forehead.

"Get him that terry-cloth robe. He can't go to the hospital that way." Linda Cobb says that. "Holits! Holits, it's us." She waits and then she takes the glass of whiskey from Holits's fingers and drinks from it.

I can see people at some of the windows, looking down on the commotion. Lights are going on. "Go to bed!" someone yells.

Finally, the long-hair brings Connie's Datsun from behind the building and drives it up close to the pool. The headlights are on bright. He races the engine.

"For Christ's sake, go to bed!" the same person yells. More people come to their windows. I expect to see Harley come out any minute, wearing his hat, steaming. Then I think, No, he'll sleep through it. Just forget Harley.

Spuds and Connie Nova get on either side of Holits. Holits can't walk straight. He's wobbly. Part of it's because he's drunk. But there's no question he's hurt himself. They get him into the car, and they all crowd inside, too. Betty is the last to get in. She has to sit on somebody's lap. Then they drive off. Whoever it was that has been yelling slams the window shut.

The whole next week Holits doesn't leave the place. And I think Betty must have quit her job, because I don't see her pass the window anymore. When I see the boys go by, I step outside and ask them, point-blank: "How's your dad?"

"He hurt his head," one of them says.

I wait in hopes they'll say more. But they don't. They shrug and go on to school with their lunch sacks and binders. Later, I was sorry I hadn't asked after their step-mom.

When I see Holits outside, wearing a bandage and standing on his balcony, he doesn't even nod. He acts like I'm a stranger. It's like he doesn't know me or doesn't want to know me. Harley says he's getting the same treatment. He doesn't like it. "What's with him?" Harley wants to know. "Damn Swede. What happened to his head? Somebody belt him or what?" I don't tell Harley anything when he says that. I don't go into it all.

Then that Sunday afternoon I see one of the boys carry out a box and put it in the station wagon. He goes back upstairs. But pretty soon he comes back down with another box, and he puts that in, too. It's then I know they're making ready to leave. But I don't say what I know to Harley. He'll know everything soon enough.

Next morning, Betty sends one of the boys down. He's got a note that says she's sorry but they have to move. She gives me her sister's address in Indio where she says we can send the deposit to. She points out they're leaving eight days before their rent is up. She hopes there might be something in the way of a refund there, even though they haven't given the thirty days' notice. She says, "Thanks for everything. Thanks for doing my hair that time." She signs the note, "Sincerely, Betty Holits."

"What's your name?" I ask the boy.

"Billy."

"Billy, tell her I said I'm real sorry."

Harley reads what she's written, and he says it will be a cold day in hell before they see any money back from Fulton Terrace. He says he can't understand these people. "People who sail through life like the world owes them a living." He asks me where they're going. But I don't have any idea where they're going. Maybe they're going back to Minnesota. How do I know where they're going? But I don't think they're going back to Minnesota. I think they're going someplace else to try their luck.

Connie Nova and Spuds have their chairs in the usual places, one on either side of the pool. From time to time, they look over at the Holits boys carrying things out to the station wagon. Then Holits himself comes out with some clothes over his arm. Connie Nova and Spuds holler and wave. Holits looks at them like he doesn't know them. But then he raises up his free hand. Just raises it, that's all. They wave. Then Holits is waving. He keeps waving at them, even after they've stopped. Betty comes downstairs and touches his arm. She doesn't wave. She won't even look at these people. She says something to Holits, and he goes on to the car. Connie Nova lies back in her chair and reaches over to turn up her portable radio. Spuds holds his sunglasses and watches Holits and Betty for a while. Then he fixes the glasses over his ears. He settles himself in the lounge chair and goes back to tanning his leathery old self.

Finally, they're all loaded and ready to move. The boys are in the back, Holits behind the wheel, Betty in the seat right up next to him. It's just like it was when they drove in here.

"What are you looking at?" Harley says.

He's taking a break. He's in his chair, watching the TV. But he gets up and comes over to the window.

"Well, there they go. They don't know where they're going or what they're going to do. Crazy Swede."

I watch them drive out of the lot and turn onto the road that's going to take them to the freeway. Then I look at Harley again. He's settling into his chair. He has his can of pop, and he's wearing his straw hat. He acts like nothing has happened or ever will happen.

"Harley!"

But, of course, he can't hear me. I go over and stand in front of his chair. He's surprised. He doesn't know what to make of it. He leans back, just sits there looking at me.

The phone starts ringing.

"Get that, will you?" he says.

I don't answer him. Why should I?

"Then let it ring," he says.

I go find the mop, some rags, S.O.S. pads, and a bucket. The phone stops ringing. He's still sitting in his chair. But he's turned off the TV. I take the passkey, go outside and up the stairs to 17. I let myself in and walk through the living room to their kitchen — what used to be their kitchen.

The counters have been wiped down, the sink and cupboards are clean. It's not so bad. I leave the cleaning things on the stove and go take a look at the bathroom. Nothing there a little steel wool won't take care of. Then I open the door to the bedroom that looks out over the pool. The blinds are raised, the bed is stripped. The floor shines. "Thanks," I say out loud. Wherever she's going, I wish her luck. "Good luck, Betty." One of the bureau drawers is open and I go to close it. Back in a corner of the drawer I see the bridle he was carrying in when he first came. It must have been passed over in their hurry. But maybe it wasn't. Maybe the man left it on purpose.

"Bridle," I say. I hold it up to the window and look at it in the light. It's not fancy, it's just an old dark leather bridle. I don't know much about them. But I know that one part of it fits in the mouth. That part's called the bit. It's made of steel. Reins go over the head and up to where they're held on the neck between the fingers. The rider pulls the reins this way and that, and the horse turns. It's simple. The bit's heavy and cold. If you had to wear this thing between your teeth, I guess you'd catch on in a hurry. When you felt it pull, you'd know it was time. You'd know you were going somewhere.

Robb Forman Dew

from

Dale Loves
Sophie
To Death

Housekeeping

MARTIN HAD NO idea that he had accumulated over the years — say all his years past age ten — so many alternatives to an apology. It would have been especially unusual for him to turn to anyone, particularly a woman, and simply say, "I'm sorry." It was not because there was anything of his pride at stake; it was because men have other ways than women do of making amends. Not many men have ever understood how disarming, how unarguable, an admission of guilt and culpability can be. Martin could only stand at the window tap-tapping his fingers on the sill and look out while Claire sat on the floor of his living room, cutting and wrapping and tying ribbons on the presents she had selected for her daughter, Katy. In this instance, anyway, sorrow, or even guilt, might not have been the precise sentiment he would have had to accommodate. Nevertheless, he remained preoccupied. At other times in his life he had rubbed two fingers over his lower lip, abstracted; he had put his hand over the late-evening stubble of his beard and gazed out of some other window to avoid an issue. In none of this behavior was there intentional deceit; there was really only an element of reticence and tradition and simple clumsiness. Martin couldn't have thought of any way to say to Claire that when they had entered his house, and he had watched her spread out the wrapping paper and ribbons and go to work with the tape, his immediate impulse had been finally to put his hands at her waist, with his thumbs pressed against that vulnerable cleft just below her winglike rib cage. It was all he had thought about as he watched her, because over the summer weeks his house had become a neutral territory, empty of his wife and not under the influence of Ellen. Summer after summer, he had experienced the same melancholy during the absence of his family, but his dejection always took him unawares. It had never become a habit. He hadn't caught the knack of nestling gloomily into it so that it might even have been of some use to him. Vic and Ellen had always been his mainstay during the two and a half months his wife and children were away, but never before had he been offered any other distraction than simply that of their calm company. But now, since Claire and Katy had come to live with them, and even the Hofstatters' lives were becoming complicated, he was drawn more and more into a new and separate domesticity.

The souvenirs of Dinah and his children, dispersed throughout his house, had lost their significance, and the usual communal state of the household had gradually elapsed into an entirely personal order controlled only by himself, and he was seldom there. He had taken to sleeping on the couch many nights at the Hofstatters' house in the country and staying in town only on the two days he had to teach. There was so little gas, and the cost of going back and forth was too great. He had forgotten, in some respects, that he was responsible for any house at all. And night after night he had thought about Claire, and he had convinced himself that she expected and desired just what he expected: that at last, like children growing up and leaving home, they could do just as they liked, now that they were alone together. Thus the lingering feeling that he should explain something to her, since they weren't doing anything at all but wrapping packages. But she worked with incurious concentration, and not only could Martin not have said anything to the point or even formulated what was to be said, but his mind adapted with singular beauty to the situation and leaped over his original intentions. He was only looking out the window wondering where they could get all those balloons filled with helium.

He and Claire had waited an hour in line at the gas station to fill Martin's car, and he had expected to be able to have the balloons inflated at the same station, but he had found that they didn't offer that service, and, in any case, this was a poor time to make the request. In answer, he had been given only a vacant stare. But Martin had latched on to the idea of helium balloons for Katy's party, and he was not to be persuaded that they weren't necessary. He had become privately morose, standing against his car waiting for gas and listening to people insult each other. The poor, gangly attendant burst into apprehensive perspiration under the accumulated fury of his customers. In the unusual heat the cars glistened ominously, and Martin even became fearful. All summer he had protected himself from the sudden desperation of a previously complacent society by steeping himself in what he considered to be the remarkable serenity of Ellen's house. It was a balm for his spirit. One could remain convinced, in that carefully contrived environment, of one's relevance in the world. But in that gas line the only things that seemed important, all at once, were fuel and food and sex. And — also — the helium balloons.

He turned to Claire, who was still working with ribbons there on the carpet. "I think we might be able to get them filled at Newberry's," he said.

Claire didn't care about the balloons so much, but she looked at him with an expression of resignation. "Look, why don't I phone first? It's so hot to drive around, and we'll only waste gas. Where's the phone?" Martin showed her through the house into the kitchen and rinsed their beer glasses while she telephoned discount stores and any dime stores she could find listed in the book, but she had no luck. Finally, they gave up and carried all the presents Claire had bought and wrapped out to the car, leaving behind them a litter of tiny slivers of paper and odds and ends of ribbon strewn across the rug where she had been sitting. It hadn't occurred to either of them to sweep them away; the house didn't seem to be anyone's property. Their plan was to take the party, completely assembled, out to the farm, because it had become apparent over the week that Ellen had no intention of making an exception to her habit of noncelebration, even for Claire's daughter, Katy, of whom she was very fond, and who would be five years old on Saturday. In fact, Ellen had seemed cross and edgy all week, and Martin had boxed himself into the position of being Claire's conspirator.

One evening Martin had been sitting down on the grass with Katy and Claire so that they formed a triangle. Katy was talking about her birthday. "Well, Katy," Martin said then, "you're probably feeling very sad. In a few days you'll have the very last evening of ever being four years old. Think of that! It will be the last time you'll look over and see those horses with four-year-old eyes, the last time you'll go swimming in your four-year-old skin. And you'll never wake up four years old again!"

His own children usually took this up wildly: "And the last time I have to go to bed at an eight-year-old hour! The last time I'll get an eight-year-old allowance!" But sitting there in the grass at age thirty-eight, and looking around him at Claire, who was frowning, and Katy, who watched him with alarm, Martin realized what he was saying, and he was ashamed of himself.

"So," he went on, "your mother and I will go into town Saturday morning and buy everything that's simply too old for a four-year-old but just right for someone as old as five. When you still had so long to go before you would be five, I didn't want to tell you how much better it is than being four. You'll be much smarter, and you'll be able to swim faster, of course. And you'll be surprised at how soon you'll even be much taller!" But all the while he talked to Katy with her tiny wedge of a face and wispy, colorless hair like her mother's, he was plagued with sorrow that year after year he had remorselessly inflicted on his own children the desolate message of their mortality. Why had he done that? And as though it were a joke? Perhaps he had thought that they could avoid it if they knew about it, because that was what he wished; they were the repository for all his life's care.

Claire looked up at him, relieved. "If you really would drive me to town on Saturday, it would be a big help. I haven't wanted to ask Ellen or Vic. I'm not so sure they're too enthusiastic about this party."

As a rule, the Hofstatters did not give parties, but their summers went like this: People arrived in the morning or after lunch on some days and didn't leave until late evening. If Vic was at work on his own writing, or if he was going over material for the *Review*, the company might not see him at all. He would have settled himself into the big upstairs bedroom for the day, only appearing now and then to make a sandwich or get some more coffee. If this was the case, the visitors would register their arrivals and departures with Ellen, who moved around the downstairs rooms to attend to many and various small tasks. Sometimes she would sit at her desk in one corner of the dining room and work at her poetry, and then people came and went without disturbing her. The wide front door, mortised in a traditional double-cross pattern, stood open. The central hall was illuminated on sunny days, or if the sky flew with clouds, it was as though the shining wood floor was darkening and lightening of its own accord. The guests arrived dressed to swim, or they changed unabashedly in the long grass at the edge of the pond. Some simply took off what they had on and waded in. It was established that no visitor judged any other as to their apparel.

Some of the company were friends who just came out to enjoy the pond, and others were carpenters or plumbers or rural neighbors who stopped by on farmers' errands. People brought gifts. They brought cakes, tomatoes, cut flowers, books.

Martin had a niche in that house into which he settled customarily, and of which he was the sole occupant. He and Vic could consult each other if need be, but otherwise they could weed in peace through the unsolicited manuscripts sent in to the *Review*. They could work well in the tranquillity of a busy house that nevertheless functions methodically. The two of them could work with the assurance that other things were being taken care of.

Ellen was their protection. She had almost made Martin believe in the feasibility of living a life that was only immediate. One night, as they sat watching the news in the Hofstatters' small sitting room off the kitchen, they had suddenly been confronted with the plight of the Vietnamese boat people set afloat precariously on dozens of swaying, tottering ships. The people were packed so tightly aboard that they could only stand, and they looked out at the camera with apparent apathy. In that instant Martin was overawed by sorrow. His instinct was to cover his ears and close his eyes, although he only sat there looking, filled with hopelessness, and then also affected with fear for his own children, who would be, who must be, eventually, threatened by the world's condition. But Ellen rose from the floor where she had been sitting and turned off the set. She sat back down to the crocheting she was doing, and her features were so bleakly determined in her anger that Vic was surprised into alarm. "Ellen . . ." he began, and Martin, too, thought that she was so saddened that she couldn't bear it.

But, in fact, he hadn't understood. "It's an obscenity," she said, "to have that on the air. What can we *do* about it? Why do we need even to know about it? For God's sake, why do they tell us?"

Anyone could have answered her, and might have if she had not been so angry — and her anger was at the people themselves, all those people crowded on board those bathtublike boats. Martin was shocked; he saw that her empathy was so far away, so isolated from any external influence that she would not be touched. From that moment he would regard her more warily, and yet she had given him a peculiar comfort. She managed to sanction a life lived within the bounds one delineates for it. In some way Martin was absolved of responsibility by her attitude, and yet his affection for her was subtly diminished.

But it was Ellen's determination to live her life within her own house that made Martin's summer a respite from normal cares, and made it a time in which he could do work that was important, for the most part, only to himself. He set himself up in the large living room and spread his material on the coffee table, while he stretched out comfortably over one or the other of the huge, matching butterscotch leather couches. When he and Dinah had first visited this house and sat in this room, Ellen had been very charming and precise in explaining it.

"Well," she said, "when we decided it was time to buy some furniture we were in Boston, and we simply walked into a store that seemed to be completely filled with very swank, leather furniture. You know the sort of store. Chrome lamps and glass tables. There was brown leather, black leather, white leather, beige leather . . . well . . ." She shrugged helplessly. "I became very taken with it all. I just walked around and around that store loving the smell of all that leather, and we bought these two couches and those three armchairs and quilted leather pillows! I was carried away." She tilted her head down with a deprecating smile. "And then, as we were leaving the store — after we had arranged for delivery and so forth — a man was coming in, and I just stopped dead still and put my hand out to make him stay there at the door. I was astonished, you see. I just couldn't grasp it. He had on one of those sports-car hats — suede — and I said, 'But, Vic, we've forgotten the hats! We haven't got any leather hats!'"

Martin and Dinah had been delighted, and a little mesmerized, to discover such furtive and superior humor let loose in their midst, and they were all four complacent in their mutual grasp of each other's wit.

The vast leather sofas continued to be exotic and misplaced there in the living room of the old house, where the floor was still covered with black-and-white linoleum. Sometime during the summer Vic and Martin would pull up those tiles, however, because they had removed a small section and found grand, wide, primitive walnut boards beneath. They would pull up the tiles and strip off the glue and varnish. They would sand the floor and perhaps they would stain it, and then they would cover it over with a final coat of polyurethane. Meanwhile, Martin didn't mind the black-and-white linoleum at all, he was so used to it. And when the heat and humidity grew intense and hung for a long time in the little valley where the Hofstatters lived, Martin pitched in and helped remove the film of greenish mold that blossomed overnight on the exposed surfaces of honey-colored leather.

Each summer Martin accomplished the greatest portion of what he considered to be his work. Not his job, because his job was teaching, and he enjoyed it, but the *Review* was his work. The four of them, Vic and Ellen and Dinah and Martin, had conceived the idea; they had planned it as a collective editorial effort, but both women had drifted away from the project and from each other. Martin had never taken time to ponder this; it hadn't seemed unusual as it had happened. Dinah was increasingly involved with the Artists' Guild shop, and Ellen became more and more wrapped up in her own writing, which she regarded as strictly her own affair. She did not intend it for publication, in any case, so the *Review* could not be a useful instrument for her, and Vic and Martin never even saw her work. She did mail it off to a few friends across the country, and to favored ex-professors. The *Review* became a thing of Vic and Martin's making, and it gave them great satisfaction, but the work was often tedious. So Martin thought of his summer as a time in which he truly labored.

This summer, though, a new intensity of purpose suffused the air like pollen. Ellen moved about these days taut-limbed and with severe and controlled intentions — setting up for herself more and more arduous tasks and insisting on completing them by her own arbitrary schedule. Her tension was picked up by everyone in the household, even the visitors and carpenters and plumbers, who did their work in half the time and departed. Her tension was picked up by all but Claire and Katy. Therefore, Martin gradually realized that there was an eccentric insistence in Ellen's behavior that had as its focus Claire's blithe disregard for the gravity of everyday life. Claire proceeded through each day as need be. Of course, she cooked and ate and cleaned and cared for her daughter. She did all the irritating or pleasant chores of any day, but she went along with comparative frivolity; she never acknowledged or even seemed to think of any long-term goal.

Martin had always watched Ellen with wonder as she ran her household. She laid out her days like playing cards, he thought, so that one felt she must be bound to complete the deck. Each task was carefully thought out in relation to something else. "You know, I can't bear it — it almost makes me ill — to have anything in my house that isn't beautiful of its own accord," she had said to Dinah one night years ago. So she persuaded herself of the beauty of things which had always seemed quite ordinary to Martin. She even insisted that Vic mow the lawn with an old-fashioned push mower she had found in a junk shop, because she said it pleased her by its simplicity. "I don't see why all the objects we're forced to live with, just because of a sort of imposed civilization, shouldn't have aesthetic value. Well, the thing is, I think I'm diminished in some way if I allow myself to use inferior tools — or inferior methods." Martin had known at the time of that discussion that Dinah would be intimidated and irritated at once by even such a notion. As it turned out, the reverse was true, also. Ellen had been ill at ease in Dinah's house with its almost systematic chaos. In those early days, when the two women had been friends, Ellen visited Dinah at the shop, where tranquility reigned. But this summer

Martin observed Claire and Ellen and began to think that Ellen's passion for perfection amounted to an obsession. As this came home to him, he realized that Ellen herself perceived his slight disenchantment, and it seemed to drive her into a frenzy of worthwhile activity.

She kept at her writing, but she also applied herself relentlessly to harvesting blueberries and strawberries and all the garden vegetables, and laboriously canning and pickling and making jam. She baked loaves and loaves of bread — oatmeal, whole wheat, pumpernickel.

One afternoon, while Martin sat in the cool living room halfheartedly making notes on a manuscript, she called to him from the kitchen with such urgency that he thought there must have been an accident. He went to help and found Ellen standing in the center of the room looking forlorn — as he had never before seen her.

"What's wrong? Are you all right?"

She was standing, slowly shaking her head, and in her shorts and halter top she was too thin, too muscular. She looked like a drawn bow.

"Well, just look!" she said. "Oh, just look at that!" And she gestured at the window, where there were at least a half-dozen loaves of bread sitting on waxed paper on the sill.

Martin was at a loss. He stared and stared at them and then back at her, only to see her face turned to him with that widened look of expectation, so that the tension had left her features, and her expression had gone blank in anticipation of his sympathetic reaction. But he was so baffled and so naïve that his face, too, went blankly quizzical, and it infuriated her.

She seemed to Martin to leap in one bound like a cat over to that window, and she slapped her hand lightly across each little bread loaf as she spoke. "Well, just *look* at them! I like them all lined up and glistening like a little train. They sometimes look like a little train in the sun, and with the copper pots hanging over them they're just right. But *look!* They've all sunk in the middle! I took them out too soon, or the damned oven's off again. And they're too brown on top, too. They're ruined! They're just ruined!" And it ended up that Martin moved over and embraced her, and she just leaned into him in limp despair. Claire came in, too, from the garden, where she had been working, and sat down at the table to rest, while Martin stood at the window with Ellen.

"The bread's gone wrong, I think," he tried to explain, although Claire hadn't seemed the slightest bit curious. She got up and inspected the little loaves, and then turned to her sister with concern.

"But they'll be delicious, Ellen. They smell wonderful. They're only a little scorched on top." She finally understood that Martin was holding on to Ellen because she had gone absolutely still in despondency. "Oh, but, Ellen," she said plaintively, putting a hand on her sister's back as it was turned to her, "it doesn't make any difference. It just doesn't matter." But Ellen gave no response at all. She disengaged herself from Martin and left the room.

In the evening, when Martin was sitting by the pond with Katy and Claire, who both lay nude in the fading sunlight — their bodies not so dissimilar — on towels they had trampled down over the high grass, he finally asked her about it. "Is Ellen all right? Is that bread all right?" Claire didn't answer for a little while, and Martin thought she wouldn't. He just let his question drift out over the pond, but then she turned her head to the other side to look at him.

"Maybe she's just surprised that she's getting older," she answered finally. "She likes to be in charge. Well, I'm not sure. I'm not sure what it is. The bread's fine. I don't know what that was all about."

Martin was looking down at Claire's young skin and her narrow, childlike body as she lay there on her stomach next to her daughter, with her head buried in her arms and her wet hair splayed out over the towel, and so he wasn't listening, or caring, really, what she answered. But when he glanced up the hill and saw Ellen in her lawn chair snapping beans, he understood with perfect clarity that things had not gone as she had expected them to this summer. He knew now to expect a greater, a more dogged ferocity in the weeks to come. He remembered that at the first of summer, shortly after Claire and Katy's arrival, Vic had spoken out into their small company one evening almost in the manner of a warning. "All the people in the house," he had said, "anyone who comes by, they are all, for the time being, property of Ellen's."

Ellen had looked around at him severely and said, "Oh, yes? And you, too?"

"I come with the furniture," he said lightly, and after a moment she had smiled at him, pleased.

But when Martin saw Ellen looking down at the three of them there by the pond, then he himself suddenly saw Claire as an intruder and himself as her ally. She was a purveyor of propaganda simply by the resolute meaninglessness of her everyday existence. The reality she made for herself was both alluring and threatening, and Martin, looking up the hill, saw that he might suddenly find himself an alien in that house.

But the morning he drove out to the Hofstatters' in his old, blue Chevrolet to pick up Claire for their birthday shopping spree, he was optimistic; he was almost joyful. He liked giving presents. When Claire came out of the house, however, to meet the car, he was a little disappointed that she had on her usual khaki shorts, so that her thin legs projected from them like parentheses, and that she wore her old T-shirt with the subway system of Paris stenciled on its front. He was dressed as usual, too, in old jeans and a faded shirt, but he had been thinking of this as an occasion.

"You've never seen Dinah's shop, have you?" he said to Claire, because he often spoke of Dinah; he had told Claire a lot about her. "She has wonderful children's toys. Why don't we drive into West Bradford?"

"The Artists' Guild, you mean?" Claire asked in a dubious tone, and was thoughtful for a moment. "Okay. That'll probably be fine."

When they arrived, it was disconcerting to see Claire make her way around the shop. She looked more than ever like a waif, especially since Martin was accustomed, in this building, to the influence of Dinah's disheveled elegance and her authority. Claire handled a beautifully carved wooden train as thought it were not, in fact, amazingly sturdy; she behaved as though she could damage it. She did linger for a while over the hand-sewn stuffed animals made in Vermont by three women who took care to embroider with great thoroughness all the eyes and noses on their creations. But she walked away from the toys while Martin still inspected them, and she drifted around the shop and stood on its small balcony, which was cleverly cantilevered out over the Green River. Wind chimes rang faintly under the eaves, and inside, every object was beautifully displayed on blond-oak platforms with raised edges so that the pottery and hand-blown glass could be set down on a bed of white crushed stone.

Martin joined her out on the balcony. She was leaning against the railing. "You know," she said, "the whole shop is really more beautiful than anything in it. Your wife is the best of the lot. As an artist, I mean." She paused and looked out at the river and the little park on its other side. Her voice was oddly toneless. "Well, I'm not much of a judge, probably, but it's a beautiful place. But, you know, all Katy really seems to want is a toy plastic shopping cart she's seen advertised on TV." She looked at him to see if he knew what she meant, but he didn't. "You must know the thing I mean. It's junk, but it has all those little pretend cans and bottles in it. It's the only thing she's asked for." She smiled at him but took up her large leather purse, ready to leave, and Martin felt as if he had betrayed his wife, even though he was somewhat mollified by his notion that Claire's smile was one of apology.

They went to a shopping center five miles away in Bradford and hastened through the oppressively dark mall lined with benches, where a great many old people sat waiting for someone or simply keeping their places in that air-conditioned tunnel and nursing some private and unspoken fury. Martin had to be especially invigorated whenever he put himself up to shopping here for the special bargains they advertised.

Claire had made her selection with what seemed to be slight consideration but great satisfaction, and Martin had bought all sorts of things. He had been carried away with the whole thing. They found the little cart Katy had requested and then brought all those toys back to Martin's house to wrap in birthday paper.

When they finally finished that chore and left his house, they stopped at the bakery to pick up a cake Claire had ordered, and then they drove slowly out of West Bradford in the summer tourist traffic back toward Vic and Ellen's. They progressed hesitantly along the main road and then through Bradford once again, stoplight by stoplight. While they sat still in the sun waiting for one light to change, Martin gazed ahead at a broad, grassless churchyard on the corner, in which some large activity was taking place. It looked like a children's fair, and he realized with a rising, gleeful ebullience that everywhere there were grubby, dust-covered children running around with helium balloons attached to their belt loops or wrists by a taut string.

"Let's stop, Claire," he said. "We might be able to fill the balloons here." He was terribly enthusiastic, thinking how excited Katy would be to run all around the meadow with a mass of party balloons bobbing high over her in the air.

"God, Martin. It's so hot. It isn't that important, really, do you think?" But his delight was so intense that he turned at the corner and parked the car in the church lot. He and Claire wandered through the crowd looking for the source of helium. It was a frantic group in that depressed section of town; the children moved about with a cocky authority that his own children did not possess. These children knew how to fend for themselves. The only advantage Martin and Claire had was their height; their status as adults brought them no special consideration. The other adults were mostly sad and pasty-looking women, hot and disheveled and defeated, who clearly had relinquished control long ago of whichever children were their own. But Martin spotted the helium dispenser and took hold of Claire's arm to propel her in the right direction. The man filling the balloons was enjoying a letup in their popularity, and he stood leaning against the outsized plastic clown which encased the cylinder of gas. He gave them a glum look as they approached with their two cellophane bags of birthday balloons.

"I can't fill all those balloons. This thing is for charity. I just hire out for a fee." He looked at them sullenly like an ill-treated dog.

"Well, what if I gave you ten dollars to fill them? Would that seem fair to you?" Martin asked, and Claire just lagged back, seemingly offended by the whole event going madly on around her.

"I told you, this is a charity thing. The kids get the balloons free. The church pays me."

"But we can't find anywhere else to get these filled. They're for a birthday party."

The man didn't seem to have any particular greed and no sympathy on which to play, but when he realized that Martin was going to continue to stand there arguing, he straightened himself and held out his hand resignedly for the balloons, which he fitted over a spigot protruding from the clown's grotesque smile. He turned the knob that released the pressurized gas. Martin took on the job of tying off each balloon and attaching it to a string, handing them to Claire as they accumulated. When the balloons had all been blown up, Martin turned to her to see that she was holding at least twenty balloons in each hand, and that she was absolutely radiant with the unanticipated pleasure of their buoyancy. He looked at her carefully; he had never seen her face so devoid of reserve, and

55

when he turned to pay the man his ten dollars, he felt as if he might cry. But at the same moment, he realized that what he was feeling was an unexpected and nearly mournful lust.

It took them some time to arrange themselves in the car. Ten or twelve balloons fitted in the back seat, pressing against the ceiling. The others were left to Claire to hold on to tightly by their strings as they were suspended outside her front window. People honked at them and waved as they resumed their slow progress, with the balloons perilously in tow.

Martin drove along slowly, thinking of Claire when he had seen her nude, swimming and floating and diving in the deepest part of the Hofstatters' pond. Her coloring was so odd that as she had become tanned, her skin, and even her hair, had taken on the same muddy opaqueness as the water. All those times he had not really desired her. She was a friend; she seemed very much like a tall child. But he was suddenly feeling that he was in the process of experiencing a pervasive loss that could not be appeased. It had been made clear to him, when he had turned to Claire and seen that his enthusiasm for those balloons — for the celebration inherent just in the having of them — had been communicated to her, that all those summer days without his wife he had been thoroughly bereft. Now he would have stopped the car and made love to Claire in any field, but instead, of course, they continued sedately on, with the balloons buffeting about and squeaking against each other above their heads and out the window.

When they arrived at the Hofstatters', Martin drove up the long driveway in sudden embarrassment. It had only just occurred to him what an imposition they might be making on Vic and Ellen's careful schedule. But Ellen had seen them approaching, and she met them in the driveway full of goodwill. She immediately appropriated the party and made of it her own invention. She abandoned herself to its organization, although she insisted that it be held outside, so that any amount of running around would not matter. She brought out onto the grass an old wooden coatrack and went about the business of attaching the balloons closely to its several arms. In the end she had created a glorious, multicolored, and bulbous tree, so the rest of the group sat down beneath it and left the arrangements to her. She dashed in and out of the house, and at some point she changed from her shorts into a long, flowered chintz skirt with a wide flounce at the hem, so she weaved and bobbed over the lawn as intriguingly as the beautiful balloon Katy had appropriated from the original bunch.

After they had all had a piece of cake and Katy had opened her gifts, Vic and Ellen and another couple who had dropped by to swim sat with Martin and Claire in the yard drinking champagne that Martin had bought for the festivity.

The balloons had been untied from their tree trunk and given over to Katy, who, just as Martin had expected, did drift through the meadow with all of them tied by their strings to her wrists. But it was somewhat disappointing, because the balloons were apparently too porous to be inflated with helium, and they floated limply now, not so far above her head. An obscure memory flickered through Martin's mind just then. One year when he had been in New Orleans during Mardi Gras, he had been edging through the crowds on Canal Street with friends when they realized that they were being bombarded with water-filled balloons dropping from many stories up by some drunken revelers. He had thought that they were balloons, but when he noticed one broken on the sidewalk he realized that they were, in fact, condoms. Now he had driven twenty long miles from Bradford to the Hofstatters' with balloons that had had a remarkably prophylactic effect on his own rather doleful desire.

When he looked at Claire and poured more wine, he discovered that his desire had dissipated, that he felt instead overwhelmingly depressed, with a longing for his own home, his own wife, his own children. He had a heartsick need for that quiet and continual celebration of the spirit when it is bound fast by the expectations and wants and demands of other people whom one desires above all else to please and cherish and be nurtured by in turn.

Michael Dorris

from

A Yellow Raft
In Blue Water

I HAD WALKED into the wrong bar on the right night, and the experience left me temporarily insane.

In the days that followed I barely recognized myself — I acted like women I had never understood or believed. Living for February 18, the day Elgin was to be discharged, I went to work and came home and waited for his nightly call from the base. Neither of us was good with phones, but our three minutes passed like no time at all. Sometimes I simply listened to Elgin breathe while I squeezed my eyes closed and went over him, one part at a time, in my mind. Afterward, when the operator came on and we hung up, I became a high school girl again, made designs out of our initials with my purple felt-tip pen, covering the borders of the slick pages of *Cosmopolitan* and *Bride*. I told myself Elgin was my change of luck, and believed every promise he made. I even believed his guarantee could bring my brother back in one piece.

I was so sure, I thought of writing home that Lee was okay, but Dayton wouldn't trust my intuition, and Aunt Ida would claim I was just wishful thinking. She took inklings and feelings seriously only when they spelled trouble. I decided to wait until Lee returned, safe and sound, then break the news I had known all along.

After the first surprise at finding myself involved with a black man, I took it for granted. I bought myself new underwear and a pair of high white boots. Three times a week I filed my nails into perfect ovals, pushed every sign of cuticle out of sight, and laid on two coats of Revlon's finest. I lost eleven pounds in three weeks. I went to the Indian Health Service hospital in Seattle and had my sore tooth filled, and I got friendlier than I ever had been before with the black women on line with me at the airline caterers.

Yet I kept a secret edge of doubt like a card up my sleeve. I trusted Elgin more than any boyfriend I had before, but I didn't want to be a fool, to be another sad story. I told myself I could take any man or leave him. But Elgin wasn't just any man.

I took the eighteenth off to clean my apartment, to go to the market. I fixed Indian pinto bean chili like you never tasted. I was ready at four o'clock, though Elgin wasn't due till five-thirty. I was ready at six, but still not worried. I was ready at seven-thirty when I called to make sure the bus from Fort Lewis had arrived on time. And I was ready at nine when Elgin, beer-breathed and smiles and carrying a bouquet of live flowers in one hand and his suitcase in the other, blew through my open door.

The chili burned to the pan and then got cold, and the flowers wilted for lack of water. Our first days together had just been practice, Elgin said, and he was right. We were out of our minds. The lovemaking between us was so different from anything I knew before that I found myself wondering if we were under some kind of a spell, or making one. There was nothing we didn't try, and nothing that didn't work.

Tacoma in those days was not yet urban renewed, but we never noticed. Elgin had enough money saved for me to quit my dead-end job and stay home to study him full time, and every new feature about him gave me pleasure: his long sighs as he fell into sleep, the tease of his breath in my ear, the blunt shape of his cock, and the sensitivity of his nipples. He loved to be touched under his arms, and he stretched like a sleeping cat when I kissed the back of his neck. Some mornings he'd pull the shades down, then beg me not to dress at all. He had this game where he inked his index finger with his tongue, and then wrote on the bare skin of my breasts and stomach. He made me guess the words. The prize if I was right, and the penalty if I was wrong, were the same.

Elgin could make perfect hashed brown potatoes and could carry a tune when he sang. He read our horoscopes in the newspaper before he checked the want ads for work. He complained he had no skills, but I just laughed until he laughed too, low and sly and proud of himself.

Nobody can predict the future, but some things you can take into your own hands. For the first time in my life, I didn't take precautions. Every grown woman I knew had a child, and I wanted mine to be Elgin's. I imagined what he'd be like, a boy who took after his father. It never occurred to me that I wouldn't get pregnant.

Some women say they know just the moment their baby is made, and I'm among them. One spring morning too nice to stay inside, we got the idea for a picnic. We stopped at Mr. Chicken down the street and bought two box dinners, then took the Number 11 bus to Point Defiance Park, overlooking Puget Sound. I don't know where everybody was, at their jobs I guess, but the place was deserted. We hitched short rides and climbed the road, carrying our lunch and hanging on every word the other said. Elgin laughed at the sign on one lookout about how in 1841 some navy captain had said that with guns placed there and on the opposite shore he could control the world. I was so happy I could almost hear background music, and I took my steps to the beat.

Elgin wore a green T-shirt and rust-colored cotton pants. I had bought him a present from some hippies on the street corner, a bracelet made of three different kinds of metals — iron, copper, and brass — twisted together. A girl I used to work with had one, and she told me that in Africa it was supposed to bring good luck. Elgin wore it all the time, and that day it glinted in the sun where it hung low on his wrist. He was a strong man, tall. I rushed to keep pace with his long legs, but every so often I'd hang back for a full-length view.

He watched me too. I had my hair gathered in back with a beaded clip, my legs were bare below my cutoffs, and the flip-flops kept slipping off my feet. Elgin had gotten me a sweatshirt at the PX that said PROPERTY OF U.S. ARMY and I wore it without a bra, even though my breasts were large.

When we came to a private place with a good view of the Sound, we spread the horse blanket I had brought from the bed and opened our Mr. Chicken. Everything tasted better than it was. The sun was so bright on the water I had to squint my eyes to look across, and the heat soaked into my skin. I lay back on the warm, springy wool and pulled my shirt over my head. Then I unbuttoned my cutoffs and pushed them down. I took a deep breath and looked at Elgin. He faced me, his elbows on his knees, his arms in a steeple, his chin resting on his hands, his eyes quiet and dark as the night sky. Time passed while we stayed like that, only touching with our minds, then he lay beside me without a word and there, in a public park on a workday, in plain view of the ships that moved north and south in the waves far below us, we loved each other.

Later, while we caught our breath, as he trailed his thin brown fingers over my thighs and I cupped him gently in my palm, I told him we had made a baby.

"You're pregnant?" He stopped his hand, propped up on his elbow. His face became alert and tense. "How long?"

"Five minutes."

He didn't believe it, drew back as if to see me from a greater distance. "You can't be sure."

I made my mouth into one of those mystery smiles you see women on the soaps give when they know what only a woman knows. He could question it if he wanted to, but a month from now there'd be no doubt in his mind.

"You didn't use anything, really?" Elgin still hadn't moved his hand, and it grew heavy on my body.

"It's *okay*." I wanted him to be quiet, not to spoil how I felt. "I don't expect anything extra from you. You don't need to be married to have a baby."

Elgin thought about that awhile, and then his hand began to move again. His fingers traced a word on the smooth, low curve of my stomach. He leaned over me to place his cheek against it. Finally he sat and looked at me.

"Yes?" I guessed.

"Yes, you do."

"Yes, I do what?"

"Yes, you do have to be married to have *my* child. You have to be married to me."

If you had told me, three years before, that at twenty-five I'd be living in Tacoma, engaged to a black veteran, carrying his child of my own free will, ready to settle down — I'd have laughed in your face. And if you told me that nine months later in the Seattle IHS hospital I'd give birth, married, halfway deserted, and near broke, to a slim, dark girl, as unlike me as a baby could be, I wouldn't have believed it.

In the beginning, my pregnancy seemed to make no difference in our lives. Being with Elgin, and morning sickness, blocked out all my bad habits, so I stopped smoking, quit drinking cold turkey, and we went to bed early most nights. Some days we never got up.

When Elgin's money ran low, we moved to Seattle to look for new jobs. Elgin had seen in the *Post-Intelligencer* that there was a call out for mail carriers, and he thought that would be decent temporary work while we figured out what to do next. But the first day he came home dressed in his uniform he looked so good I told him he had to quit. The pale blue-gray gabardine strained over the swells of his body, rough against the dark cream of his skin. I made him promise no C.O.D.'s.

With Elgin on the street every day, I was bored and lonesome. I never had been good company for myself. I didn't want to get trained again, so I went back to my first job in the city, making black boxes. The final design was a secret — I didn't even know what they looked like when they came off the line — but I had a picture all worked out in my mind: the surface was polished to a shine and there was no visible way to open it. It made no sound, no tickings or buzzing. Attached beneath a plane's instrument panel, so simple and plain that the crew would forget it was there, it was a silent witness to everything that took place. Day in, day out, the bolt I screwed would hold the spool that wound the tape that recorded every sound, every joke, from Seattle to Japan, from Japan to Hong Kong. If something went wrong anywhere in the rest of the plane, the box would know. Even after an explosion, it sent out silent beeps that could be traced to the deepest part of the ocean or the emptiest stretch of land.

There were times that I thought of my stomach as a black box. I wondered what the baby heard, what sounds took hold in its brain. It was my memory, so I let myself sleep as the honeymoon with Elgin slowed down. I got through the nights that no excuses of special delivery letters or working late could explain. Sitting home, huge and alone, I pretended that mail got sorted on Sunday afternoons. My baby, not me, recorded the jokes Elgin's new friends made about his Indian squaw and how he had got himself scalped before he made his last stand. My baby, not me, was the eyes that saw the biting, jealous stares of skinny black women, following us when Elgin and I went out in public. Like the pilot of an airplane with a slow fuel leak or low oil pressure, I sailed above the clouds, planning for tomorrow, never fearing that something important had broken and thrown the trip off course.

We were living in a hotel over on Ninth Street, the Excelsior, which suited me fine. The place had an elevator that worked, and our room had a sink and a tiny unit that contained a refrigerator and stove combination. It was handy for cooking, since the burners were built in on top of the small freezer, but whenever I fried anything for more than ten minutes, all the ice cubes melted. We slept in two soft narrow beds. At first we pushed them together so we could curl against each other, but often before morning one of us, usually me, would slip through the crack and get wedged in. I'd lie there like baloney in a sandwich, making little movements to wake Elgin without startling him. I learned early on that he would jump in panic if I shook him or called his name when he was asleep, and I was afraid his thrashing arms would hit me when I couldn't defend myself. I blamed his nerves on the army, since I'd known more than one vet who woke scared.

As my baby grew inside me, though, I left the beds apart. That way, when I had to get up during the night or when Elgin came back after the light was out, as he did more and more, we wouldn't bother each other. I liked to rise early and eat a good breakfast, but if he didn't have a route, Elgin would sleep until eleven o'clock. After he got used to my habits, he could tune out any sound I made on a regular basis.

One day, getting ready to go to the market, I couldn't button my raincoat across my stomach. I stopped trying and sat on the side of my bed, wondering what to wear. It was a Saturday, the end of the best week between us in some time. Elgin was delivering a neighborhood he enjoyed, not too hilly and no loose dogs, and I had finally settled on a name for our child: Raymond, after the actor who played Perry Mason and never lost a case. I felt one hundred percent, and when I caught my reflection in the mirror over my bureau, I liked what I saw. My skin was clear, my hair shone black after a brushing, and my shoulders were broad and strong. I even appreciated the sight of my high round stomach, big enough to support a TV dinner tray.

Elgin and I had filed for a marriage license in Tacoma, but my life had become so cluttered with trappings — a man, maternity clothes, a steady job — that I neglected to arrange the actual wedding. There were too many things to think of every day to plan for invitations or clothes or a big dinner. Now my raincoat made me remember.

"So when does the knot get tied?" I asked Elgin. I planted my arms behind me for support.

He was on the floor in his old army undershirt, shining his work shoes, and at first he looked at the laces as though I was talking about them. Then he gave it up, raised his head.

"You worried I'm going back on my word?" His voice was tight.

I hadn't, before that minute. I figured Elgin and I had to plow through some rough times before we got used to each other, but that was only normal. I spent my teenage years glued to *The Newlywed Game* and heard Bob Eubanks laugh off everything from husbands who dressed in their brides' panties to couples who got the measles on their wedding night. Compared to a lot of them, we weren't so bad. But it sounded as if the idea of not marrying me had occurred to *Elgin*, it sounded as if he had to fight that idea hard.

"Fuck your word," I said, struggling to push myself upright. "Fuck you."

Elgin dropped his shoe and jumped to kneel over me on the bed. All I really wanted to do was hold him close, but that wasn't how the game worked. He had to pin my arms and make me surrender. I was nearly a foot shorter, but he was afraid of my pregnant body and that evened the odds.

I spoke into his face, only inches above mine. "I want to wear . . . a long white . . . dress and . . . have a three-foot . . . wedding cake and . . . go to Hawaii . . . on my honeymoon . . . with Paul Newman." My words were forced out in bunches, as I strained my muscles against his strength.

"You're a crazy woman," Elgin said when, breathless, he rested his forehead on mine. He smelled like wintergreen Lifesavers. "Crazy." He dropped his body next to mine, folded me to him.

A long time ago I had stopped saying aloud how good our lovemaking was. I didn't want Elgin too sure of himself. But that time, that morning, I saw in his eyes that same look that hooked me at Barclay's, the same desperate stare that eclipsed the public park in Tacoma. It was an expression that had never been in anybody's eyes but his, and I'd kill to keep it there.

We married at the federal courthouse, with no witnesses that we ever saw again except each other. I chose a beige dress because it was on sale and it made me look darker, as though Elgin and I were closer to the same shade. Elgin dug out his dress army uniform, even though we thought that might be illegal. It was either that or the blue satin cowboy shirt I got him with my last black box paycheck. The woman judge wore a tweed pantsuit and pearl earrings. She smiled at us and wished us good luck.

Once we were outside again, Elgin put his hand under my elbow to help me negotiate the stone steps, then we stood on the sidewalk, letting the crowd flow around us while we decided what to do. Finally, we ate an early dinner of salmon steaks and rice, huckleberry pie for dessert, at a seafood restaurant, and went next to a C&W club everybody said was the place to go. We sat at a table, suddenly shy with each other, until the band started playing "Sweet Dreams." That song made me want to cry, and I reached for Elgin's hand. We moved out and danced close and clumsy, the baby inside me wedged between us, our arms around each other's backs, and we stayed that way, barely moving our feet, after the music stopped and the other couples sat down. When I opened my eyes and saw a middle-aged Indian woman spying on us with a question in her mind, I broke free.

"Today's my wedding day," I announced to that roomful of strangers, "and we're celebrating."

The woman was mortified that I had seen what she was thinking, and joined in when everybody gave us a hand. Those people acted like they had never heard of married before, they made such to-do. All the men wanted to stand Elgin a drink and the women asked me when the baby was expected. The manager of the place wouldn't take our money, and when we scraped back our chairs to go home, the whole crowd whistled and pounded on the tables.

The chill of the damp night air outside that club was a shock. After hours of noise and music, the late silence made us whisper and then fall quiet as we crisscrossed the abandoned streets toward the Excelsior. We started with our hands clamped tight on each other in excitement, but by the time we had gone a few blocks we let go, tired from being the center of attention and I, at least, amazed to find myself a married woman. Elgin was wrapped in himself, a closed door to me.

You'd expect tonight we could coast through another hour, but it was clear we were heading for a fight. Elgin walked too fast for my new white heels, and I hung back even more to make him take a husband's responsibility. The gap between us widened. Under a streetlamp almost a block ahead of me, he halted and looked from side to side. When I wasn't there, he whirled around, then waited while I took my time catching up to him.

"I lost track," he said, and put his heavy arm around my shoulders.

I forgot about our fight. What mattered right then was the feel and smell and sight of him, and the fact that I knew I'd better not pass something when it was handed to me on a silver platter. I smiled and snaked my arms around his waist.

"Slow down, Mr. Taylor. Save some energy to carry me over the threshold."

Elgin's laugh, all warm and thick and bubbling from inside, colored the night. "I'll show you a threshold," he said.

He lifted me into his arms, supporting my back and under my knees, and held me to him like a sleep child — with a beach-ball in her stomach.

"You're out of your mind," I cried, but he walked with me that way the last two blocks to our hotel, through the dimmed lobby, and onto the creaking, gilded elevator. I pulled at my skirt and hid my face in his chest so I wouldn't see the night clerk's face. When we got to our floor, Elgin carried me down the hall, shifted my weight while I searched in his pocket for the key, then he kicked the door shut behind us.

Aunt Ida didn't have a phone so I sent her a postcard with the Seattle skyline by night on the back. "I have a husband who's not an Indian," I wrote. "His name is Elgin Taylor and now I'm Christine Taylor. We didn't have to get married but I'm going to have a baby. I hope you're fine. Did you hear anything new about Lee? I'll write a long letter soon. Love from your *daughter*, Mrs. Christine Taylor." If I could be somebody's wife I could be Aunt Ida's child. I wrote the address of the Excelsior Hotel in the corner, zone and all, and sent it off to Montana.

Days and weeks passed without any word from her. I didn't know whether to be worried or mad, so I was both. My weight confined me by that time, and I had to leave my job. The mail was all there was to look forward to, but what I got were flyers and advertisements, mostly addressed to another Mrs. Taylor, who must have lived in the hotel before me.

Elgin was off before dawn every morning, and some nights he didn't come back until I was in bed asleep. Maybe I should have asked more questions, but I preferred not to suspect him. Men cheated on wives who gave them no peace or understanding, never wanted to have fun, and probably fooled around themselves. In my mind those wives merged into a fat, mean, money-mad woman. I had never blamed those husbands when they left her for a date with me.

One wet Friday afternoon the manager had been at the door twice wanting our rent, and I couldn't go out in public because I didn't have a raincoat that would fit. Hour after hour, I looked for Elgin. He could get us a pizza so I didn't make myself any dinner. Finally I went to bed, a ticking bomb.

Elgin waltzed in at eleven o'clock, no excuses, no how was your day. Beer marked him like aftershave.

I gave him a chance for the first word, but when he didn't take it, I spoke from the dark.

"Where the hell have you been?"

"I had to work late." His voice had a hurt tone to it, as if I had accused him of something he was ready to deny. He flicked a light and slowly hung his uniform pants on the metal hanger with two clips for the creases. Finally he turned toward me.

"I didn't know they had a tap in the sorting room," I said. "You run out of Lifesavers?"

Elgin's full lips firmed to a line, and he stared hard into the surface of the bureau against the wall, letting his reaction build.

"So what if I stopped off," he yelled at last. "What's there to come here for anyway? You sit around making lists of things to bitch about."

Now I was the one unjustly convicted. "It's not my fault," I said. "You think I like that fish-eyed desk clerk hounding me for what we owe? Did you cash your check?"

Elgin was drunker than I had realized. He moved, knocking a chair over backward, reached into his suspended uniform pants and emptied the pockets onto the kitchen table. Loose change, dollar bills, Kleenex pressed into tight clumps by his hands spilled across the surface.

"Does that satisfy you?"

I saw myself through his eyes. I was that fat, mean woman. He was one of those husbands.

"Who is she?" I asked in a quiet voice.

He didn't answer. He snatched his pants off the clips and put them on, then banged the door so hard behind him that it ricocheted ajar. I heard his steps hammering down the fire stairs, not even bothering to wait for the elevator. I heard the door open on the ground floor, and then nothing, just a hollowness, empty as a deep tunnel.

I got my unemployment. I got my Indian Health. I got by. Elgin didn't return for three days, the whole weekend, and when he did come back, something was missing. There was no time to fight before the baby was due, and I didn't want to scare Elgin away, so I didn't ask where he'd been. He paid our hotel bill, in the evenings told me stories of his day, stayed around more. Sometimes he watched me, and I knew what he was thinking because I thought it myself: what have I got myself into? I was too far along for our bodies to work their full magic, and it got harder and harder to trust that they'd ever be able to again. My stomach seemed to grow and stretch with every lying word and regret.

The baby poked and simmered night and day. Its hiccups made my body bounce. It stuck out a foot or a hand and held it firm until I rubbed it back into place. Sometimes I thought the heartbeat was loud enough for anyone to hear, and when the baby dropped and its round, heavy head rested low, I couldn't take a step without remembering it. It took me over and held me in its time, and I was a prisoner of my own body.

My due date was December 3, and I was a week past on the morning the desk clerk delivered a letter addressed to me in Dayton's handwriting.

It was eleven o'clock and I was still in my gown, still in bed, waiting for my water to break. My wedding ring cut into my swollen finger. I had felt the first fluttery contractions before dawn, nothing I couldn't handle, and I didn't mention them to Elgin as he dressed to go to work. On my last visit to the hospital, the doctor said this stage, when it started, would last for six to eight hours. Elgin would be long back from his route before anything was ready to happen, and if he wasn't, I'd leave him a note to meet me at IHS. The baby was only inches above the path it would follow into this world, and birth seemed easy and hopeless at the same time. I had a bag packed for the hospital, and the doctor's telephone numbers were written on a card in my purse. Alone this morning, I had French braided my grown-out hair tight against my scalp.

I studied the envelope a long time, as if I had X-ray vision. It was the kind you buy at the post office with the stamp printed on, and Dayton's script was large enough to fill the whole space. He used my new name, so I knew Aunt Ida had received the postcard I sent. I had never written her the long letter I promised.

Finally, I slit the flap with a nail file and unfolded the lined white stationery inside.

"Lee is dead . . ." seared my brain before I knew what I was reading. I crushed the paper, holding it with both hands against my chest, but it was no use. I panted, my breathing shallow and useless, my eyes closed. I turned to glass, I turned to shale. My mouth moved in automatic prayers until my tongue began to flap Lee's name, again and again, soundless, clacking in time with my breath. Pictures raced through my mind like snapshots, a newsreel of Lee's face, talking, sleeping, angry, joking, young, hair cut short, all ending with the flashing of Dalton's words. I raised the letter again, held it in front of me, opened my eyes.

It poured like rain into a cave, striking here and there, forming puddles, running down the walls: ". . . fell behind enemy lines . . . all along . . . reported on a list of casualties . . . They won't give back his body until . . . No reason for you to come . . . Ida is taking it . . . Yours truly."

I threw my arm over my eyes, arched my back. I couldn't form a thought, couldn't cry. I gasped the air around me, swallowed it, drew more in. My body was a turtle shell and nothing could touch me. I pushed it all down from my head, down my arms, down my chest. My legs shivered, but I pushed harder. A warm flood washed from me, soaking my gown and the mattress. I looked, expecting blood, but I couldn't see beyond the mountain of my stomach. Everything below had disappeared. And as I watched a dent form beneath my gown, changing my shape as if an invisible fist had driven into me.

When the cramping pain released, I rolled to my side and reached for my purse. I fumbled for the card with the numbers, grabbed the phone and dialed the hotel operator.

"This is Mrs. Taylor," I said. "Get a cab."

The ache overtook me again, and I gripped the receiver and watched my fingers turn thin. I dug my nails into the skin of my palm as if that could take the place of all other feeling. I drew back my lips, bit on nothing, and waited it out. Finally I could notice the female voice speaking from the phone, asking, over and over, was I all right?

"It's the baby," I said, and read her the doctor's number to call. I dropped the receiver onto its cradle and looked around the room to locate my clothes. I wanted to be ready to move after the next contraction. My purse lay open on the floor, and as I sensed, far away but coming fast, the pinching drag of my muscles, I took Dayton's letter and stuffed it deep inside.

As soon as I reached the hospital, the labor slowed. I sat in a wheelchair in the hall for hours, answered the questions of a woman seated behind a glass window who typed them onto a printed form and checked me in. Three times that endless afternoon I called the hotel to leave messages for Elgin, but he never showed to receive them. I was pushing by the time they finally brought me to my first examination in the delivery room.

In maternity I had an idiot for a nurse, a woman who nagged, "Don't bear down until the doctor comes," and then, when he finally arrived, she stood at the side of my electric bed, fed me crushed ice, and wouldn't shut her mouth.

"Be a brave girl," she said as I seized her hand. "Don't be in a hurry."

I lost any sense of time, the limits of the world the space between my pain, my only guides "push" and "rest," until I heard someone say, "She's ready."

I paused for a turquoise instant, preparing to squeeze the baby from my body, but the nurse broke in.

"Do you ever watch *The Price Is Right* on TV?" she demanded. I was dumb from exhaustion, my hair damp with sweat, my face streaked in tears, and I knew no better than to nod that I had.

"Well, come on *down*," she said. "Make this a real push!"

Before I could tell her to go to hell, to shut her face, I lost myself in the force of the contraction. I dug my chin into my chest, held my breath, and pressed so hard my eyes felt as though they'd burst from my skull. Alarm bells went off in my brain. The baby was too big for me, something was wrong. If I bore down again, even a little, my body would rip apart.

The doctor was a white mask, a pair of gloved hands. "Now," he told me, but what did he know? I gritted my teeth and to satisfy him, pretended, but I protected myself.

"It's worse if you won't help," he said, impatient and far away. "I don't want to use forceps."

"Just get *mad* at the baby," said the stupid nurse. "Just say, 'Bad baby, bad baby,' and shove it out."

76

I could have killed her at that moment. The force of my hate almost wrenched me off the table, and it gave me strength. When the next contraction came I put common sense away, tightened and loosened everything I could feel. I held my eyes on the nurse's face. "Good baby," I managed. "Good baby, good baby, good baby."

"Hold it. Hold it," the doctor said.

There was nothing but my pain. I gave myself to it, drowned in it. My thoughts were a white screen in a black room.

"That's the head. One more. Yes."

My muscles obeyed their own will. I fell back in relief, my body collapsing against empty space as the baby slipped from me. My mind left with it, losing the memory of every hurt, needing only to know the child was safe. I stared at the light above the bed, waiting to hear a cry, and when it came, reedy and high as a Cheyenne war dance song, I answered back, echoed the exact sound.

"Raymond," I demanded, holding out my arms to the doctor and nurse busy at my feet. My neck strained for a look. "Give me Raymond."

"That's a funny name for her," the doctor said, and lifted my daughter for me to see. I felt the heft of her in my hands and brought her to my breast.

She was a long dark shape, smeared with white cream. Thin black hair rose in straight, slick lines from her head as if she were a cartoon baby and had just been frightened. She had stopped crying but still moved her mouth, flexing and flexing her deep bowed lips. Her nose was large for her face, so broad. I took one of her hands, uncurled the fingers against my own. Her palms were a lighter shade than the rest of her, golden against rich brown. The clamped cord, which had joined us, stuck from her stomach, and below that, her legs were thin, curved in below the knee as if made out of rubber. Her toes bunched in a knotty line, each nail flawless, smooth, clean.

I guided her mouth to the hard nipple of my left breast, and she knew what to do, drew me into her, took what she needed. As I watched, she opened one eye, piercing, squinting in even the shaded light of the room, to search for me. The iris was muddy green, camouflage, the tint of a shallow lake. We stared at each other, strangers. I inhaled her damp, salty smell, my breath elevating and lowering her weight, as the heat of our bodies flowed together and once again became the same.

I hated the hospital. The nurses wouldn't leave me alone. They wanted to wash my baby, measure her, put drops in her eyes. They wanted to put my baby in the nursery and keep me in the ward, but I yelled when they tried to take her, and scared them with my will power. They thought I was insane, whispered about me among themselves, but gave me my way, put us together in a private room they said I had no right to use. I forgot them the minute they were out the door.

Elgin came to see me later. Nobody gave him word, he said, nobody at the hotel knew where I had gone. It was lucky he had found me at all. He stood at the far end of the bed, his hands turning his hat, his eyes darting to the hallway. He was full of things he couldn't tell me, full of his secrets, but I had lost interest in them.

"They say it's a girl."

"They're right." I turned back the yellow blanket to reveal her face, and, as though she heard us talking, she opened those strange angry eyes and studied Elgin.

"She could stare down a train," he said.

I had a flash of my feeling for Elgin, a surge of wanting him to hold me in his big hands, a picture of the three of us, mother, father and daughter, smiling on a Christmas card. He sensed my softening and moved in, sat on the bed, touched the baby with silk fingers.

"She's got my mother's mouth," he said. "Little Diane."

"Diane?"

"My mama."

Elgin's parents and a couple of sisters lived in California, but he didn't talk about them. When he called them on the phone he never mentioned me at all. I wasn't going to have my baby named after some mystery woman, much less looking like her.

"I already picked out the name," I reminded him.

He raised his eyebrows. "Raymond." He said it flat, like it was a joke.

"Didn't you ever hear of Ray for a girl?"

"Ray short for what?"

I thought fast. Rayburn. Rayton. "Rayon," I said. "Rayona."

He couldn't believe he had heard right. "Like nylon?"

"Like nothing." I wasn't going to argue with him.

Elgin shook his head. "Well, her middle name's Diane."

I didn't care. Nobody used their middle names, and I'd never tell her.

"Did you call anybody?" he asked.

"There's nobody to call." I reached for my purse, dug out Dayton's letter, and handed it to him without another word. I hadn't looked at it again, but I hadn't forgotten it. It was on the back burner, keeping warm, ready to boil. Elgin unfolded the paper and read under the light. His eyebrows drew together in a frown.

"Damn."

He had been my last hope. Deep inside, I had been waiting for him to tell me not to worry, that it was a screwup. I wanted him to say the army made lots of mistakes and Lee was alive, like he had promised. But he let Lee die right in front of me.

I snatched the letter from Elgin's hands and balled it back into my purse. I glared at him while he told me he was sorry, he understood how I felt. I wanted him to get out, to leave me alone with my baby, but he wouldn't quit.

"This Dayton says they're not going to turn back the remains yet," he said. "It could be a while before they work it out."

"I can read."

"That's shit," he went on. "What do they want with his body?"

I thought of Lee's body, lean and loose on a rodeo horse, his left hand thrown high in the air, his right hand on the belt, his long hair flying with every buck.

"Liar," I said.

The night nurse came into the room and Elgin was embarrassed that she might have heard. He spoke quietly, like he was talking to the baby, as he rose to leave.

"It's all going to change. Starting today, all new. Give me a chance." But when he fumbled for my hand, I pulled it away.

As my shock wore down, I let myself turn to Elgin for kindness — when I didn't need it too badly. I let him father the baby through her first months, let him walk with her through the halls of the Excelsior when she couldn't sleep. Some nights I let him push our beds together and blanked my mind to everything but his touch. But I never let down my guard, never believed him the way I used to, and when once again his days at work got longer, when his nights got later, I wasn't surprised and I wasn't too unhappy. I got a sitter for the baby, and met new people myself. I was still young and I had good times. Finally, when Rayona was nine months and I was back at work at a new job, I packed a bag and moved to a place of my own.

Even then, Elgin was gum on the sole of my shoe. Every once in a while he phoned late at night, lonesome and sad, to say we should start over. Sometimes I opened my door to his knock, sometimes not. And sometimes I was the one who called.

Clyde Edgerton

———

from
Raney

DR. BRIDGES agreed for us to stop therapy after seven sessions and see how things go for a while. We don't stay mad so long at a time as we did and we're able to say how we feel better than we were before.

I've got a new part time job.

Daddy's store — the Hope Road General Store — is at the intersection of Crossville and Hope Roads. It's a normal general store with a porch on the front and a feed room built onto the side and three gas pumps out front. Daddy's had it as long as I can remember. When I was little I used to go with him out there some nights and help. I'd wait on a few people while he watched and he'd let me make price signs with crayons and meat wrapping paper. And I would go into the feed room where the feed sacks were as big as me and tight as ticks and smelled musky and I'd climb up on them and crawl around until Daddy came in and got me and we started home.

I stopped in yesterday morning when I was coming back from the dentist. I walked in and stood just inside the door.

In the back, behind the stove, was Uncle Nate's wicker bottom chair — with the little flat navy blue pillow. It hit me all of a sudden that I could take Uncle Nate's place — in a way. I had been thinking about doing some part time work. Daddy gives Charles and me money — he insists. I hate to *keep* taking it, but he won't talk about it, or else goes on and on about how he don't want us to have the same hard times that him and Mama had when they started out.

The store definitely needs a woman. First of all, right in the middle of the bread section — which is just inside the door — is this great big minnow tank which they don't keep cleaned out good. The water's so muddy you could drive a fence post down in it. And it smells. Who's going to want to buy a loaf of bread standing there beside that mudhole with several dead suffocated minnows floating on top?

The thing to do is clean that thing up and move it to the back where the overalls and water buckets and wash tubs and stuff like that is. Then we could put a sign up in the bread section saying MINNOW TANK IN BACK.

Sneeds Perry, who as I said is running the place, will sit with a toothpick in his mouth watching the air move while the floor fills up with cigarette butts and the bottle cap holder on the drink box gets so full that your bottle cap just plings down onto the floor and rolls up under something.

But Sneeds is generally nice. That's why I think I could work with him. And Daddy said the other day that it was going to be hard to find part time help to take Uncle Nate's place. I could take care of the stuff inside while Sneeds pumps gas. Like I say, this all hit me out of the clear blue. It seemed like just the thing to do.

Sneeds was working on a radio that was sitting on a shelf over behind the cash register. He had the front off and was doing something to it with a screw driver.

I spoke to him. He looked over his shoulder and said, "Howdy, Raney." Then I walked along the canned and boxed food aisles. Some of the food had just about disappeared under dust: there were cans of corn that could *grow* corn.

Then there are all those shelves built into the front windows. They're so stuffed you can't see out. Or in. There are hats and boots and oil cans all stuck in there. And combs and hand-kerchiefs on these dusty cardboard displays. I figured I could have all that cleaned out and windexed in a afternoon. Just that little bit of work would change the whole atmosphere.

I knew I'd be a real asset to the place and if Sneeds and Daddy and Charles all said okay, I'd be in.

I walked over to the cash register and said, "Sneeds, you need a woman's touch around this place."

"That's for sure," he says. He put down his screw driver, turned around and shifted his toothpick. "What you got in mind?" Sneeds always wears a little black toboggin, engineer boots, rolled up dungarees, and a flannel shirt — summer or winter.

"Well, if I worked in here part time for a while I could have this place looking real nice. What I mean is I got some ideas about moving things around, you know: rearranging a bit. To help sales go up. Then, too, when you have to go out and pump gas I could stay in here and watch things."

"Fine with me," he says. "I'll tell you there's plenty of woman's work around here and like I always said: a woman's work is for a woman. I hate it. Talk to your Daddy."

I'll say he hates it. "Then it'd be all right with you?"

"Sure."

That was easy enough. So I drove to Mama's and Daddy's. Daddy's truck was out front. He was in the kitchen drinking a cup of coffee and eating a piece of pound cake like he's done just about every day of his life.

"Afternoon," he says. "Where you been?"

"I've been to the dentist. Fourteen dollars — just for a cleaning. Listen daddy, I've got a idea: why don't I start working at the store?"

"What's the matter with you, honey? You don't need a job."

"Daddy, it would just be part time. That store is a mess. And with Uncle Nate gone now — you need somebody part time. If

I move a few things around in there and get it cleaned up, you'll do a better business. I guarantee it."

"Honey, don't nothing much but farmers come in there. We sell more cigarettes, drinks, chicken wire, fence posts, and such than anything else. No need to try to make it into something that won't have no market."

"I don't mean change it. I mean make it better. That fish tank stuck in the bread section is just awful. It ought to be moved to the back. The place needs a woman's touch. All I want to do is go in there a few afternoons a week after I get the housework done. It'd give me a chance to talk to people and make a little spending money." Daddy didn't say anything. "Don't you think it'd be all right, Mama?"

"Well, I don't know. Maybe. Until you all start thinking about raising a family." She was drying the last dinner dish.

"Now, honey," said Daddy, "I told you not to worry about money for a while. You know I don't want you going through the troubles me and your mama had."

"Daddy, I'm getting bored at home. I need a place to work — part time at least."

Daddy stuck the last piece of cake in his mouth and put down his fork. "I'm not so sure it'll be as much fun as you think it will," he said with his mouth full of cake, losing a couple of crumbs; "but if you've got your mind set on it, go ahead. I'll tell you what, try it for one week and then let me know what you think."

I hugged his neck and told him to brush the crumbs off his chin.

Next, Charles.

It was Friday, so Charles had cooked: pork chops, new potatoes, and some early turnip salet Aunt Flossie had brought by. He's been cooking on Friday nights because he says it helps him unwind from the library.

"Charles, this pork chop is delicious," I said. "I declare, we're going to have to open you up a restaurant."

"Thanks."

"Listen, Charles, not to change the subject, but I want to work at Daddy's store. Full time." (I figured I'd give myself room to compromise down to three-fourths and finally to half time.)

"Raney, we don't need the money. Your father said he'd help us get on our feet. You know he wouldn't want you working at that store."

"He said it would be fine. I asked him this afternoon."

Charles sat there looking at me and chewing on a piece of pork chop long after it was chewed up. "Your daddy said okay?"

"He sure did. You're so cute."

"Raney, you'd get tired of it. Why do you want to work at that store?"

"It needs a woman's touch. And it'd be fun. I stopped in there this afternoon and that's exactly what it needs — a woman's touch. That place could be fixed up real nice, so housewives would enjoy shopping in there. That minnow tank had two dead minnows in it and there's Sneeds Perry working on a radio; and most of the time he's sitting out by the front door, leaning up against the side of the building with a toothpick in his mouth, counting to see which is most that day: Fords or Chevrolets."

"Raney, you can't just walk in there and change that place around. And you know what kind of people go in there all the time."

"No, I don't," I said. "What kind of people go in there all the time?"

"Well, housewives don't — much. They go to the Piggly Wiggly in Bethel."

"What kind of people do go in there then?"

"A bunch of men who . . . who stand around and spit on the floor."

"Charles, there are three oil cans with dirt in the bottom over by the stove for people to spit in."

"It's not the clientele you should be around all day."

"Please tell me what that is supposed to mean."

"What it means is: the people who hang around that store are a bunch of rednecks — in the truest sense."

"Charles, Uncle Nate used to work out there, and my own flesh and blood daddy happens to own it, and he 'hangs around' out there."

"Look, Raney, it would never work. It would never work. I just don't want you stuck in that store all day. Especially with Sneeds Perry."

"Charles Shepherd, you've got to be kidding. Sneeds is as harmless as a flea. The main reason Daddy has him there is Sneeds knows everybody and has a real easy way about him with the customers. It's his cousin Sam that causes all the problems. And he's honest. That's what I've heard Daddy say. And for heaven's sake, he's got rotten teeth and wears the same clothes all the time." (The thing is, I've never actually *smelled* Sneeds. Daddy says he has just three shirts and that he'll wear them for two or three days each and then he'll wear this sweater one day — the day he's getting the shirts cleaned. Then he starts over again. But he's never actually smelled as far as I could ever tell.) "I'll tell you what, Charles: if you're so worried, I'll work just three-fourths time."

"Raney, we don't need the money."

"I'm getting bored staying home and I don't feel right about keeping on taking handouts from Daddy, Charles."

Charles chews for a while. "Your Daddy wouldn't be happy unless he was helping us out."

"Maybe so, but that's off the subject. . . ."

"Raney, I don't think —"

"Okay, okay, okay. Half time — but then I might as well not be working at all. Half time; I'll do it half time."

Charles chewed some more. "Go ahead. I don't want to be the one to stop you. But don't say I didn't warn you."

"Warn me about what?"

"You won't like it."

"I bet I will."

While Charles cleaned up after supper, he left the strainer out of the sink and the water turned on, but I was so happy about him saying yes about me working, I didn't say anything about it. But I do need to mention it next time. In marriage counseling we talked about how you shouldn't carry around little grudges because they grow bigger and uglier while you carry them around. Next time he leaves the strainer out, I'll mention it.

* * *

Sneeds and me got along fine the first week at the store. Monday — the day I started — he let me do the candy order. I had to check the items on the order sheet. The salesman says, "Two boxes Baby Ruth, two Butterfingers, one Powerhouse." He was going so fast I had to keep stopping him. Sneeds said that was the thing to do. He said a delivery man gypped him out of some potato chips one time and some magazines another time.

The part I like best about working in the store is finding something for somebody when I know where it is and they don't. Somebody will come in, look around for a minute, then come over and say, "Do you have any Kleenex?" And I say Sure do, and come around from behind the counter and go straight to it. It's like being in a spelling bee and getting the easiest word.

Right off the bat — that first day — I told Sneeds that the minnow tank had to be moved.

He says, "Do you know how much that thing weighs?"

"No, but if you'd scoop out all the dead minnows and mud it'd probably be down to about twenty pounds and you could slide it wherever you wanted to."

He laughed. He's got rotten teeth and he's about thirty-five or forty I think, and he moves real slow. But he keeps the books and Daddy says he's accurate and he just hopes he can keep him.

"Well," says Sneeds, "besides the fact that that tank weighs about a thousand pounds, you've got the problem of that big wall socket for the filter and light and all that. There ain't another one anywhere except on that post right there beside the tank. You'd have to put in another wall socket."

"I'll talk to Daddy about that," I said.

Also on that first day I found a feather duster under the counter. But you will not believe what else I found under there. There were these boxes of preventatives. There were all kinds of makes and models. It embarrassed me to death.

Well, that's okay. People have to get them somewhere.

I tried to dust off the canned food with the feather duster but what I needed was a vacuum cleaner. All the feather duster did was move the dirt somehwere else. So Thursday morning I brought my Kirby and by lunch I had the canned and boxed food cleaned up and by Friday I had the windows squeaky clean and all the junk cleaned off those shelves. Even Sneeds was pleased. The whole place looked like you'd opened window shades on a sunny morning. I moved out those oil cans from around the stove and got three brass-colored spittoons from Pope's, cleaned the ceilings, the bathroom, the shelves, and threw out nine big garbage bags of pure-t trash.

The only problem was that even before I finished, one of Sneeds's buddies, Lennie somebody, came in and said, "Hell, I might as well be in the g. d. Seven-Eleven, Sneeds!"

Monday, when I put the feather duster back under the counter I noticed these stacks of magazines under there. Girlie magazines. *Playboy, Penthouse,* and some other one. In my daddy's own store. I could not believe it. My mind shot ahead six or seven years and I saw a little boy or girl of mine rustling under that counter and seeing a picture of a unnatural act which would stick in their mind forever as the way it's supposed to be. In my daddy's own store.

"Sneeds, why do you have those magazines stuck under the counter?" I said. "Why don't you put them out on the rack with all the others?"

"They ain't your regular magazines," says Sneeds. "We might get a little trouble from some of the church people."

I've already heard two or three men around the store talking about "the people down at the church."

"Well," I said, "how does anybody know about those magazines if they're stuck behind the counter?"

"Oh, they know. They know. There's regular customers who come in here as soon as we get in a new shipment."

"Well, don't expect me to sell any."

"Okay, I won't. Just holler for me."

That beat all. Here this had been going on under the whole community's nose for no telling how long. In my daddy's own general store. I figured I'd just have to say something to Daddy about it.

I finally had a chance after Sunday dinner when he went back to the bedroom to take his usual Sunday nap; I followed him.

"Daddy, I know about them magazines under the counter at the store."

"Honey, now you leave those magazines alone."

"Daddy, that's not what I'm talking about. How can you go to church and still sell those magazines? I can't do it. Everytime somebody wants one I call Sneeds. Why do you sell them?"

"Honey, Sneeds manages all of that. I give him free rein in ordering and the whole magazine idea is his. I asked him about those magazines myself and he said their profit margin is higher than anything in the store. If you want to talk to Sneeds about stopping the magazines — fine. I just hate to put a man in control of something and then pull the rug out from under him. Plus, they're out of sight. He keeps them out of sight."

"I just think it's wrong, Daddy."

"Well, let me think about it. That's all I know to say now. I hate to let Sneeds do something and then tell him not to do it."

So I decided I would try to talk to Sneeds again. Monday afternoon — of the second week — during a lull, I'm sweeping inside and Sneeds is sitting out front in the sunshine. I go out and stand in front of him, putting the shadow of my head across his eyes.

"Sneeds, don't you think those magazines under the counter are filthy?"

"They ain't filthy — necessarily," he says. "They don't hurt nobody as far as I can tell. These people'll buy them somewheres. We might as well make the money as somebody else."

"Well, I just don't think it's right. If it was, they wouldn't have to be under the counter. You know the expression 'under the counter'?"

"Well, yes, but if you put them out where everybody can see them, old Mr. Brooks is liable to have the sheriff on us."

"Well, I just think it's wrong to sell them at all and I wish you'd think about stopping."

"Do you know how much money they bring in?"

"No."

"A lot. One heck of a lot."

There didn't seem to be much I could do. I put out some tracts — "What the Bible Means to Me" — but they didn't go very fast. The magazines sold steady. (I must admit that I couldn't help laughing at some of the cartoons in *Playboy*. That's all I looked at though — for any length of time. The pictures of the naked women are hazy like they're in a dream. And I cannot believe they show *everything* like they do — so the men can go off somewhere and look at the pictures. I mean you don't ever see some man sitting on the front porch or out in the yard looking at *Playboy*, do you? No. They're too embarrassed.)

Madora told me about *Playgirl*, but I don't care to see one. I wonder if they have the men all hazy like in a dream like in *Playboy*. I think it would be better if they had them sweaty — kind of shiny, maybe like they just got off working in the fields on a hot day. But I haven't seen one and I don't plan to.

For two days I'd noticed this brand new broom — with a piece of thin cardboard around the thistles — sitting by the cash register, but I hadn't thought anything about it until Mrs. Johnson, who had just bought three bags of groceries, took a look at her receipt after Sneeds had torn it off the cash register.

"What's this here?" she said, pointing to the receipt.

"Oh. That's the broom," says Sneeds.

"I didn't get no broom," says Mrs. Johnson.

"That there ain't your broom?" says Sneeds.

"Oh, no. I didn't get no broom."

"I declare, I'm awful sorry, Mrs. Johnson. Let me put this back where it belongs. I imagine somebody must have left it standing here," Sneeds says, real puzzled like. He carries the broom to the back of the store and leans it up against the other new brooms. "I'm awful sorry, Mrs. Johnson. I just saw it standing there and I thought it was yours. Let me give you your money back." He dings open the cash register. "There you go."

Mrs. Johnson got her purse out of her pocketbook, snapped it open, folded the bills and stuck them in and dropped the change in and clamped her purse shut and smiled at Sneeds. "I don't even need a broom," she says. "I got three."

Sneeds followed her to the door, saying he was sorry. But do you know what he did then? He walked to the back of the store, got that same broom and leaned it up against the cash register. *Again.*

"Sneeds Perry," I says, "you tried to cheat her."

"Oh, no. It was an honest mistake. I didn't mean to charge Mrs. Johnson for that broom."

"Well, Sneeds, you went and got it and set it right back up there! What for?"

"There's people, Raney, plenty of people — but not Mrs. Johnson — who come in here and charge stuff. Right?"

"Right."

"Well, some never pay it off. Paul Markham has a bill you wouldn't believe, and nobody knows about it but me and your daddy, and Paul'll pay *on* it, sure, but he won't pay it off. Well, it ain't right. It simply ain't right, and I tell your daddy and he won't do a thing about it. So, I collect interest — I'll have a broom this week and a jar of pickles next week — one of them giant jars. Now that there with Mrs. Johnson was a accident. I didn't mean to ring up that broom. But Paul was in here yesterday and Fred Powers today and I'd just rung it up for both of them and so —"

"Sneeds, two wrongs don't make a right."

"I might as well get them both while they're here."

"No, no. I mean *your* wrong don't make *their* wrong right."

"Oh. Well, maybe not, but charging them extra ain't wrong because it cancels out their wrong. In other words, one wrong can cancel out another wrong."

"Sneeds. Sneeds, what if I tell Daddy? I mean I can't just ignore this."

"If you have to tell him, tell him. But I think you ought to remember that I agreed to you working in here in the first place, so if it hadn't been for me you wouldn't have known about this anyway, so it's my own doing, in a way. And what I'm doing is helping out your daddy, so you telling him would actually hurt him moneywise. But do what you have to do."

"Well, if it's something definitely wrong, like cheating, I'd have to tell him." I don't know what to do. I doubt Daddy would do anything. He's always making excuses for Sneeds.

* * *

We have two cars. The Dodge Dart and the Chevrolet Daddy gave me. The Chevrolet was in the shop yesterday and so Charles had to come get me at the store on his way home from the library. It's the only time he's picked me up in the three weeks I've been working there.

I'm in the back of the store when he walks in with Sneeds right behind him. He gets a Pepsi at about the same time I start up front. When he gets over to the cash register, where Sneeds is waiting, Sneeds reaches under the counter and pulls out this slick, shiny *Penthouse* magazine and slides it across to Charles at about the time Charles looks at me and I look down at the magazine and then right into Charles's eyes which are not looking back into mine but are instead staring at the cash register.

Sneeds rings up the magazine and the Pepsi and says, "Did you bring a bottle?"

"I don't want the magazine," Charles says, shaking his head.

"What's the problem?" says Sneeds, who, I all of a sudden realize, don't know that Charles is the Charles who is my Charles. Charles hardly ever goes in the store. *Or so I thought.* Live and learn.

Well, listen: I won't born yesterday. I just took my pocketbook from underneath the counter, walked out front and got in the Dodge.

Charles comes out with*out* the magazine, drinking on that Pepsi. He comes up to the car window and do you know what he says? He says:

"Is there an empty bottle under your seat?"

"I don't know, Charles — there's no telling what might be under there. Where's your magazine? I came out so you could buy it."

"What magazine?"

Sneeds sticks his head out the store door. "I'm sorry, man, I swear. I am *sorr-y.*"

"*'What magazine?'*" I say to Charles. "That slick, shiny *Penthouse* magazine, full of filthy pictures of naked girls that Sneeds slid across the counter to you just as natural as . . . as . . . selling a . . . a . . . shiny red chicken to a black snake. *That's* what magazine."

"That's none of your business, Raney."

"Well, if it's none of my business, how come you clammed up like God was watching you?"

"I said it's none of your business. Don't change the subject."

"I swear, you must go in there as regular as meals to pick up a copy of that magazine. And Lord only knows where you hide them at home. Where *do* you hide them?"

"Raney, I said it's none of your business. It's absolutely none of your business. We happen to be living in a free country which tells me in its own constitution that I am free to read what I want to, when I want to, without reporting in to you."

"If you're so free, Charles — where's the magazine?"

"I'll tell you one thing, Raney: it wouldn't hurt you to pick up a few pointers from *Penthouse*."

"Charles, you son of a . . . , if you've got something to say to me then say it. Don't hide behind a stack of filthy magazines."

"Raney, they are not filthy magazines. Filth is in the mind of the beholder."

"You can say that again. And that's what I mean, Charles — you are filling your mind with filth."

"That's not what I'm talking about. I'm talking about how you define what you see. I do not define it as filth and you do define it as filth so what I'm saying is: speak for yourself."

See how he is. Here I am trying to say how I feel. That's what Dr. Bridges kept saying: "Get in touch with your feelings. Get in touch with your feelings and express them. You'll only be telling the truth." I know exactly how I feel about this magazine business but as soon as I express that to Charles, he gets off on some dictionary definitions. It's just like him. I'm concerned about this whole issue of sex in a consecrated marriage. How am I supposed to carry on a normal sex life with somebody who is reading these filthy magazines and coming up with no telling what in his mind. That was the whole problem on our honeymoon. I'll bet you five hundred dollars.

"Charles," I said, "the problem is this: I don't know what to do in a marriage that has this extra ingredient of filthy sex in it."

Charles didn't answer. He got in the car and we drove on home without saying one solitary word.

When we walked through the front door I said, "Charles, where do you keep all those filthy magazines?"

"Raney, it seems to me we could just leave this whole discussion off — cancel it, forget it."

"That would be fine with you, but what happens when you catch *me* doing something wrong?"

"Raney, you don't. . . ."

"What?"

"Don't you see that. . . . Listen, when I read one of those magazines, you tell me who is being hurt."

"First of all, Charles, you don't just read the magazine, you look at it."

"Okay, okay — whatever. What I want you to do is tell me who's getting hurt."

"Charles, the Bible warns against lusting in your heart. That's all I need to know about the subject. That's all I'm supposed to know about the subject. That's all I want to know about the subject. That's all there *is* to know about the subject."

"Raney, don't you see what that does to me? Don't you see how that leaves me without a chance to communicate anything about this to you? Don't you see there is no way I can talk to you now, and I have things inside me that I want to say — that I want to explain?"

I could tell he was serious. It seemed like he really did want to talk — like he needed to explain something, and Lord knows we're not all perfect, so:

"Okay, Charles," I said. "I'll listen. You go ahead and talk and I promise I'll listen." Dr. Bridges would have been proud.

"Raney, I can live a perfect sex life in my body, a faithful sex life. No problem. But not in my mind. Why did God give me this kind of mind if he —"

"Charles, you can't —"

"Raney, you *said* you would listen."

You know it's really hard to listen to somebody when they've got something completely wrong. It's almost like you want to mash them out, do away with them, clean them up.

"Okay," I said. "Go ahead."

"Well, for some reason — I guess because we reproduce biologically — I have an attraction for the opposite sex. I didn't put it there. It was there when I came along. Now what am I supposed to do with that?"

"Well. . . ."

"No, wait. That was a rhetorical question."

"I was just going to answer it."

"No, a rhetorical question doesn't need an answer."

"Then why do you call it a question? I never heard of a question that don't need a answer."

"It's a statement in question form."

"Well, why don't you just —"

"Wait a minute, Raney. Let me finish? Okay? Okay?"

"Okay."

"Now, I can't hide what flows around in my mind — and furthermore, I don't intend to. And I believe we should both be entitled to certain privileges of privacy. I believe that with all my heart, Raney. That does not mean anything about my soul going to hell. It does not mean anything about my having a filthy mind. It does not mean anything about my being unfaithful. It does not mean anything about committing adultery. It does not mean *anything* but that I am practicing my freedom, in a free country, with a God-given mind that has fantasies sometimes for God's sake."

"Charles, I don't think I can talk about this."

"Raney, please. I'm not asking you to talk about this. I'm asking you to listen. To try to understand my point of view. You don't have to agree. Listen, you don't have to agree with any of this. I'm asking you to try to understand something which you don't necessarily agree with. And then we can be different. We can be different about some things, Raney. It's okay. The world won't fall apart. If we could just agree to disagree and not get all bent out of shape. That was one of the main things we decided in therapy."

"I'm not all bent out of shape." I was thinking that if I could hold off, not get mad — go ahead and let Charles get all of this *out*, then maybe down the road somewhere we could solve the problem, and in the meantime, he'd have to listen to my views on all this. "I'm okay. I'm glad you're getting all this out, Charles. I think that's a good idea . . . and . . . Where do you keep all those filthy magazines?"

"Raney."

"Well?"

"Raney, I —"

"I just don't want to stumble over one of those filthy magazines some day when I'm looking for some reading material for our son or daughter."

"Raney, have you listened to — or heard — anything I've said?"

"I think so."

"I hope so."

I don't mind us disagreeing so much. It's just *what* we disagree over. And I do wish we could disagree over things it's *okay* to disagree over. This sex business is one of the few areas in the universe, it seems to me, that we ought *not* to disagree over. What kind of car you want — okay. Whether to get the freezer on top or on the bottom of the refrigerator — okay. Whether or not to plant corn in the garden — okay. But there are some things. And sex is one of them. But I do think Charles and me have got to give each other a chance to talk about things. Next time he'll have to be quiet and listen to me. I did my part this time.

Some of what he said did make some sense somehow. I've just never thought about it along the lines of living in a free country.

* * *

There is this hussy in Listre — Thomasina Huggins. She lives five or six miles down Route 14 and she comes by the store about three times a week. Her husband left her and moved to Alaska. She's after Sneeds — anybody could tell — and I guess she's caught him.

Daddy gave me a key to the store in case I need to get in for any reason when it's closed. Last Saturday night, when I needed some eggs for Sunday morning, was just such an occasion. When I drove up I noticed Sneeds's pickup truck and Thomasina's black and orange Thunderbird parked around at the side of the store. The store closes at six on Saturdays, and it was about nine-fifteen when I pulled up.

Well, I'm not one to pry, but I absolutely had to have a dozen eggs. I unlocked the door and went in. I didn't try to be noisy and I didn't try to be quiet. The light from the street light was strong enough for me not to have to turn on the overhead light.

They were in the feed room. I heard them. And the light was on in there. The door was cracked. And the eggs happened to be by that door. So I *had* to see what they were doing. I couldn't help it.

They were sitting on three stacked bags of feed amongst all the other bags on the far side of the feed room with their feet on another bag and they had on *just their underpants* and were reading this magazine — just thumbing through it. It was one of those you-know-what magazines. And there was Thomasina's dinners just hanging there as big as day. I was absolutely shocked that something like this could be going on in my own daddy's store. I felt like I was in a trance. Her lipstick was as red as a candy apple and she had on dangly shiny ear rings. Tacky.

Sneeds poured her something out of a bottle into a *plastic cup* and she says, "Not too much, Sneeds," and giggles.

Well, what was I to do? I stepped — and the floor squeaked as loud as a creaking door. When I lifted my foot it squeaked again. They looked in my direction and I started for the front door and said real loud and innocent, "Is anybody here?" There was nothing else to do. There was this scrambling and the feed room door slammed shut.

I hollered, "Sneeds, is that you?"

"Yes. It's me. Is that Raney?"

"Yes. I just had to come get a" — I looked to see what was close — "flashlight battery. See you later." And I got out of there. I had the eggs, too.

Well, I have never. Sneeds Perry, of all people. Who I work with. What could I do? Talk to Sneeds? Charles? Daddy? I didn't see how. Aunt Flossie? Dr. Bridges? I guessed not.

Well, Monday morning Sneeds acted nervous and jumpy. Who wouldn't? I didn't say one word. I didn't even look at him. I just went about my business, and at about ten A.M. when I'm back wiping off the drink box, he comes up behind me and says, "Did you know Thomasina Huggins and me are getting married?"

"Lord, no," I said, and kept polishing.

"Yep, we are. But we ain't told nobody."

I turned around and leaned up against the drink box.

"Yep," says Sneeds, "we were having a little engagement party when you came in Saturday night. But we don't want to tell anybody, so don't mention it yet."

Sneeds was lying bigger than a house. He wadn't a bit more engaged than me. He had had his fingers in the cookie jar that very weekend in the very feed room we were standing beside and was trying to mask it all over by lying to me about being engaged.

"Well, Sneeds, it's none of my business what you do in that feed room."

"What do you mean?" he says.

"Just that. It's okay whatever you do."

"Did you look in there Saturday night?"

"In where?"

"In the *feed* room."

"I certainly didn't." I felt my cheeks and neck getting hot. "Sneeds, I'm real happy you're getting married and I just suppose I think a feed room is an unusual place to have an engagement party." I started wiping the drink box again — with my back to it.

"Well, the truth is, Raney — we keep a little bottle back there and we just stopped by for a little harmless nip. And I'll tell you something else: you only live once."

All this was too much. I got the conversation stopped, went back to polishing the drink box, and Sneeds went back up front.

Engagement party my foot. It was a party all right, but not an engagement party. They were having a mighty good time and it came back to me about what Charles had said about nobody getting hurt making something all right. Just because nobody is getting hurt does not make something right. Nobody was getting hurt when Hitler *started* making speeches before World War II or when the Japanese were *on their way* to Pearl Harbor.

If Sneeds and Thomasina had been married, maybe it would have been different.

Monday night I'd decided to talk to Charles about the whole incident when Sandra and Bobby Ferrell (who've been saying they were coming to see us) knocked on the door.

Charles gets furious when somebody decides to just drop by and he refuses to go see anybody unless they know for sure he's coming. I say that takes all the surprise out of it, which is one of the best parts of a visit anyway. Charles thinks it has to do with manners and he can't understand that since Sandra and Bobby were raised around here they don't have all these insights into Emily Post that he has. And never will, or want to, or should have.

Anyway, they came on in and sat down and asked us to sing a song. We sang a bluegrass arrangement of "Bless Be the Tie that Binds" which I worked up last week. We both like it and plan to start finishing all our gigs with it.

When we finished, Bobby and Sandra clapped. Then Bobby started asking Charles questions like he was getting to know him. He asked Charles if he ever did any hunting. I've heard Charles talk about hunting just enough to know he don't like it.

"No, I can't say as I have," said Charles. "Never had the heart to."

"Never had the heart to?" says Bobby.

"That's right. Never had the heart to."

"Well, the way I always look at it," says Bobby — "Do you eat chicken?"

"Yeah, I eat chicken," says Charles.

"Well, the way I always look at it is this: somebody has to kill the chicken, and the chicken is meat and the way I look at it is — I might as well kill my own meat. I mean what's the difference?"

"Well, the difference is —"

"I mean it all comes out the same."

"Well, I'd never thought about it exactly that way. I think —"

"Most people don't. I mean if a person absolutely refuses to eat meat for some reason then I don't have no argument, because it's a fact that I do eat meat and if they don't, I can understand them being against killing it. It's just that if *I* eat it, then I don't see that it makes no difference who kills it — me or the butcher."

"I don't have any problem with eating it," says Charles, "but I think I would have some problem shooting it — whatever it is: a squirrel or something. The idea of my taking away life just happens to bother me."

"Charles," I said, "you don't seem to mind catching fish. That's not exactly logical is it? You're taking away a fish's life as much as a squirrel's."

"It bothers me more with animals because —"

"Wait a minute," says Bobby, and laughs. "Animals kill each other, you know."

"People kill each other!" says Charles. "That doesn't mean I'm supposed to kill people!"

I was getting embarrassed. Here was Charles already raising his voice, but on the other hand I could see why. I realized I hadn't ever talked to Bobby very much — or he hadn't ever talked to me very much. He was insisting too hard on this subject of hunting all of a sudden; and in a way I didn't blame Charles for raising his voice. I couldn't figure out exactly what Bobby was getting at.

Daddy asked Charles to go hunting once and Charles said no and that's all that was ever said about it. I figured I ought to say something on Charles's behalf:

"But, Bobby, what if you don't like to shoot things that are alive?"

"Well, not only do these animals, and fish, kill each other for a purpose, unlike people — I mean hawks killing quail and rabbits and stuff — but you've got the natural environment doing the same thing. I mean flash floods and so forth wipe out millions of animals a year. And another thing: money from hunting licenses helps preserve wildlife, which is one of the reasons it's good to hunt."

Charles was getting fidgety, so I tried to remind Bobby what I was talking about. "But what if you don't like to shoot things that are alive? Charles don't like to shoot things that are alive and I don't think I would either, even though my daddy does it."

"Well, have you ever shot a quail on the wing?" Bobby says to me.

"I never shot one anywhere."

"No, I mean flying."

"No, I never even shot a rifle."

"You don't shoot a quail with a rifle. You use a shotgun."

"Oh, no, I never have and I don't think I'd want to. I feel like Charles in that respect. We've talked about it before."

"Well. Whatever. But there's a great deal of sportsmanship and marksmanship involved. I mean you have to have very good reflexes, and good eyesight, and be very quick."

"You're probably in the NRA," says Charles.

"That's right," says Bobby.

"What's the difference between having good reflexes and being quick?" I said. I didn't now what the "NRA" had to do with it.

"Well, with reflexes you're speaking about accuracy, and with quickness you're talking about speed. But I mean, really, each to his own. I guess I just see it as a sport and darn exciting at times and a way to put meat on the table, unless of course you're some weirdo vegetarian or something."

I looked at Charles, wondering if he'd say it. Charles looked at me. "Charles's mother is a vegetarian," I said. "But she ain't weirdo."

I must say I felt right good about that. Bobby shrugged his shoulders and looked like he was looking with his eyes for something to say. I just hadn't ever talked to Bobby and I hadn't realized he'd be so insistent. Sandra came in on our side — at least more on our side than on Bobby's.

"What I can't stand," she said, "is *cleaning* quail. Bobby expects me to clean them. He'll come in and —"

"You don't clean your own game?" says Charles.

"Well, I clean them sometimes."

"When did you ever clean the first bird?" says Sandra. She was looking at Bobby like she didn't like him.

Bobby was getting a little fidgety now. "I've cleaned them before." He looked at Sandra like he could shoot *her*. I noticed that that was the first time he'd looked at her at *all*.

"Well, I can't remember when," says Sandra.

"Your daddy is a big hunter," I said to Sandra. She certainly deserved a right to be included.

"Oh, yes. He's been hunting with your daddy before, and he goes with Sneeds Perry right much — the one who works out at your daddy's store."

"Do you know if Sneeds is engaged?" I said.

"No. I hadn't heard. Why?"

"I just wondered. I guess I ought to ask him. I'm working part time out at the store now and I was just wondering. Somebody said something about it."

"How do you like working out there?"

I went on to talk about the store for a while. They didn't stay a whole lot longer and I must admit I understood a little more about how Charles could feel about Bobby.

When they left me and Charles laughed about how Bobby's face looked when I said Charles's mother was a vegetarian. And I felt a little bit sorry for Sandra — for how she's bound to feel left out sometimes. I asked Charles if he noticed and he said he did.

I forgot to bring up about the feed room until we were going to bed, but then I decided not to — in case it developed into a long conversation with Charles going on and on about his views on all this sex and so forth.

* * *

Well, here's how this feed room business turned out. My soul is still reeling about the whole thing. I've prayed about it, with some success, I suppose.

Two nights ago, Thursday, me and Charles were driving back from supper at the Ramada Inn and I had to get a half gallon of milk. It was about eight and the store was closed.

Something I must explain first is this: Charles has got me to sip his white wine at the Ramada a few times — to show me how much better it makes the food taste. One night I tried a whole glass. Just to make the food taste better because it can make the food taste some better, depending on what you're eating. Thursday night when we stopped by the store I'd had *two* glasses. For the first time. I don't think I'll ever do it again, and I shouldn't have then. I can't decide what I think about it exactly. It does make the food taste some better.

Charles followed me into the store and I got the milk and while I was leaving a IOU note by the cash register I told Charles about seeing Sneeds and Thomasina in the feed room. Being there in the store helped me tell about it.

Charles walks on back to the feed room and turns on the light and starts looking around. I followed him.

Well, I don't know how to explain what happened. What happened to me inside. It was like something was melting to a gold-yellow color — and I just don't know how to explain this, but I wanted to sit on a feed bag in my underwear. I don't know where it all came from, unless from the very Devil himself, but I thought to myself: Charles and me are married. There's nothing in the Bible about what married people can't do together. It's a free country.

But I don't know how to explain this feeling inside me. It seemed like such a cozy room. It was warm and those feed bags had this smell which was kind of musky, and they had this rough texture, and Charles found the magazine and I felt as awful as I've ever felt in my life but at the same time just as good. Honest. Both together.

I decided to go with the good. I didn't say a word.

"Here's the magazine," Charles said, "and the booze — Southern Comfort."

I didn't say a word. I walked over to Charles and he looked at me and he must have seen what was happening inside me because he just simply gave me this little kiss on the lips and let it linger for a while longer than it should have and I wasn't thinking about what was going on in his head, but what was happening inside me and it was like I had to give over my insides to the Devil but I couldn't fight it and for heaven's sake we are married I said to myself.

"Charles, let's sit down. My knees are a little weak."

Charles's cheeks were flushed. I can always tell.

So we sat on that tight bag of feed and Lord have mercy I did want my *bare* fanny on it and Charles says:

"Now Raney, you just relax. I want you to see that . . . look, there are stories in here, and advertisements and —"

And I'm sitting there wanting to take my skirt *and panties* off for heavens's sake, and I don't care what's in the magazine. Charles and me are married. So:

I stood up and Charles stopped thumbing through the magazine and everything was melting inside and jumping around getting excited and I said to myself, "Lord, please excuse me for a minute." And that almost broke what was happening inside but it came right back so I figured the Lord had done so: excused me — and Charles was looking up at me like he didn't know *what* to expect. So I just — very slowly, to get it right, to give it the best effect which would fit what was going on inside me — I just unbuttoned the three buttons down the side of my skirt, slowly, and let my eyes droop to about half mast, and let the skirt drop, and then popped the elastic on my panties and pulled them right off over my ankles and put my warm fanny down beside Charles on that tight, rough feed bag and said:

"Hand me a warm-up of Southern Comfort, Charles — my fanny's getting cold."

And after that it was me, Charles, and the feedbags. And I'd just had my hair done that afternoon. But I didn't pay a bit of mind to that. I was happy and it was wonderful.

I've reconciled myself to it.

Louise Erdrich

from
Love Medicine

from
The Plunge of the Brave

(1957)
NECTOR KASHPAW

I NEVER WANTED much, and I needed even less, but what happened was that I got everything handed to me on a plate. It came from being a Kashpaw, I used to think. Our family was respected as the last hereditary leaders of this tribe. But Kashpaws died out around here, people forgot, and I still kept getting offers.

What kind of offers? Just ask . . .

Jobs for one. I got out of Flandreau with my ears rung from playing football, and the first thing they said was "Nector Kashpaw, go West! Hollywood wants *you*!" They made a lot of westerns in those days. I never talk about this often, but they were hiring for a scene in South Dakota and this talent scout picked me out from the graduating class. His company was pulling in extras for the wagon-train scenes. Because of my height, I got hired on for the biggest Indian part. But they didn't know I was a Kashpaw, because right off I had to die.

"Clutch your chest. Fall off that horse," they directed. That was it. Death was the extent of Indian acting in the movie theater.

So I thought it was quite enough to be killed the once you have to die in this life, and I quit. I hopped a train down the wheat belt and threshed. I got offers there too. Jobs came easy.

I worked a year. I was thinking of staying on, but then I got a proposition that discouraged me out of Kansas for good.

Down in the city I met this old rich woman. She had her car stopped when she saw me pass by.

"Ask the chief if he'd like to work for me," she said to her man up front. So her man, a buffalo soldier, did.

"Doing what?" I asked.

"I want him to model for my masterpiece. Tell him all he has to do is stand still and let me paint his picture."

"Sounds easy enough." I agreed.

The pay was fifty dollars. I went to her house. They fed me, and later on they sent me over to her barn. I went in. When I saw her dressed in a white coat with a hat like a little black pancake on her head, I felt pity. She was an old wreck of a thing. Snaggle-toothed. She put me on a block of wood and then said to me, "Disrobe."

No one had ever told me to take off my clothes just like that. So I pretended not to understand her. What robe?" I asked.

"Disrobe," she repeated. I stood there and looked confused. Pitiful! I thought. Then she started to demonstrate by clawing at her buttons. I was just about to go and help her when she said in a near holler, "Take off your clothes!"

She wanted to paint me without a stitch on, of course. There were lots of naked pictures in her barn. I wouldn't do it. She offered money, more money, until she offered me so much that I had to forget my dignity. So I was paid by this woman a round two hundred dollars for standing stock still in a diaper.

I could not believe it, later, when she showed me the picture. *Plunge of the Brave* was the title of it. Later on, that picture would become famous. It would hang in the Bismarck state capitol. There I was, jumping off a cliff, naked of course, down into a rocky river. Certain death. Remember Custer's saying? The only good Indian is a dead Indian? Well from my dealings with whites I would add to that quote: "The only interesting Indian is dead, or dying by falling backwards off a horse."

When I saw that the greater world was only interested in my doom, I went home on the back of a train. Riding the rails one night the moon was in the boxcar. A nip was in the air. I remembered that picture, and I knew that Nector Kashpaw would fool the pitiful rich woman that painted him and survive the raging water. I'd hold my breath when I hit and let the current pull me toward the surface, around jagged rocks. I wouldn't fight it, and in that way I'd get to shore.

Back home, it seemed like that was happening for a while. Things were quiet. I lived with my mother and Eli in the old place, hunting or roaming or chopping a little wood. I kept thinking about the one book I read in high school. For some reason this priest in Flandreau would teach no other book all four years but *Moby Dick*, the story of the great white whale. I knew that book inside and out. I'd even stolen a copy from school and taken it home in my suitcase.

This led to another famous misunderstanding.

"You're always reading that book," my mother said once. "What's in it?"

"The story of the great white whale."

She could not believe it. After a while, she said, "What do they got to wail about, those whites?"

I told her the whale was a fish as big as the church. She did not believe this either. Who would?

"Call me Ishmael," I said sometimes, only to myself. For he survived the great white monster like I got out of the rich lady's picture. He let the water bounce his coffin to the top. In my life so far I'd gone easy and come out on top, like him. But the river wasn't done with me yet. I floated through the calm sweet spots, but somewhere the river branched.

So far I haven't mentioned the other offers I had been getting. These offers were for candy, sweet candy between the bedcovers. There was girls like new taffy, hardened sourballs of married ladies, rich marshmallow widows, and even a man, rock salt and barley sugar in a jungle of weeds. I never did anything to bring these offers on. They just happened. I never thought twice. Then I fell in love for real.

Lulu Nanapush was the one who made me greedy.

At boarding school, as children, I treated her as my sister and shared out peanut-butter-syrup sandwiches on the bus to stop her crying. I let her tag with me to town. At the movies I bought her licorice. Then we grew up apart from each other, I came home, and saw her dancing in the Friday-night crowd. She was doing the butterfly with two other men. For the first time, on seeing her, I knew exactly what I wanted. We sparked each other. We met behind the dance house and kissed. I knew I wanted more of that sweet taste on her mouth. I got selfish. We were flowing easily toward each other's arms.

Then Marie appeared, and here is what I do not understand: how instantly the course of your life can be changed.

I only know that I went up the convent hill intending to sell geese and came down the hill with the geese still on my arm. Beside me walked a young girl with a mouth on her like a flop-house, although she was innocent. She grudged me to hold her hand. And yet I would not drop the hand and let her walk alone.

Her taste was bitter. I craved the difference after all those years of easy sweetness. But I still had a taste for candy. I could never have enough of both, and that was my problem and the reason that long past the branch in my life I continued to think of Lulu.

Not that I had much time to think once married years set in. I liked each of our babies, but sometimes I was juggling them from both arms and losing hold. Both Marie and I lost hold. In one year, two died, a boy and a girl baby. There was a long spell of quiet, awful quiet, before the babies showed up everywhere again. They were all over in the house once they started. In the bottoms of cupboards, in the dresser, in trundles. Lift a blanket and a bundle would howl beneath it. I lost track of which were ours and which Marie had taken in. It had helped her to take them in after our two others were gone. This went on. The youngest slept between us, in the bed of our bliss, so I was crawling over them to make more of them. It seemed like there was no end.

Sometimes I escaped. I had to have relief. I went drinking and caught holy hell from Marie. After a few years the babies started walking around, but that only meant they needed shoes for their feet. I gave in. I put my nose against the wheel. I kept it there for many years and barely looked up to realize the world was going by, full of wonders and creatures, while I was getting old baling hay for white farmers.

So much time went by in that flash it surprises me yet. What they call a lot of water under the bridge. Maybe it was rapids, a swirl that carried me so swift that I could not look to either side but had to keep my eyes trained on what was coming. Seventeen years of married life and come-and-go children.

And then it was like the river pooled.

Maybe I took my eyes off the current too quick. Maybe the fast movement of time had made me dizzy. I was shocked. I remember the day it happened. I was sitting on the steps, wiring a pot of Marie's that had broken, when everything went still. The children stopped shouting. Marie stopped scolding. The babies slept. The cows chewed. The dogs stretched full out in the heat. Nothing moved. Not a leaf or a bell or a human. No sound. It was like the air itself had caved in.

In that stillness, I lifted my head and looked around.

What I saw was time passing, each minute collecting behind me before I had squeezed from it any life. It went so fast, is what I'm saying, that I myself sat still in the center of it. Time was rushing around me like water around a big wet rock. The only difference is, I was not so durable as stones. Very quickly I would be smoothed away. It was happening already.

I put my hand to my face. There was less of me. Less muscle, less hair, less of a hard jaw, less of what used to go on below. Fewer offers. It was 1952, and I had done what was expected —

fathered babies, served as chairman of the tribe. That was the extent of it. Don't let the last fool you, either. Getting into the big-time local politics was all low pay and no thanks. I never even ran for the office. Someone put my name down on the ballots, and the night I accepted the job I became somebody less, almost instantly. I grew gray hairs in my sleep. The next morning they were hanging in the comb teeth.

Less and less, until I was sitting on my steps in 1952 thinking I should hang on to whatever I still had.

That is the state of mind I was in when I began to think of Lulu. The truth is I had never gotten over her. I thought back to how swiftly we had been moving toward each other's soft embrace before everything got tangled and swept me on past. In my mind's eye I saw her arms stretched out in longing while I shrank into the blue distance of marriage. Although it had happened with no effort on my part, to ever get back I'd have to swim against the movement of time.

I shook my head to clear it. The children started to shout. Marie scolded, the babies blubbered, the cow stamped, and the dogs complained. The moment of stillness was over; it was brief, but the fact is when I got up from the front steps I was changed.

I put the fixed pot on the table, took my hat off the hook, went out and drove my pickup into town. My brain was sending me the kind of low ache that used to signal a lengthy drunk, and yet that was not what I felt like doing.

Anyway, once I got to town and stopped by the tribal offices, a drunk was out of the question. An emergency was happening.

And here is where events loop around and tangle again.

It is July. The sun is a fierce white ball. Two big semis from the Polar Bear Refrigerated Trucking Company are pulled up in the yard of the agency offices, and what do you think they're loaded with? Butter. That's right. Seventeen tons of surplus butter on the hottest day in '52. That is what it takes to get me together with Lulu.

Coincidence. I am standing there wrangling with the drivers, who want to dump the butter, when Lulu drives by. I see her, riding slow and smooth on the luxury springs of her Nash Ambassador Custom.

"Hey Lulu," I shout, waving her into the bare, hot yard. "Could you spare a couple hours?"

She rolls down her window and says perhaps. She is high and distant ever since the days of our youth. I'm not thinking, I swear, of anything but delivering the butter. And yet when she alights I cannot help notice an interesting feature of her dress. She turns sideways. I see how it is buttoned all the way down the back. The buttons are small, square, plump, like the mints they serve next to the cashbox in a fancy restaurant.

I have been to the nation's capital. I have learned there that spitting tobacco is frowned on. To cure myself of chewing I've took to rolling my own. So I have the makings in my pocket, and I quick roll one up to distract myself from wondering if those buttons hurt her where she sits.

"Your car's air-cooled?" I ask. She says it is. Then I make a request, polite and natural, for her to help me deliver these fifty-pound boxes of surplus butter, which will surely melt and run if they are left off in the heat.

She sighs. She looks annoyed. The hair is frizzled behind her neck. To her, Nector Kashpaw is a nuisance. She sees nothing of their youth. He's gone dull. Stiff. Hard to believe, she thinks, how he once cut the rug! Even his eyebrows have a little gray in them now. Hard to believe the girls once followed him around!

But he is, after all, in need of her air conditioning, so what the heck? I read this in the shrug she gives me.

"Load them in," she says.

So the car is loaded up, I slip in the passenger's side, and we begin delivering the butter. There is no set way we do it, since this is an unexpected shipment. She pulls into a yard and I drag out a box, or two, if they've got a place for it. Between deliveries we do not speak.

Each time we drive into the agency yard to reload, less butter is in the semis. People have heard about it and come to pick up the boxes themselves. It seems surprising, but all of that tonnage is going fast, too fast, because there still hasn't been a word exchanged between Lulu and myself in the car. The afternoon is heated up to its worst, where it will stay several hours. The car is soft inside, deep cushioned and cool. I hate getting out when we drive into the yards. Lulu smiles and talks to the people who come out of their houses. As soon as we are alone, though, she clams up and hums some tune she heard on the radio. I try to get through several times.

"I'm sorry about Henry," I say. Her husband was killed on the railroad tracks. I never had a chance to say I was sorry.

"He was a good man." That is all the answer I get.

"How are your boys?" I ask later. I know she has a lot of them, but you would never guess it. She seems so young.

"Fine."

In desperation, I say she has a border of petunias that is the envy of many far-flung neighbors. Marie has often mentioned it.

"My petunias," she tells me in a flat voice, "are none of your business."

I am shut up for a time, then. I understand that this is useless. Whatever I am doing it is not what she wants. And the truth is, I do not know what I want from it either. Perhaps just a mention that I, Nector Kashpaw, middle-aged butter mover, was the young hard-muscled man who thrilled and sparked her so long ago.

As it turns out, however, I receive so much more. Not because of anything I do or say. It's more mysterious than that.

We are driving back to the agency after the last load, with just two boxes left in the backseat, my box and hers. Since the petunias, she has not even hummed to herself. So I am more than surprised, when, in a sudden burst, she says how nice it would be to drive up to the lookout and take in the view.

Now I'm the shy one.

"I've got to get home," I say, "with this butter."

But she simply takes the turn up the hill. Her skin is glowing, as if she were brightly golden beneath the brown. Her hair is dry and electric. I heard her tell somebody, where we stopped, that she didn't have time to curl it. The permanent fuzz shorts out here and there above her forehead. On some women this might look strange, but on Lulu it seems stylish, like her tiny crystal earrings and the French rouge on her cheeks.

I do not compare her with Marie. I would not do that. But the way I ache for Lulu, suddenly, is terrible and sad.

"I don't think we should," I say to her when we stop. The shadows are stretching, smooth and blue, out of the trees.

"Should what?"

Turning to me, her mouth a tight gleaming triangle, her cheekbones high and pointed, her chin a little cup, her eyes lit, she watches.

"Sit here," I say, "alone like this."

"For heavensake," she says, "I'm not going to bite. I just wanted to look at the view."

Then she does just that. She settles back. She puts her arm out the window. The air is mild. She looks down on the spread of trees and sloughs. Then she shuts her eyes.

"It's a damn pretty place," she says. Her voice is blurred and contented. She does not seem angry with me anymore, and because of this, I can ask her what I didn't know I wanted to ask all along. It surprises me by falling off my lips.

"Will you forgive me?"

She doesn't answer right away, which is fine, because I have to get used to the fact that I said it.

"Maybe," she says at last, "but I'm not the same girl."

I'm about to say she hasn't changed, and then I realize how much she has changed. She has gotten smarter than I am by a long shot, to understand she is different.

"I'm different now, too," I am able to admit.

She looks at me, and then something wonderful happens to her face. It opens, as if a flower bloomed all at once or the moon rode out from behind a cloud. She is smiling.

"So your butter's going to melt," she says, then she is laughing outright. She reaches into the backseat and grabs a block. It is wrapped in waxed paper, squashed and soft, but still fresh. She smears some on my face. I'm so surprised that I just sit there for a moment, feeling stupid. Then I wipe the butter off my cheek. I take the block from her and I put it on the dash. When we grab each other and kiss there is butter on our hands. It wears off as we touch, then undo, each other's clothes. All those buttons! I make her turn around so I won't rip any off, then I carefully unfasten them.

"You're different," she agrees now, "better."

I do not want her to say anything else. I tell her to lay quiet. Be still. I get the backrest down with levers. I know how to do this because I thought of it, offhand, as we were driving. I did not plan what happened, though. How could I have planned? How could I have known that I would take the butter from the dash? I rub a handful along her collarbone, then circle her breasts, then let it slide down between them and over the rough little tips. I rub the butter in a circle on her stomach.

"You look pretty like that," I say. "All greased up."

She laughs, laying there, and touches the place I should put more. I do. Then she guides me forward into her body with her hands.

Midnight found me in my pickup, that night in July. I was surprised, worn out, more than a little frightened of what we'd done, and I felt so good. I felt loose limbed and strong in the dark breeze, roaring home, the cold air sucking the sweat through my clothes and my veins full of warm, sweet water.

As I turned down our road I saw the lamp, still glowing. That meant Marie was probably sitting up to make sure I slept out in the shack if I was drunk.

I walked in, letting the screen whine softly shut behind me.

"Hello," I whispered, hoping to get on into the next dark room and hide myself in bed. She was sitting at the kitchen table, reading an old catalog. She did not look up from the pictures.

"Hungry?"

"No," I said.

Already she knew, from my walk or the sound of my voice, that I had not been drinking. She flipped some pages.

"Look at this washer," she said. I bent close to study it. She said I smelled like a churn. I told her about the seventeen tons of melting butter and how I'd been hauling it since first thing that afternoon.

"Swam in it too," she said, glancing at my clothes. "Where's ours?"

"What?"

"Our butter."

I'd forgotten it in Lulu's car. My tongue was stuck. I was speechless to realize my sudden guilt.

"You forgot."

She slammed down the catalog and doused the lamp.

I had a job as night watchman at a trailer-hitch plant. Five times a week I went and sat in the janitor's office. Half the night I pushed a broom or meddled with odd repairs. The other half I drowsed, wrote my chairman's reports, made occasional rounds. On the sixth night of the week I left home, as usual, but as soon as I got to the road Lulu Lamartine lived on I turned. I hid the truck in a cove of brush. Then I walked up the road to her house in the dark.

On that sixth night it was as though I left my body at the still wheel of the pickup and inhabited another more youthful one. I moved, witching water. I was full of sinkholes, shot with rapids. Climbing in her bedroom window, I rose. I was a flood that strained bridges. Uncontainable. I rushed into Lulu, and the miracle was she could hold me. She could contain me without giving way. Or she could run with me, unfolding in sheets and snaky waves.

I could twist like a rope. I could disappear beneath the surface. I could run to a halt and Lulu would have been there every moment, just her, and no babies to be careful of tangled somewhere in the covers.

And so this continued five years.

How I managed two lives was a feat of drastic proportions. Most of the time I was moving in a dim fog of pure tiredness. I never got one full morning of sleep those years, because there were babies holed up everywhere set to let loose their squawls at the very moment I started to doze. Oh yes, Marie kept taking in babies right along. Like the butter, there was a surplus of babies on the reservation, and we seemed to get unexpected shipments from time to time.

I got nervous, and no wonder, with demands weighing me down. And as for Lulu, what started off carefree and irregular became a clockwork precision of timing. I had to get there prompt on night number six, leave just before dawn broke, give and take all the pleasure I could muster myself to stand in between. The more I saw of Lulu the more I realized she was not from the secret land of the Nash Ambassador, but real, a woman like Marie, with a long list of things she needed done or said to please her.

I had to run down the lists of both of them, Lulu and Marie. I had much trouble to keep what they each wanted, when, straight.

In that time, one thing that happened was that Lulu gave birth.

It was when she was carrying the child I began to realize this woman was not only earthly, she had a mind like a wedge of iron. For instance, she never did admit that she was carrying.

"I'm putting on the hog." She clicked her tongue, patting her belly, which was high and round while the rest of her stayed slim.

One night, holding Lulu very close, I felt the baby jump. She said nothing, only smiled. Her white teeth glared in the dark. She snapped at me in play like an animal. In that way she frightened me from asking if the baby was mine. I was jealous of Lulu, and she knew this for a fact. I was jealous because I could not control her or count on her whereabouts. I knew what a lively, sweet-fleshed figure she cut.

And yet I couldn't ask her to be true, since I wasn't. I was two-timing Lulu in being married to Marie, and vice versa of course. Lulu held me tight by that string while she spun off on her own. Who she saw, what she did, I have no way to ever know. But I do think the boy looked like a Kashpaw.

Perry Glasser

---

from
MEXICO
(a novella)

WHEN DORALEE Jackson was nine years old her Momma one night gathered her and her two younger brothers up in her arms, ran them out of the house to a taxicab, and took them to the shelter where they lived for two whole months before Momma was sure enough the injunction she got from the judge would really and truly keep Poppa away. Doralee didn't miss Poppa one little bit, and she never told Momma or anybody else about the two times he'd come to her in the night when she was eight and explained exactly what good girls did and kept their mouths shut afterward. Momma didn't miss Poppa much, neither. The swelling on her face went down and she turned into a downright pretty woman once she learned how to take care of her hair, got some clothes, and quit the beer.

The people from the shelter got them an apartment on the southeast side of Des Moines, what was called the Bottoms, and they must have given Momma some training because Momma got a job first as a waitress and then as a cashier at the Denny's out near the interstate. Doralee didn't remember much about those times right after the shelter, just especially how she would be alone and had to take care of her brothers Jimmy and Daniel, making peanut butter sandwiches and when she got to be a little older defrosting fried chicken TV dinners night after night. It wasn't so much taking care of the boys she remembered, but the being alone in the darkness waiting for Momma, the boys asleep, watching the black-and-white television that stood on the kitchen table, expecting anytime that Poppa would show up at the front door and take them away. But he never did, and Doralee never learned just where he'd gone to, and that was just fine with her.

Momma slimmed down, and by the time Doralee was thirteen she understood why there were nights Momma didn't come home at all, or if she did come home made it in at three or four o'clock in the morning. She was having her time, and she was entitled to it, didn't Doralee think? Momma would ask her when they both had a cup of morning coffee in the half-hour before Jimmy and Daniel got out of bed, Momma's lipstick leaving rings on the rim of the cup that later Doralee would have to scrub to get rid of. Momma told her about the truckers that came into the restaurant and how nice some of them were, the Southerners the most gentlemenlike, fellas who'd been to faraway places with names that sounded to Momma (and to Doralee) like places from a storybook. Iron City was Pittsburgh, Bean Town was Boston, and the Music City was Nashville, of course. And there were places that didn't have nicknames, like Des Moines, but sounded nice when you said or heard them (not like Des Moines which didn't sound to Doralee or Momma like nothing at all). Joplin, Missouri. Wichita, Kansas. Bakersfield, California. And the cabs of some of the trucks in the little space behind the driver's seat were fixed up like little apartments, with stereos, a place to sleep, pictures on the wall, even. It was a wonder how those truckers got so much into so tiny a space.

A body might expect all of this to have gotten in the way of Doralee's schooling, but the fact of the matter was that it didn't make much difference at all. Doralee and schooling never had all that much to say to each other. She could read good enough, and she could do her arithmetic, but beyond that school somehow seemed not to be the main thing. They called her "Dumb Dora," of course, but she took that in stride because it came from the kids who didn't know much about real life, like how to cook what you bought at the 7-Eleven, what to do when your little brother burned his hand on the radiator, or how to give your Momma just enough brandy when she had the cramps. *That* stuff never showed up on those tests where you had to fill in the itty-bitty circles with your pencil. She knew what she knew, and she suspected that if the tests had questions about things that mattered, she'd do just fine.

The day she turned seventeen she went to the counselor at school and said she was ready to quit, and the counselor sort of shrugged his shoulders like that might not be such a bad idea. Momma thought it was all right, too.

She went on mornings at the supermarket and looked for an afternoon job, and quick enough got one at the Burger King right near the South Ridge Mall. She hated the stupid polyester uniform, and she had to cut her hair because she wouldn't wear a net on her head, but it was another twenty hours a week. She brought home french fries to reheat for Jimmy and Daniel — they were growing up pretty good and she didn't worry about them anymore, Jimmy good enough at varsity football there was a chance he might go to college the coach said if he didn't hurt himself, and Daniel getting along in junior high. Momma seemed to be slowing down, a steady fellow that had lasted more than a year, now, though Doralee had a hunch he was married someplace or other because Momma clammed up about him whenever Doralee hinted around that. She waited six months and then announced to Momma that she was moving into her own place.

"I'm nearly eighteen," she said.

"You're a baby."

"I ain't never been a baby, ever."

That remark made Momma cry, something she did more and more lately. Doralee was sorry for that, but she couldn't help any, now could she?

But she hadn't been asking permission or for approval, and so soon enough she found an apartment on the third floor of a five-story walk-up. Two rooms that weren't much, but they were furnished, they wanted only a half-month's rent security which would leave her some left over to get linens and plates and whatever, and the place was real close to the bus lines she needed to get to her two jobs.

There had been boys, but they had not been important, what with her not having a lot of time on her hands to go riding in some redneck's pickup and park by Gray's Lake or the Saylorville dam. She knew she didn't look like any damned Hawkeye cheerleader whose shit smelled like ice cream, but she was far from ugly. Her figure was all right, her belly flat, and it seemed to stay that way no matter what she ate. She might have asked for a little more on top, but she did all right with what she had.

Ricky Laughton took her out now and then, a boy she knew from when she was in high school who one day when she still lived with Momma had walked through her checkout aisle and recognized her. He came back a day later to buy just a loaf of bread, and she knew right away he was sweet on her because he could have gone through the speed aisle but instead waited on line with just the one loaf of bread under his arm. He'd take her bowling, they'd have some beers, and once he took her roller-skating, but after a little time they would run out of things to say, and she could predict that soon as the conversation dried up he'd take her home and park a half-block from the building where Momma lived, and then he'd try to kiss her. She'd let him, now and then, but she didn't get any feeling from it, and he never tried to do much else, which was fine with her.

Art Phillips tried to do more. He worked with her at the supermarket, and the very first time he was with her got himself so worked up she almost laughed. He was so serious, smelling of Aqua Velva and hair tonic but still smelling green and wet as the lettuce and cukes he worked with all day long in produce, and he spent the whole Clint Eastwood movie fiddling with the buttons of her blouse, trying to jackknife his hand under her bra, and her all the time keeping her eyes straight ahead on the movie, making like she didn't even know his arm was wrapped like a snake around her neck. When he took her home she practically jumped out of the car before he could turn off the engine, ran into the building where she lived, and leaned against the door while she laughed. He asked her out again, and the second time she played hard-to-get, not so much because she wasn't sure if she liked Arthur well enough, but because she had spent a week trying to figure out if she were a virgin or not. Did what her father had done count? So the third time Arthur took her out — another movie, it was the only thing he could think of — after the movie he bought a six-pack and she let him take her north of the city, halfway to Fort Dodge. It was May, and it was warm. There was moonlight of sorts. They drank the beer, and she let him do it to her in the back seat of the car so she wouldn't have to wonder about it anymore. She liked it all right, and she did it with Arthur one more time to be sure, and while he was going at it she was thinking about the green-checked café curtains she had seen at Montgomery Ward that might go nice over the little window she had in her bathroom.

Two years passed. There were a few other boys, even one or two she could properly call a man, and while she gave herself away now and then, she kept a rein on it, too. She hoped for a man who offered a little excitement. Some part of Doralee still heard the music in those names of places that were far off, those places that Momma's truckers had talked of. Tulsa. Yuba. Chino. Denver. Houston. Corpus Christi. Albuquerque. Doralee Jackson was mired in Des Moines, Iowa, the heart of the toolies, which wasn't the end of the earth, but if you had a mind you could throw a rock off the edge.

The jamokes she came across chewed tobacco and wore adjustable hats that said John Deere on the crown, and it seemed if she let them into her pants they all either disappeared or started right away talking about children and putting in one hundred fifty acres of soybeans and did she want to settle down? Which she most certainly did not. She was not one of these fluff-brained beauties that thought of a man as something that would take care of her forever and ever. No, thank you very much, Doralee Jackson would damn well take care of herself. She wasn't good at much, but she was damned good at that.

She was nineteen when Kirk Dugan came into the Burger King and she was working the second register on the right. He ordered the chicken sandwich, a Dr Pepper, and the large fries, and she hardly looked up, would not have noticed him at all, except that when she gave him change for a five he said,

"I gave you a ten."

She checked the register — she was careful with money — and there was no way he had given her a ten-dollar bill. If he thought so, he was wrong. But she checked, then did a check of the register tape against the cash drawer, running totals, and told him he had given her a five.

He raised his voice the slightest bit, said he would call the manager, what did she think she was doing to him?

"Listen," she said and noticed his black hair, stubble of beard, and blue eyes, so when she started out stern despite herself her voice got soft, "I'll get you the manager if you want. His name is Duncan, but he's going to do what I just did which is to check the receipts against the drawer, and I'm telling you, you gave me a five. Why don't you just sit down and enjoy your sandwich? There're other people waiting."

And that was when he smiled and muttered, "Shit, can't blame a man for trying," and she'd had to laugh when he walked away, looking more sorrowful than a dog in a drought.

She forgot about him, but two hours later when her shift was up and she was ready to leave, she stepped out in front and there he was, still sitting at a table, still sucking on the straw in the same Dr Pepper.

"You need a ride home?"

"The buses run."

"You don't have to be like that."

"I sure do," she said and went to the bus.

While she walked to the bus stop he drove a white Ford flatbed real slow right next to her, the window rolled down so he could talk, him leaning all the way across the seat not watching at all where he was going, the other cars coming around the truck honking their horns, but he didn't seem to mind. She noticed the truck had Illinois plates.

"You're not from around here," she said.

"How'd you know that?"

"I could tell."

At the bus stop he parked and she stood, waiting. She thought he was cute in a rough way. She wasn't at all scared.

"I'm just passing through town for a day or two. Made a delivery. My name's Kirk. Kirk Dugan. You're Doralee."

There was no sign of the bus. It was due in a minute. "You read my name tag."

"That's right. What's your last name?" The flatbed's bad idle made it rattle and cough. Kirk bent toward her and the door swung open. "I could take you home, Doralee."

The bus rumbled up to the stop, and the driver gave Kirk a blast of his horn. Doralee got on the bus, and the whole ride home kept herself from looking out the bus windows to see if the flatbed was following the bus, and when she got off she expected to see it, but it was not there. Walking up the three flights of steps to her place, she didn't know if she was relieved or disappointed.

A month or so later, about fifteen minutes before quitting time at the Burger King, Kirk Dugan showed up again, waiting on line at her register even though the one next to hers was open and twice the girl said, "Can I help someone?" He ordered just a Dr Pepper, smiled at her, and gave her the exact change. Never said a word except to order. At quitting time she walked into the parking lot, her uniform stinking of the smell of cooked beef, and she looked for the flatbed, but it wasn't there, so she started out for the bus stop and that was when she heard her name called. She hadn't seen him because he was in a blue Chevy Nova, slouched way down low in the seat. The Chevy had Iowa license plates. She went to the car.

"You remember me?" he asked.

"Fella from Illinois. Kirk Dugan," she said, and the minute she said his name realized it was a mistake to do so, because then he knew she'd thought about him. He smiled broadly, knowingly. There wasn't any point, then, to stalling, so she went right around the car and got in. The front seat was covered all over by cigarette ashes and crumpled pieces of cellophane. He started the car, making the tires squeal just like she knew he would, and she directed him to her place.

They parked right in front of the walk-up where she lived and he asked if he could see her the next day, now that he knew her address.

"You just passing through?"

"Noper. I'll be here a bit, this time. Got a job. Knew a fellow who knew a fellow, so here I am."

"Doing what?"

"Pump gas. A little mechanical work. Been in town couple of days, got this car, and the guy lets me bunk in this trailer they got out back, until I find a place, he says. How about it? You want to go for a ride with me tomorrow?"

"Ride where?" Doralee knew she was going to say yes, but not quite yet. She saw no harm in it, and the car did have Iowa plates.

"Well, I don't know. I don't know. I was hoping you'd have some ideas about that. I don't know my way around here at all."

He looked so damned confident she wanted to scream, but he was acting like a gentleman, so she said it would be all right if he called for her at 7:30, and he did, the next night. That first time together she let him put his hand in her pants after they kissed some, and in a week he was coming by for her at work every day at the end of her shift, and pretty soon she believed she was in love with him, not for anything he said or did, but just because he had a way about him that made her feel easy with him. He told her about his times in Illinois, how he had been in what he called a boys' school because when he was sixteen — he was twenty-four now — he had gotten caught with three other fellows in a car they had borrowed just to go for a ride, and that was where he had learned to do some mechanical work. It was where he had gotten the Zig-Zag man tattoo with a straight pin and a Bic pen. The Zig-Zag man was the trademark on a brand of rolling paper.

The night she took him up to her own place, he rolled two marijuana cigarettes, and she smoked one, and then they "got it on," which was what Kirk called making love, and it was terrific, the first time she ever got so far into it that afterward she could not remember what had happened, only that she had been rocked and sweaty and exhausted and turned this way and that. His body was hard and lean, all strain and muscle, and his strong hands on her here and there knew just what to touch for how long and exactly how hard to press. She let him spend the night. It was strange to lie beside a man, strange but nice, and sometimes even after he was asleep she'd get the quakes and these little tingles, even though they'd stopped making love hours before. It made her smile, and she was amazed. While he slept, she rolled to her hip and touched his long, black hair, longer than her own, recalling how it had flared out about him, wild, as he had gripped her with his skinny arms. You could give yourself up to a man like that.

In the morning they made love again, but it wasn't as good

because he'd awakened her and started right in, and all she could think about was that she had to pee.

A week later he moved in with her. It was sort of understood.

Kirk knew things, things you could not learn from a book, and Doralee Jackson respected that kind of knowledge. If you're hard up for a drink, you pour hair tonic through white bread, and to check you put a match to it. If it burned red, don't drink it; burned blue, it was okay. She couldn't believe anyone would be that hard up for a drink, but it was good to know a trick or two. He'd traveled a lot, and could tell her how to get from anyplace to anyplace else, reciting the interstate roads and where they came together or went apart, like the whole country was his backyard to play in. And she liked how sometimes they would go in a place and Kirk would get stared at for his hair, and he would stare right back, facing down the crackers, he called it, and she was glad to be stared at as the woman who was with him. Special. Different. She'd never known how much she needed that.

So when after two months of living with Kirk Dugan he said to her one day that he was ready to take off, her heart caught, but then she nearly wept when he asked if she wanted to go along. She did. She did, indeed.

He laughed at her when she said she needed a few days to settle things, especially to say good-bye to Momma and the boys. "That shit just holds you down," he said, but she insisted, and she felt even better about him when Kirk said it was all right, a day or two more would make no never mind.

Doralee was sure Momma didn't believe her story about a job she got in Denver, but Momma gave her fifty dollars and said to be sure to call if she got into trouble and needed more. She seemed tired, tired in a way that had nothing to do with working long hours. Lying to Momma didn't sit well with her, but she took the money. Daniel gave her a big hug and she promised to send him picture postcards of wherever she went, and as soon as she got settled they could all come visit her. And Jimmy listened to her talking to Momma, and then late that night while Momma was drifting off asleep in the big old living room chair, Jimmy took Doralee to the kitchen and while he drank a whole quart of milk straight from the carton told her that she must have thought their Momma was awful stupid. Doralee told him she loved this fellow, Kirk, and Jimmy nodded his head, wiping the milk mustache from his upper lip, understanding especially the part about how she needed to get out, there was nothing here for her anymore, never was, how she was sick of taking care of herself and just wanted a rest, and while Kirk Dugan wasn't some hero out of a book, he was not the villain, either. "If he treats you bad," her brother the all-state tackle said, "you let me know." He hugged her then, and that was all there was to good-byes.

So when Doralee Jackson got into the blue '78 Chevy Nova with Kirk Dugan way up in Iowa, she did not have many doubts, and if the truth was she did not have a pile of good reasons to go along, she did not have many reasons to stay behind. The doubts came quick enough, though, miles before they reached Mexico and the beach at Puerto Peñasco, but by then it was too late, she'd taken her chance, and she had to ride her play out.

The shower stall's blue tile was cracked and chipped from the floor to the ceiling, the grouting, brown and rotten, fell out in chunks, the double bed's springs squealed everytime you rolled over so that you woke up three, four times every night just from moving, and if you made love the damned thing made enough racket you expected every Mexican for two miles around to come by to peek through the raggedy cloth curtain that was nailed into the plaster and hung across the window that faced into the courtyard. The walls were a sickly yellow, the paint was peeling, and right above the bed was a hole you could see clear through to the beams, a hole that looked to Doralee like a horse, or maybe a camel. Over the beat-up bureau was a mirror, and beside that was a lamp with a three-way bulb that only worked at the lowest illumination.

But Doralee Jackson liked the room. And she liked that Kirk made slow love to her that first night, good as old times, and damn! how she liked that shower, rotten tiles, spiders, and all. The water was a miracle, hot as could be, so she came out with her skin tingling and when she pinched her hair she'd washed with the motel's soap, her hair squeaked and she felt her scalp breathe.

They took their meals in a small restaurant just outside the motel's gate, one of the dark luncheonettes they had wandered past that first morning. Eggs for breakfast and a hamburger at night. Doralee wanted to try shrimp Vera Cruzana, or shrimp in butter and garlic, but she kept her mouth shut because they had to pay cash in the restaurant. They were out of cigarette and beer money, so Kirk cursed up a storm and then pried off his boot heel and took out one of the hundred-dollar bills. Getting the heel back on he stomped around the room like a man gone crazy with roaches. It made Doralee laugh, and when Kirk first looked up at her, he glared angry, but then he laughed, too. And the clerk in the motel office gave them change without batting an eyelash, but Kirk threw the deadbolt lock on the door that night and pulled the bureau to block the entrance, convinced they'd have their throats slashed while they slept.

Doralee might have wanted a bathing suit, but her cutoffs and a T-shirt worked okay. She might have wanted some tanning oil for the long afternoons on the beach, but she could do without, her skin naturally darker than Kirk's. All they did was sleep, swim, eat, make love, and sleep some more.

Four days in Rocky Point, and it was clear that no one was going to sell them dope. It would take Kirk a little longer to see that, or at least admit to what was already obvious. Well, it wasn't a bad vacation, and she'd be all right if he'd give it up and they would either head back to the border or to the south, maybe to a place called Mazatlán Doralee had seen on the map where they might have better luck. And if that didn't work, then Mexico City. Whatever it took.

The problem with men was you had to get them to think that everything was their own idea, and Kirk just didn't know how to admit he might have been wrong. He became cranky as a wet baby, hardly speaking to her at all.

Sometime after noon on the fourth day, the sun so hot and white a body couldn't even lie out on the beach, Doralee was in the room. Kirk was who knew where — probably asking dark-eyed little boys who had nothing to eat where the cocaine dealers were. An awful clanking came from the courtyard. She lifted a corner of the maroon curtain and saw a battered old bus pull up beside the Chevy. The bus was the kind that hauled kids to school, but it was grayish-blue, not a bright proper yellow. Mexico. Nothing was right in Mexico.

The men that got off the bus all wore open-necked sport shirts and slacks, bright reds and blues or yellows that were startling in Mexico where everything was sun-bleached to the same no-color washed-out dusty brown or gray. Each of them carried a duffel bag, and they laughed and cursed like men did when they liked each other and were having a good time. Mexicans. But there were three — the three who got off the bus last — taller than the others, paler, and no doubt about it, American boys. She saw them only a second, and then they walked toward the motel office, under the terrace in front of her door, and they were gone.

Later she was with Kirk out on the beach at a round concrete table that had an umbrella that probably once had been painted with colors but now was just metal-colored. They drank beer. The tide was out. All along the beach gulls and pelicans picked at whatever had been left by the tide along the rocky shore.

"You know what's wrong with Mexico?" Kirk asked. "You can't tell what's what. We were in the States, I would know what to do. Find a bar with a pool table, talk to a couple of people, and pretty soon we'd score and be gone. But fucking Mexico, man, fucking Mexico. I bet there's not a pool table in this town."

"Maybe we should head back."

"No way. We have to wait it out. They'll find us, soon enough. They'll find us. If I knew what was what, I'd find them, but I don't, so we'll wait."

"Maybe we should go south."

"South? What in fuck is south?"

"Other towns. Different people."

He chewed a thumbnail. "No. It'll be the same."

"You scared?" She stared out to sea, but felt his eyes on her.

"What's that supposed to mean?"

"Kirk, I'm bored. We're not *doing* anything."

"If you'd done time, you'd have learned patience."

"You did time?"

"Easy time. I told you. The boys' school."

"That's not like jail."

"Shows what you know. Juvey Hall could have been a fucking penitentiary."

She sipped her beer. In the south there'd be cool green jungles and blue parrots. What would that be like? You took a man from what he knew, he closed up. But she was unafraid to wonder. A woman would wonder.

One of the three American men she'd seen come off the bus was emerging through the archway of the cinder-block wall that divided the motel from the beach, trudging across the sand. He carried a towel, and he wore a proper bathing suit. He started going down to the water where some other people were clustered, people with children and coolers, fold-up chairs and fruit, but Doralee saw him notice her and Kirk, and he changed direction, easy as you please, coming toward them across the sand, taking confident strides with his long muscled legs, his bare feet sinking in the white sand, his straw-yellow hair falling over his eyes, a white country-boy smile big as the sky on his face. She kept her head tilted way back and her eyes open, the beer still cold enough in her throat, though she lost a bit that flowed over her chin and dripped to her T-shirt. She wished to God she had a bathing suit.

"Hi," he said, standing just outside the puddle of shade cast by the metal umbrella. "You folks are Americans."

"That's right," Kirk said.

"It's hot."

"Sure is," Kirk said.

"Why don't you sit down in the shade?" Doralee said, and Kirk looked at her sideways, his eyes squinted, but she made as though she was Dumb Dora and did not see him glance at her.

"Thanks, I think I will." He sat between them, closer to Dora than to Kirk, but not so close you had to think anything of it. "I'm Bobby Kelly." He held out his big hand to Kirk, the back of his hand all covered with fine white hairs, the knuckles big and red, rough hands that had known work.

Kirk hesitated, then took Bobby Kelly's hand. "I'm Kirk Dugan. This here is Doralee."

"Doralee Jackson."

"Pleased."

Bobby Kelly was smiling at her, so hard she had to smile back. He was soft-spoken, and his voice had something in it she did not recognize, not Southern or Eastern, but something else that was maybe sorrow and made a girl want to take him home and keep him safe.

"You folks on vacation?" Bobby Kelly asked.

"Yupper."

"Staying at the old Hacienda, huh?" He laughed at some private joke.

Doralee had said nothing since she'd asked him to sit and told Bobby Kelly her whole name, and she knew that if she spoke she risked Kirk's anger later on, but to hell with him. Four days. He didn't know how to make things happen.

"I'm from Iowa," she said.

"Is that right? I've got a cousin in Iowa. In Davenport."

"I know Davenport."

Kirk sniffed as he wiped his lips after draining the last of his beer and throwing the brown bottle onto the sand.

"I'm from Oregon."

"You on vacation?" Kirk asked.

"No." Bobby Kelly swung his legs around and under the table, settling in. He put his elbows on the table. He kept right on looking hard at Doralee while he spoke, and she kept right on looking hard back at him. It was a contest. "I throw for the Penguins."

"What are the Penguins?" Doralee asked.

"The Puerto Peñasco Penguins. Triple-A Mexican baseball club."

Kirk laughed, a mean little laugh that made Doralee want to reach over and slap his face and pull his ears, but instead she said, "How long you been doing that?"

"Three years. I played for the University of Oregon and then came down here. I thought it might be a way to the bigs." His smile was almost an apology. "You know, American baseball."

Kirk took Doralee's still half-full bottle from her and helped himself to a long swallow. "How the hell can you play for a Mexican baseball team?"

"They allow four gringos to a team. I write home about the Penguins, and my Daddy laughs, says it isn't a decent name for a baseball team, sounds like we all wear tuxedoes and waddle in the outfield. But it's not bad ball, actually. Valenzuela once pitched in a league like this."

Doralee wondered who in Creation Valenzuela was, but she just nodded her head, trying not to smile because her teeth were so crooked, and she wondered just how windblown and ugly her hair might be. This beautiful boy from Oregon who wrote letters home to his Daddy — imagine such a thing! — this boy looked like he drank milk at every meal and breathed easy in the mornings.

She said, "Sounds like fun."

"Well, I wouldn't go that far. It's not much fun anymore. I just want to play a while, and I can do that here. Came down for one season, and here I am in my third. The money isn't great, but I get to play."

"If there's no money in it, it's bullshit."

"Kirk, don't be such a downer."

"Shut up."

"I'll say what I please."

"You usually do."

"Hey, I'm sorry . . . ," Bobby Kelly began.

"No problem," Kirk said.

They were silent a minute, watching the ocean, listening to the crash of the waves.

"I don't get to see many American girls down here. Thought I'd come over to talk a few minutes. Practice is at four o'clock and I've got just enough time for a quick dip." He smiled that big good-old-boy smile that made Doralee think of home. "You two are married, right?"

Kirk whooped, his head back and his long hair flying. Bobby Kelly's hair was short, longest in front.

"No, we're not married," she said, and added softly when she was sure Kirk was laughing so hard he wouldn't hear, "We're just traveling together."

"I see," he said and then smiled even more broadly at her, not leering, but glad, Kirk so busy laughing a gut-buster that he couldn't notice, and for the first time Doralee wondered how Bobby Kelly would become her ticket out of here.

Kirk wiped his eyes when he stopped laughing. "I used to play baseball myself," Kirk said. "Second base."

"That right?"

"Sure. In Illinois. At this school I was at for two years. Batted four-twenty-two."

"Is that right?" Bobby Kelly said, and smiled even wider before he pursed his lips and nodded like a man that knew a secret. "Heavy hitter like you would probably like to come to the game tonight. Eight o'clock. I'm pitching. Get you two seats right behind our dugout. Freebies."

Doralee said, "Yes," before Kirk could say a word.

Bobby Kelly smiled and said that he had to be off, shook both their hands — his hand really was rough, but nice — and headed right back for the motel without taking his swim.

"What the hell did you ask that cracker to sit here for?"

"Why not?" Doralee said. "I thought maybe he'd know somebody who might sell dope," she tried, knowing just from having looked at Bobby Kelly that he would never in a million years know anybody like that. But Kirk chewed on that notion a second. She watched his eyes cloud and then get clear. So she added, "And he probably speaks Mexican."

Kirk said, "That asshole probably doesn't know shit."

"Maybe he does."

"Maybe." Kirk threw an empty bottle at a gull that fluttered up and then landed right back, undisturbed.

"So we'll go to the game?"

Kirk drummed his fingers on the table. He looked out to the ocean where the wind made whitecaps on the waves, so strong it brushed foam into the air. "Sure. Why not? We'll have to find out where the damn ballpark is."

"We can find out."

"I hate guys like that."

"Guys like what?"

"Like that. Like that guy. So dumb. He thought I was married to you."

"You want to swim?"

"I want to fuck."

"I want to swim. First."

Kirk smiled, and as she stood he reached to pat her ass.

The tide was coming in and even though it was hot as could be the wind made her feel cool. She walked out a bit, stepping carefully on the rocks ready to hurt you, so unlike Iowa lakefronts where soft bottom mud sucked at your feet, and she bent to splash herself with the water, cold and smelling of salt, and then as a wave came at her she jumped straight up and when she came down she let herself sink, bending her knees, pinching her nose closed. Beneath the surface she opened her eyes and saw motes of light glowing from the sun, bubbles rising around her, and she listened to the total silence, so abruptly different from above the surface, and then she heard a roaring which was her own blood in her ears. She stayed under as long as she could, then exploded up, straightening her legs.

On the concrete terrace before the room Kirk said, "You swim like a shit."

"I never learned to swim."

"Well, you swim like a shit."

"'Bout as good as you play baseball."

"What in fuck does that mean?"

But she didn't have to answer because they were going into the room and on the floor they found a little white envelope with two tickets and on the envelope in pencil was a map to the ballpark. Kirk picked it up and threw the envelope on the bureau. "Are you going to take a shower again?" he said and from behind her put his hands on her hips, pulling her toward him.

In fact, she wanted to. But she had figured out she would have to spread her legs enough to keep him happy, he was too damned dangerously close to being unhappy. She wanted him to want to go south with her, score the dope, make the money, buy the good life, have the good times, but Kirk could never be that bold. He was a mean, petty little crud. But there was no way she could piss him off if she wanted to go to that baseball game. She knew diddley-shit about baseball, had never once in her whole life seen a game except on television, but now she wanted to see a baseball game more than anything. Bobby Kelly might be her chance.

It pissed her off. Kirk Dugan or Bobby Kelly. How did Dora-lee Jackson's life become a matter of this man or that? Damn! She'd fucked up this time.

She pulled Kirk's hands from her hips under her wet shirt and onto her breasts and leaned back against him.

"I know just what you like," he whispered in her ear, "I know you better than you know yourself, woman."

Doralee Jackson was still in love with Kirk Dugan the day they left Des Moines, heading east because he wanted to show her Illinois where he had been raised. But in the car Kirk became silent, and before they got as far as Iowa City he all of a sudden twisted the wheel, bumped the Chevy over the grass divider of the interstate so hard her teeth rattled in her head, and told her that it would be better if they headed west. She loved him for that, the quickness of it, the unthinking swift willingness to allow events to take a course, and she was sure that afternoon that she was onto a good thing because even as her jaw snapped together when the car bounced over the divider she thought of the men she had known who knew nothing of horizons and could never have done anything with less than a month to think, weighing changes and judging prospects, until they'd bled the joy from it, thinking a thing to death. So she was sure she was along for a good ride.

They went to Omaha where Kirk knew some people, and they stayed there in a small apartment above a hardware store on the east side near the Missouri River for a few days with Lee Harkin, a woman named Sherry Anne, and their six cats. Lee and Sherry Anne would be out during the day, so Doralee and Kirk had the place to themselves, to make love on the sofa with the cats looking on, the sunlight strong in the windows, with Kirk so cocky that he left the window shades up, which embarrassed her some until she saw it excited her, too. In the evening they would all smoke a little dope and then walk in the Old

Town or down along the riverfront, the gray river clogged with rusted barges and cranes taller than the office buildings against the western sky.

She liked Sherry Anne all right — she was a washed-out blonde woman older than herself who must have been pretty once — but Lee Harkin frightened her a little. A big man going bald, he had small eyes and a lot of dark hair on his arms. Kirk and he did some business, and Kirk told her later he had expected to do more, but that never happened. One night Kirk argued with Lee Harkin — she didn't know what about — and the next day they were in the car so early in the morning she was half-asleep, and all that day the car took them across Nebraska to Denver, Kirk not saying a word, just smoking one Marlboro after another, the Chevy filling with blue smoke, until late in the afternoon when the Rocky Mountains in front of them were like a wall that meant you couldn't go no further, Kirk punched the seat and said that Lee Harkin was a chicken-shit son-of-a-bitch mother-fucking asshole who'd lost whatever balls he might have ever had.

They didn't stay long in Denver, just a night and a day, and they slept in the car to save some money, something Doralee didn't mind a whole lot because Kirk was smart enough first thing in the morning to get to a roadside restaurant with a bathroom and what was a pretty good breakfast of eggs and home fries. He said he'd been in Denver lots of times, but he got lost on the highways until he finally found Larimer Square. He was sweet that day, standing by her as they walked in and out of the fine stores and she made believe she could afford the dresses and makeup, even in one place trying on this frilly red skirt with a white lace border that actually cost more than three hundred dollars. Another man might have gotten bored and antsy, but Kirk admired the clothes along with her, patient as could be, sitting in a chair near the try-on room sort of staring up at the ceiling and buffing his fingernails against his jeans.

They left Denver near four o'clock in the afternoon, and Doralee was all turned around, but they must have been heading south and east, because by eight o'clock they were in Kansas, and that was when Kirk pulled into the darkest part of a Stuckey's parking lot and told her to wait in the car, he'd be just a minute. Then he smashed the Chevy's interior light before he opened the car door, and with the motor running and the door left wide, he walked to where she could see him in the store's bright glare. He was carrying something heavy and black in his right hand just behind his leg. He came back five minutes later, and even by the dim green and amber glow of the dashboard she could see the heat in his eyes and the sweat on his face. He threw a brown paper bag at her, slammed shut the door, and the Chevy hugged the darkness back out onto the road half a mile before he put the headlights on, pumping the accelerator the whole time.

"You should have told me," she said when they were finally out on the highway and he was watching the speedometer, making sure he stayed right on 55. "You didn't have no right to assume."

"Honest, Doralee, I'd have told you except I was afraid you'd disapprove and leave me. I couldn't stand that."

Put that way, it was hard to argue with him, and she thought that maybe Hell was loving a thief.

She said, "It's dangerous."

"What's the difference? We need money. This is easy."

"Where'd you get the gun?" It was on the seat between them, big and black, and when she asked the question Kirk moved it under the seat between his legs. He took a beer from the back seat, steered with his knee while he popped the Bud.

"Lee. That pussy wouldn't do no work, but he sold me the gun. Two hundred dollars."

"I don't like guns."

"You expect me to go into a place and ask them sweet as pie

to give me what's in the register? And they'll do it, of course, 'cause I'm so pretty, right?"

"I don't like guns."

"You just count what's in that bag, hear?"

Two hundred and twenty-eight dollars. More than she was able to save in three months when she had worked at two jobs in Iowa. She told him.

He smiled, drained the last of the beer, and said, "I figured it right, then. End of the day, dark enough that no one can eyeball the car, and the register's got the day's receipts in it. Pretty slick."

She kept her mouth shut. They did need money — you couldn't go anyplace without it — and when they made it to Wichita late that night, Kirk took her to the finest motel room she had ever imagined. Drapery on the windows, a terrace, real glasses, big gold towels, free movies on the color TV, satin border on the blanket, and plastic wrapped across the toilet so you were sure it was clean.

They walked across the road to a restaurant with table cloths and hot rolls in a basket covered by a napkin. After dinner, the night cool and the stars all out, she realized that she didn't mind much at all what Kirk did as long as he did it so no one got hurt. If that made her a thief at heart and as guilty as he was, well, she would sure be stupid not to enjoy the fruits of his labor. But he should have told her, and she knew she wouldn't trust him anymore, couldn't, because he was sure to get them into all sorts of shit sooner or later. The first sign of trouble — and it had to come, you couldn't just walk into anyplace you wanted wherever you wanted and take money without sometime, someplace having the roof fall in — the first sign, she'd be saying fare thee well.

She loved Kirk Dugan, right enough, but that wasn't the same as saying she was ready to give over her life to him, neither. Look at that sweet girl Sherry Anne. What did she have to show for her life with a thief except six cats in an Omaha apartment over a hardware store?

They drifted south and east a while. It got so that when Kirk told her it was time to stop someplace and make a withdrawal she got only a teensy nervous, sitting outside in the car, watching moths, expecting any second to hear the gun go off. But Kirk was a lucky man — she began to realize that, and like Momma had said, better lucky than smart — and not once did the slightest thing go wrong.

A hundred and thirty-seven from a Missouri gas station, seventy-eight from a convenience store outside Tulsa. They'd sailed down the Will Rogers Turnpike and Doralee watched out the window at the country passing her by, and she was sad for her Momma who'd heard of all these places but would never get to see a one, and here she was, Doralee Jackson from Des Moines, going places. It was not bad. When they had a room she felt clean, and she was happy to wash her clothes and Kirk's in the motel sinks.

Whenever Kirk Dugan stole, that night they lived high, and he would come at her those nights like a bull in breeding season, two, three, and once four times, and afterward he would lie across her exhausted, sweaty, and she would hold him, her fingers laced in his damp hair, and she wondered at the mysterious workings of men, one day cold and so far in themselves you thought they'd forgot your name, and another so filled with force it took her breath away, and how that had to have something to do with what they'd done and how strong they believed they were, but had nothing to do at all with how they felt for a woman.

Driving west in Oklahoma, Interstate 40, Kirk pulled over into a rest area because the sun was in his eyes.

"Why don't you drive?"

"I don't know how."

He thought that was so damned funny, but this was a day he was most like the sweet boy who'd leaned over the seat of a white flatbed truck and followed her all the way to a bus stop, and so he right then and there decided he would teach her, there was so little to it.

They both laughed the two times the car stalled, and then he had her drive in circles and then in figure eights until she learned how much she had to press the brake and how much to turn the wheel, and then Kirk said to her, "You ready for the highway?"

"No way."

"Sure you are."

"Kirk, I can't do that with all those trucks and such."

"Nothing to it. You just keep her at fifty-five, point her, and go."

So he talked her into it, and she stayed in the right lane.

The tires drifted onto the shoulder once, and she raised dust, but he just leaned toward her and almost daintily touched the wheel until they were straight on the road again. Then he said, "You've got to do more than forty."

She was too scared and worried just with going straight to look at the dashboard, so she near wet her pants when he sidled next to her and with his left boot pushed down on her foot and the car speeded up.

"Stop that!"

"You just steer."

"Goddam it, Kirk. Goddam it."

But the car went faster and faster, and Doralee was in a sweat. He would get them both killed for sure, but pretty soon she liked the feel of it, how the car, a ton of machinery, responded to the slightest move she made on the wheel, or the brake, or the accelerator. She drove all the way to Weatherford, and they stopped there. It was something to know she could drive a car if she had to.

That night they were in this beer and pinball machine bar and Doralee was sitting beside Kirk on a high stool, getting more than a little cockeyed giddy on the beer and juke-box country music. He suddenly said to her, "Sit tight. I'll be right back."

She thought he was going to the men's room, and he did, but when he came back he was wild-eyed and she knew he had done something.

"Let's go, Doralee," he said and took her elbow.

"I want to finish this beer."

"Let's go sweetheart I mean right *now!*"

He practically lifted her off the stool, and they went straight out to the car, drove right by the pretty motel where they had taken a room, and out onto the highway. That was how Mr. William Krantz lost his wallet and credit card, taking a leak in a Weatherford bar they called a private club because Oklahoma was a dry state. So private you joined at the door and then drank as much as anybody else.

He showed her what he'd gotten, and explained that the credit card might do them good for two weeks.

"What did you do to get it?"

"I just took it."

"You hit him?"

"Not much."

"Damn it, Kirk. This is different."

"How's it different? I swear, I didn't hurt him much. He'll be fine. What in hell you worried about? Hey, I walked in and stood behind this guy until he got his pecker out and started to pee. You should have seen his face when I reach out and took his wallet. He must have thought he had some queer fiddling with his ass. He spins around, still pissing on the floor, and before he opens his mouth I hit him one good one in the belly. It was pretty funny."

He charged a tank of gas, and she watched carefully to see how it was done, having never owned a credit card. That Kirk Dugan certainly knew things.

They slept that night in the car beside the road, just over the Texas border. As she listened to Kirk breathing in the front seat and she lay curled up in the back, able to look up through the rear window at the stars over Texas, she knew that he was changing. Or she was. Whichever, it didn't matter. She was not so stupid that she believed he only had to hit that man once. No sir. William Krantz must have taken a few hard shots, and Kirk Dugan, the sweet boy who'd leaned across a truck seat not giving a damn about traffic while he talked to her, that Kirk Dugan had given them to him. She hadn't thought it was in him. Maybe it was that exact moment — it was hard to tell — but maybe it was that moment she became more wary of Kirk Dugan than in love with him.

The tedious long roads of the Southwest were like nothing she'd ever seen. Mile after mile of oil rigs and sky. The ride made Kirk talkative, and she found out then his real name was Alex, Alexander Wilshire Dugan, and that he'd "borrowed" cars as a boy in Illinois and spent two years in juvenile hall where he'd met Lee Harkin and a bunch of others he talked about, most of whom he'd lost track of, but he was sure they were doing fine. She had her doubts but kept her mouth shut, gazing out the windows at cattle pens and railroad tracks and the flat land, endless flat land that ran forever brown and away. They saw a sign that said 150 miles to Amarillo, and they both could not believe they were still that far from anyplace — when did Texas end? — so when Kirk said they could kill time and drive all at once, she didn't even think much about what he suggested but unzipped his fly and went down on him right there in the car, in broad daylight at sixty miles an hour. It seemed sinful, she was hot and bored, but she took no pleasure pleasing him, and so she was sure she was out of love with Kirk Dugan.

He told her she was a good girl, and that he wanted to do right by her.

The very next day, headed west into New Mexico after a dull night in Amarillo, he told her he had this idea about running dope up from south of the border to Los Angeles, and that way they'd make a lot of money fast, and maybe they could stay put for a month or two, live high, and have a hell of a time. His eyes got bright and he slapped at the wheel, all excited about what he started to call his plan.

"What will we do with the money?"

"Damn, Doralee, you ask the dumbest questions."

"Well, you answer that one for me, then."

"Why, woman, we'll live it up."

"Like how?"

"We're talking about big money here. Maybe a few thousand dollars. Shit, can't you think of what you would do with a few thousand dollars?"

"I want to know what you'd do."

"We'll get a nice room someplace. Eat good food. Maybe buy some clothes. How's that? Sure. We'll go right back to Denver and get you that red skirt. How'd you like that?"

"I'd like that fine. But I still don't know just what you want to do with so much money."

"Aw, shit. *Spend* it."

She'd wanted to hear him say something else. Anything else. But there he was with no imagination. And hell, she couldn't think of a damned thing, neither. What *did* people do with money? Maybe settle someplace, buy a business, a little card shop or something, and she caught herself, right then, it was a revelation, here she was thinking about not being on the move, just like the men she'd known back in Iowa that she'd thought were so damned lame with their heads and asses buried so deep in black Iowa dirt they'd never think to move. It was a revelation that she, Doralee Jackson, wanted a place that was hers and something to do there. Yes, it was Doralee that was changing, faster than Kirk Dugan might or probably ever could. They said that travel helped a person find herself. Well, she'd been traveling, and it had been one kick-ass journey, but already it was getting old. All Kirk Dugan was was lucky, and no one's luck held out forever, but she couldn't very well say to him, No thanks, drop me off here.

They drove day and night until they were in something called the Organ Pipe Monument in Arizona, and a few miles from the border he stopped the car, got out to take a whizz, and walked with her a dozen or so yards from the road. They were at the 3 mile marker on the west side of the road. She'd never seen so many cactuses, big things with arms just like in a picture book. And it was quiet, no sound of any kind, and she thought that was spooky for a place called Organ Pipe. Kirk told her to look around, remember what the spot looked like, and then he scratched an X on a big white rock. He lifted the rock. Two scorpions, little orange things with tails curled in the air, scuttled out.

"Jesus fucking Christ!" Kirk yelled and dropped the rock. He stamped the scorpions. Lifted his foot and brought his boot down hard, again and again, till they were so flat they were nothing but dust, and then he lifted the rock again, scraped a little depression in the spot under the rock, put the gun in the plastic wrap from a loaf of white bread, and left the gun under the rock. You don't want to go over the border with a gun, he explained, but whether that would matter if they were caught with a car full of marijuana was something she didn't ask him.

They'd been on the road three weeks.

When Bobby Kelly reared back, foot higher than his shoulder, and threw the ball, the ball sliced through the air and hit the catcher's mitt with a sound that let you know that ball had been *thrown*. Chunk! Doralee swore that it sizzled, hissing like the zipper on a winter coat as the ball traveled to the catcher and then Chunk!

You could see every bit of Bobby Kelly in that ball, him falling forward following his arm that had windmilled over his head, all that power right down to the fingers. How the catcher didn't get knocked on his ass was a wonder. It was special to be sitting right behind the dugout watching Bobby Kelly warm up right there on the third base line, sitting in Bobby Kelley's seats.

The top of the dugout gritty with dust was painted a pale turquoise. Kirk Dugan sat way back in his wooden seat beside her, his boots pressed against the cyclone fence trying to make like he wasn't impressed.

They'd found the ballpark easily enough, had parked on a dirt field surrounding the place where everyone left their cars every which way so it was clear no one could leave until everyone left together. This was Mexico, and the common sense of a lined parking lot just could never occur to no greaser, Kirk said, what could you expect?

You would not have thought there were that many people in all of Puerto Peñasco, men smoking cigars and swilling beer from bottles, women with babies in their arms, and what must have been a million children running loose. The field was no pretty patch of emerald grass like on television, but was scrubby and dusty in the infield, and nearly all dirt and pebbles in the outfield. There were no stands out there, just a scoreboard and a big old fence painted with advertisements in Mexican — mostly for beer but one for Coca-Cola — and there were big lights on tall posts that lit the place like day. Moths fluttered at the lights, moths so big you could hear them pattering into the glass, and the night was warm and sticky, the air thick with the smell of grease and fried peppers.

They played some music on the PA system, everyone stood up, and then Bobby Kelly and the rest of the team came out from the dugout, right out from under their feet, and before they started to loosen up and throw the ball around Bobby Kelly came over to the fence and said he was real glad Doralee and Kirk could make it, and when he smiled that American-boy smile so filled with perfect teeth Doralee couldn't help herself but had to smile right back, her crooked teeth and all. A fellow carried stuff up and down the aisles, and Bobby Kelly shouted in Mexican — which proved she was right, he could speak the lingo. The next thing she knew, she and Kirk each had in their hands a paper cone of ice and syrup. Raspberry for her and orange for Kirk. Cold and sweet, coating her throat, delicious. Kirk tried to give the guy some pesos for the treats, but he wouldn't take any, and Kirk bitched about that. Then Bobby Kelly said he had to go to work and he started to throw, and that was when Doralee got so impressed with the sound of a baseball.

Hissss-chunk!

"Look at these greasers," Kirk said. "They're so short no one's got a strike zone."

"What's a strike zone?"

"Boy, you are dumb," Kirk said, but not disrespectful, and he started explaining about knees and armpits, but Doralee was watching the men on the field who looked downright snappy in their uniforms, pinstripes on white flannel, blue lettering, and little caps, and she liked especially how the pants fit. Bobby Kelly had a great butt, and she wondered how she hadn't noticed that on the beach that afternoon, but she remembered it was his hands she was looking at then.

"Do you think he's any good?"

"We'll find out in a minute, I suppose."

"This is fun, Kirk."

He snorted. "Better than the motel room. Why don't they have any television in Mexico?"

She knew barely enough about baseball to follow what was going on, but once the game started she was pretty sure Bobby Kelly was doing all right. The first player he faced struck out, and the next two hit little dribbling shots that were picked up easily and thrown to first base. The Penguins trotted in and she could hear them chattering in the dugout.

"I thought he'd talk to us," she said.

"Nah. Pitcher's got to concentrate."

"He's doing good."

"He's doing all right. When I was a pitcher, I used to do all right."

"I thought you played second base."

"That, too. I played lots of sports. Basketball. Football."

Her brother played football and she knew what her brother and his friends looked like, so she just looked at skinny Kirk Dugan whose real name was Alex and she didn't say a word. He couldn't even bullshit in a straight line.

There wasn't too much excitement, it seemed to her, as the innings went on. Just once a Penguin walked to first base, and that was all that happened. Kirk leaned forward, intent on the game, and Doralee wondered just what her Momma would think of her girl now, sitting in the hot sticky night beside a robber, Doralee, a friend of the pitcher for a Mexican baseball team. She was a long ways from home, she was.

"I tell you, they are throwing smoke," Kirk said. "That Bobby Kelly has a cannon in his sleeve."

What was smoke? "Well, I guess, but I wish something exciting would happen."

"Doralee, you are dumb as rocks, I swear. We've got us two no-hitters going and you want excitement."

"I knew that." She licked her fingers where the ices had melted.

Then Bobby Kelly was standing with the bat in his hands, and he let two pitches go by, but on the third he swung and *craaaack* hit the ball a good one. She stood automatically, just like everyone else, it wasn't something you thought to do, and her fingers gripped the fence. "Go, go!" she heard Kirk yell. The ball sailed high up, past the lights, and then came down right into the center fielder's glove, right at the fence. There was a big sigh from the seats, like everyone let go their breath at the same time. Bobby Kelly was already to second base and he slapped his cap against his leg with disappointment, but came right on in to get his glove and start in pitching again just as though nothing had happened and he hadn't almost hit himself a homerun.

Bobby Kelly threw and nobody hit the ball past the infield. Twice the ball was hit sharp right at him, but both times he sweet as you please caught the ball and gently tossed it to the first baseman. People clapped. By God, she was friends with a star! Then one of the American fellows on the other team cracked the ball a good one down on the ground, and it looked as easy as the others had been, but before it got to the shortstop it hit one of the pebbles and bounced over the fellow's head into the outfield. The seventh inning, and he was the first man to get to first base. The noise was like to make you deaf.

"That wasn't good, huh?" she said.

"I'd say, Doralee. Bad luck, but that shithead should have got the ball anyway."

"You think?"

"Sure. You need reflexes good as mine to play this game."

Bobby Kelly seemed different then. He walked around the pitcher's mound a few times, his face grim, and he picked dirt out of the bottom of his shoe. He dug a little hole with his toe, walked around a few times more, stood with his hands on his hips and looked to the outfield and the darkness beyond the fence, like he was talking to God or something, waiting for an explanation, while all the time a new batter was waiting for him to get started. Then he turned and tried to seem ready, but Doralee knew he wasn't.

He kept glancing over his shoulder at the fellow on first. That fellow had Bobby Kelly's chin on a string and was giving it a tug. Twice Bobby Kelly threw to the first baseman, but there wasn't any heart in it. He threw to the batter, and it should have been a strike, and there was a hell of a groan from all the people in the stands while Bobby Kelly stood and stared at the umpire like the umpire was in on some dirty secret, the same secret that had made the ball hit a rock and sail into the outfield. But he pitched again, and this time the throw was so high the catcher had to jump up to keep the ball from getting past him. The catcher walked the ball back to Bobby Kelly, taking his time before returning to home plate. Sweat shined on Bobby Kelly's face, and he kept wiping his brow with the sleeve of his shirt, tossing the ball into his glove three, four, five, six times before a pitch. The fellow on first would run a bit to second, then scramble right back, and you could see that Bobby Kelly was going to lose it. When Bobby Kelly threw, Doralee couldn't hear any hiss on the ball.

He pitched one that hit the dirt and bounced past the catcher, and the runner hustled himself to second base, got there standing up and just grinned at Bobby Kelly. The greasers booed, but that didn't seem fair to Doralee, because while Bobby Kelly might be in trouble, it was no fault of his.

"Can he do that? Just run to second like that?"

"He sure can. I tell you, that boy is in deep shit now."

And on the very next pitch the batter hit one way, way out to a spot no one could reach. A double. They put a 1 on the scoreboard.

The manager came out, stood a while talking to Bobby Kelly, and then Bobby Kelly walked slowly in, kicking dust, his glove hanging from his hand, his head low.

She'd have thought he was angry or at least sad, but just before he walked down the steps to the dugout he looked up at her and the damndest thing! He winked at her. He winked!

The Penguins lost. 3-0.

It was only a minute or two back to La Hacienda. Kirk left her in the room while he went out to hunt up a six-pack of Mexican brew. "That Carta Blanca shit ain't half bad," he said. Doralee stood on the terrace in the hot night and saw the team bus roll into the courtyard. She'd have thought the players would be down, but they were laughing and noisy as if they'd won. She tried to pick out Bobby Kelly but couldn't because it was so dark, so she waited a bit, then went into the room to take a shower. Just as she was pulling her shirt over her head, there was a knock on the door — not like Kirk who never knocked — and she knew it was Bobby Kelly.

Dressed in regular clothes again, a red golf shirt with an alligator on it, he was with two other fellows, also Americans, also baseball players, and damn! they were handsome. Nice boys with pressed pants and neat little thin black belts around their waists. She wished to God she had some clothes besides jeans and T-shirts, but they didn't seem to mind at all, big grins on their faces, big bare arms coming out of their short sleeves down to their big wrists and hands.

"By Heaven, Bobby, you were right. That *is* an American girl," one of them said, and you could tell he meant nothing mean by it from the way he said it, and the three of them laughed. Doralee found herself laughing too, standing in the doorway of the room, glad for the dark so they could not see that she blushed.

"Where's your hippie friend?" Bobby Kelly asked, and before she could answer turned to the other fellows and added, "I swear, this guy has a ponytail."

"Naah. Nobody but assholes wears a ponytail anymore."

And she looked, and looked again, because it was the fellow from the other team that had hit the ball, gone to first, and given Bobby Kelly all that trouble, and here they were, together, and they were friends. How could that be?

That was when they all heard Kirk Dugan's boots coming up the walk, and they heard him say from the darkness before they could see him, "What's going on?"

They were delighted to see Kirk had some beer, because they had some, too, along with some tequila down in one of the rooms, and since they were having a party just for gringos would he and his lady friend like to join them?

Doralee said, "Sure we would," before Kirk could say a word — she wasn't about to let this chance pass her by — and that was how they wound up downstairs in a white-walled room with red curtains that must have been Bobby Kelly's place when the team was in Puerto Peñasco.

Kirk whispered to her, "What the hell are we doing this for?" as they'd gone down the stairs, but he settled in once one of the baseball players rolled a monster joint, big as a cigar, and in a few minutes the place was foggy with the sweet smell of dope. They had a big ghetto-blaster with tapes of American rock 'n' roll music, and Doralee realized just how much she missed home. All the Chevy had was an AM radio that once they made it to Mexico got nothing but static or Mexican stations that played nothing worth hearing. Bobby Kelly's tapes were mellow, college-boy music, and when Kirk asked if he had any country-western Bobby Kelly gave him a mournful smile as if to say he expected that from him and was sorry to have his expectations come true.

They tossed themselves about the room, on the bed or on the floor, a sweated cold beer in each person's hand, passing a bottle of Cuervo they either tilted straight up and gulped or poured a little into their beers. And the joint passed around the room, and then another. Pretty soon Doralee had herself a buzz and the tequila was making her sweat, but it was damned nice to hear American voices other than Kirk's again. Nice boys. Nice American boys.

Rick Johnson who'd gotten a hit off Bobby Kelly was from Wisconsin. He said that if Bobby Kelly had gotten some hitting from his team, there was no way they'd have beaten him and it was a shame he had to pitch for a team that gave him no help, and how in hell the scorer called that shot he himself had gotten a hit was a mystery to him. Best man on Rick Johnson's team, Rick Johnson said, was the Penguins' groundskeeper that couldn't rake off a damn rock. He said to Kirk, "You wouldn't score that a hit, would you?"

And Kirk brightened up and said, "I thought it was an error."

Stan Foley who also pitched but hadn't that night was from Maryland. He said, "No way. It was a clean hit, Kirk."

And Kirk had to say, "Maybe."

So Doralee could see what was what. They were putting Kirk in the middle, but in a way he'd never know it, baiting him, making him feel like a fool without knowing why, and Doralee figured that out because she was watching Bobby Kelly's big grin get wider and wider. These boys were so free and easy, it was a wonder. Liking each other, liking what they did, telling stories about where they came from and what they hoped to do. They drank beer and rolled another joint, and Bobby Kelly popped the tape on the box and put in another, mostly Bob Seger and the Silver Bullet Band, hot music that made the room hotter and Doralee could feel the sweat trickling down her back, making her T-shirt stick between her shoulder blades. She sat cross-legged, a bottle of beer on the floor next to her, and she was grinning as broad as Bobby Kelly.

Kirk told a story about how he once put a Cadillac engine in a Dodge, going into detail about just how it was done, and when he was finished Stan Foley looked him in the eye and said, "Why in fuck would anybody *want* to do that?" and the baseball players right away started talking about fly-fishing, Rick Johnson saying there was no place like a Wisconsin lake. Doralee saw Bobby Kelly punch Stan Foley in the leg when Stan Foley cut Kirk so short, and she saw that Kirk didn't see.

Bobby Kelly went to the bathroom and when he came back he sat on the floor between Doralee and Kirk, so she could hardly see Kirk at all.

"Do you dance?" he asked her, and she said she didn't.

The baseball players groaned at that, all saying of course she did, nice like, but she was just shy being the only girl at the party, wouldn't she try? She said she didn't know how, and Bobby Kelly said that he would teach her.

So they stood up, and Doralee Jackson from Des Moines, Iowa, who had never danced before, danced. "Just move with it," Bobby Kelly said, and the tequila, the marijuana, and the beer made it easy. She was swaying at first, and they all clapped when she gave a bump with her hips — Bob Seger screaming about that old-time rock and roll. She bumped it again, raised her hands over her head, closed her eyes, and felt the sweat pop over her face, down her neck, on her chest and belly, her skin feeling like it was alive and creeping, and when she opened her eyes all she saw was Bobby Kelly. This was dancing. They were moving like they were one person. The song ended, and Rick Johnson up and gave her a whirl, and then she was dancing with Rick Johnson and Stan Foley at the same time, and she felt like a queen, these big handsome American boys giving her all this attention. The song ended, and she had to sit down to catch her breath, and she noticed Kirk still on the floor with his eyes clouded black and mean, his lips thin and tight, and she suspected she would catch all sorts of shit later, but she refused to care. They were in Mexico where nothing made sense, least of all Kirk Dugan's big plans, and by God she would at least have a little fun.

Maybe Stan Foley had seen what Doralee had seen in Kirk's face, because when Doralee sat down he asked, "What are you folks doing down here, anyway?"

While Kirk answered him, Bobby Kelly's hand found Doralee's sweated knee, patting it in time to the music, and she did not push his hand away. Kirk said, "Business. We're here on business."

That got the baseball players laughing again. Bobby Kelly asked what kind of business could anyone have in shitty Puerto Peñasco? "If Mexico had an armpit, we'd be breathing Right Guard."

"I got business," Kirk said. "I got business. And maybe you boys can help."

Stan Foley smiled and popped another beer. "How's that?"

"I want to score some grass, man."

"He wants to score some grass, man."

"The man says he wants to score some grass. How much you talking about?" Stan Foley said.

"Bulk. A couple of bricks."

"You're talking weight, huh?"

"That's right."

Doralee could see Bobby Kelly was holding in a laugh, and Rick Johnson was rolling on the bed like he was having a fit, but Kirk was so hungry after what he wanted he couldn't notice anything else.

Stan Foley went on. "How much money you got?"

"Enough."

"Well, shit, I don't know anything about that stuff."

Rick Johnson guffawed into a pillow when Kirk muttered "Bullshit," and flicked a bottle cap across the linoleum floor.

"Tell me," Stan Foley said, "Where'd you get the ink?"

Kirk's hand went to his tattoo. "This here? I got that in a jailhouse."

He said it slow for effect, to show he was tough, but the baseball players kept grinning and looked at each other.

"I tell you what," Stan Foley said. "You come out with me for a walk to my car and maybe we'll talk a little business."

Kirk's little eyes narrowed even more, the temptation eating at him, and then you could see he yielded to it. "All right. But don't bullshit me."

"Have I ever lied to you?"

Stan Foley stood up and with some effort Kirk did, too. They went out into the night. A few minutes went by and Rick Johnson said he left something in his room, he'd be right back, and off he went.

Now Doralee was not so stupid that she didn't know what was going on, but the funny part was that Kirk did not. So she said to Bobby Kelly, "Does that fellow really sell dope?"

"No. Fact is, Stan got this marijuana from his sister when she was down here two weeks ago to visit. No problem passing customs going south. We don't fuck with the stuff much. Hell, we work here. Mexican jail is bad news."

She smiled, shaking her head still buzzing from Cuervo and music, her body still perspiring from dancing, like the beer itself was pushing out through her skin. It made her bold. "Well, are you going to kiss me or not?"

Bobby Kelly put his big warm hands around her waist and pulled her toward him. She opened her mouth and he opened his, their saliva and sweat making the kiss slippery, and her head spun with it, his hands so good on her, her leaning toward him, his hands moving on her belly and up under her shirt, a long slow kiss that took her breath away, but she was worried that Kirk might come back any second now, so she stopped him.

"What are you doing with that hippie asshole, anyway?"

"I don't know. I just don't know."

He kissed her again, this time teasing his tongue all along her upper lip before she parted her lips and his tongue explored inside her mouth. This was so good, so good. Her pants were getting wet. She kissed him back, hard, urgently, and he asked her if she wanted to do it right then and she would have said yes, taken him right there on the floor, this big old American baseball pitcher from Oregon, but she said, "Kirk might come in. Later?"

And Bobby Kelly just smiled that big American smile. She didn't know if she meant it. It was something to think about, it was.

He went to the ghetto blaster and turned over the tape which had run out while they were kissing, and right then Stan Foley and Kirk and Rick Johnson came back in, so with her and Bobby Kelly at opposite sides of the room they looked as innocent as kids at a church picnic. Kirk was still scowling, but he looked puzzled. Stan Foley must have gone on with the lie, telling Kirk what he had to to keep him interested, but not enough to let Kirk believe he had found his deal. It would be easy to fool Kirk.

They partied. Drank more beer, smoked more dope, chased the beer with tequila — the second bottle, now. Bobby Kelly had had his taste, and now with the half-promise of "later" was staying far away from her. What would it be like to have Bobby Kelly?

Nice, but it would not happen. She watched that man in his red golf shirt and pressed pants that weren't so pressed anymore, and she suddenly hated his easy confidence. He must have planned getting into her pants since the moment he saw her on the beach, thinking she'd be easy, and for sure eager to tell his buddies all about it later. And yes, she had played along, but she saw in an instant it was time to call a halt, time for Doralee Jackson to take control just like she'd always done. She should be able to handle a little tequila, a little beer, and a little desperation without giving herself to some bright-smiling Bobby Kelly. A girl had to break bad habits before they had a chance to take hold.

But Kirk Dugan wasn't for her, neither. No sir. She could do a lot better than that. She could dance now — there was nothing to it, you just up and let yourself go — and Kirk Dugan was so dumb he couldn't see past the nose on his face or think about anytime more than next week. She felt sad for him. He was getting sloppy and loud, talking how he had done this and had done that, that these guys didn't know shit until they stepped in it.

"Aww, hippie. Cut it off," Rick Johnson said.

"Who're you calling a hippie, motherfucker?"

Rick Johnson got the giggles. "What kind of ponytail is that?"

Kirk touched his head. "You fuckers think you're so smart."

"I am too tired for this," Rick Johnson said, and without another word got up and left the room.

"Asshole," Kirk muttered.

"I think he's got a point," Bobby Kelly said, and when he

said it Doralee sat up straight and took a deep breath. Here it was.

"What point is that?"

"That asshole ponytail, friend. That's bush league. Coming down to Mexico without knowing what you're doing, that's bush league. All that jailhouse shit, that's bush league. All talk."

"I'll tell you what's bush league. Playing baseball in this shithole. That's bush league."

"Hey, man," Stan Foley said. "It's baseball. What's better than playing baseball?"

"That's right," Bobby Kelly said, placing a beer to his lips.

"Lots of things. I do anything you guys can do with my eyes closed."

"Whee-hew!"

"You laughing? You laughing at me?"

Bobby Kelly nodded. "Why don't you name something?"

"Fighting."

Stan Foley laughed. "He's got you there, Bobby."

Bobby Kelly just smiled that big smile and glanced at Doralee. But she didn't smile back. It had felt good to kiss him and it had felt good to have his hands on her, but what he was about now made her less than human, some damned reward, a blue ribbon at the fair. Bobby Kelly wanted her not because of who she was, but as the sign that he had in some way gotten over Kirk Dugan.

"Tell you what, hippie boy. Fighting is out. I got to be on the bus tomorrow night and I wouldn't want to break my hand on your jaw. . . ."

"That's a pussy excuse if I ever heard one."

"But I'll take you on in anything else you want to try. Fair and square. Doralee here can be the judge."

Kirk looked at her. She looked right back. He was wondering. Well, let him wonder.

Kirk said, "You think I don't know what's what? I know what's what."

Bobby Kelly said, "You swim?"

"He swims great," Doralee said quick as she could, and Kirk looked at her suspiciously, then puffed up some. "Oh, Kirk tells me he's a fine swimmer." So she got him in, gave the push and nailed shut the door, and now she'd see how it would work.

Bobby Kelly said, "Stan, you remember our swimming contest?"

"I do."

"What we'll do, hippie boy, is swim out in the ocean next to each other, nice and easy like. Just right next to each other. And the first one to turn back is the loser. Nothing to it. No race. Just to see who's got the balls. You want to try that?"

Kirk looked at Doralee for a second, sipped his beer, and said softly, "You're on."

"Well, that's fine," Bobby Kelly said, and he gave his hand to Kirk to help him up. "Stan, you coming down to the beach with us?"

"You bet," Stan Foley said, but as soon as the four of them were out in the night heading for the concrete wall that separated La Hacienda from the broad crescent of sand, Stan Foley lost his legs, sat right down on the blacktop of the courtyard and said, "Boys, I do believe I am drunk."

They all thought that was pretty funny, but they couldn't get Stan Foley to stand, tugging on his arm but him falling back on his ass, and so they left him there, a beer bottle in his hand, and just before they passed under the arch Kirk turned and yelled, "You remember we got business tomorrow. You hear?" and they heard Stan Foley shout, "Yessir. Big business tomorrow," and he cackled with laughter.

Doralee walked between Kirk Dugan and Bobby Kelly, both of them with their arms around her waist like the three of them were old friends, the men's hips bumping hers, the sand sucking at her feet. She thought how stupid men were, trying to prove something that needed no proving, and she knew that they were going at it because somehow or other they believed she had agreed to be the prize.

She didn't like that, and she didn't care for either of them thinking that she was some damned trophy, so she kept her mouth shut, saying to herself, let the damned fools do what they will. Doralee Jackson was done going along for rides just to see where she'd end up.

They got to the shoreline and Kirk threw his beer bottle into the black water.

"We just swim out and back?"

"You got it, hippie. First one to turn around is the asshole."

"Then I got no problem," Kirk said.

Doralee sat down on a small hill of sand, cold and damp in the dark. It must have been four or five o'clock in the morning. The clear air had burned the alcohol from her blood. She was sober. The breeze at her back chilled her, drying the perspiration from her T-shirt, and she drew her knees to her chest and locked her arms around her legs to make herself tight and warm. Gooseflesh rippled on her arms.

The moon was setting, shining just the slightest crescent of silver light, a hand's width above the black water smooth as an Iowa lake. By the color-bleeding moon she saw the two men undress, not saying a word now. They sat to slip off their shoes, then stood, and she heard the ghostly jingle of keys as they stepped from their pants and then took off their shirts. In the moon's light it was hard to tell one naked man from the other, the light reflected off the water making them two silhouettes, Kirk the more wiry of the two, but otherwise completely the same. Kirk's black hair was no different from Bobby Kelly's blond in the moon's light. Two American boys who had somehow arrived at this Mexican beach. She heard them say a few words, though she could not hear what, and then the two shapes walked beside each other down to the water lapping at the shore, and there was greenish sparkle about their ankles as they walked forward. She could still see them black against the silver streak of moonlight reflected on the surface when they were waist deep, and then she lost sight of them, but she heard the gentle sigh of a splash as they began to swim away from the shore, and she thought maybe she could see flashes of phosphorescence as they swam, and then she couldn't even see that, just the darkness of the Mexican night and the flat smooth glassy black surface of the sea.

She rubbed her hands against her bare arms trying to stay warm, and she wondered where the birds went to at night. Pelicans and gulls, did they make nests? or bob around on the sea waiting for morning? A fistful of cold sand trickled through her fingers. The moon slowly sank beneath the water and the breeze at her back picked up, and then after a time behind her the sky turned pink and she watched her long shadow that went down right to the waterline get shorter. She peered out over the water and saw nothing, as she expected, felt the warming sun on her, and stood to see further, but she knew there was nothing out there anymore for her to see.

To her left was the pile of clothes. They were damp from the night air. She took the keys to the Chevy from Kirk's jeans and with the keys pried the heel off his left boot. Two hundred-dollar bills, neatly folded. She could drive the Chevy good enough, she thought, and she'd have that long drive north over the Mexican desert to get better at it. Or south. Why not? How could she get lost? There was just the one road and she would go anyplace she pleased, do anything she desired. She'd survive, and if she found the right place, she would do better than that. It would not be easy, but nothing worth doing ever was.

She thought of the credit card, but decided there was no point in asking for more troubles. She would have enough. She wondered how the waves breaking on the shore — crashing in, flowing out, crashing in again — could sound so sorrowful and lonesome. A gull fluttered to the surface of the sea and floated lightly on the undulating surface, and she thought how she was the only person in the world who would ever know that beneath a white rock with a scratch on it in the Arizona desert a gun lay hidden, and that chances were that gun would rest undisturbed forever and forever.

Gail Godwin

---

from

Glass People

Cameron
Awaits
Francesca

FOUR WEEKS later, on a Saturday, Cameron let himself into the apartment. He went straight to his study, where he sequestered his golf clubs in a corner of the closet and hung his golf hat on its hook. It was early afternoon and he was savoring this particular slice of time, the hours before he was due at the airport to pick up his wife.

He took off his shoes and ambled into the kitchen in his black socks. He liked the waxed smoothness of the linoleum skidding against this feet. He made himself a drink: a gin and tonic, replacing the portion of lime he did not use in a plastic bag, refilling the ice tray with water, sponging off the few flecks of wet from the kitchen counter.

Drink in hand, he went to the bedroom, stood in front of his open closet, his nonexistent stomach slouched forward, and with his free hand selected his welcome-home outfit for Francesca. He had made reservations at a fine new restaurant for dinner. Of course, he had gone there to sample it first. He'd taken along his faithful secretary, Paula (happily married to a TV scriptwriter), who had been honored and rather touched when Cameron confided he always liked to sample Francesca's pleasures first, to make sure she wouldn't be disappointed. Did Paula think his wife would like this restaurant?

He ran his bath. While it was running, he went back to the kitchen and made himself a chicken salad sandwich on onion rye. He had imagined himself standing here spreading home-made mayonnaise and chicken salad on the bread just like this, even the smooth swish of the waxed floor beneath his socks, while sinking the putt on number 9 this noon. He often did this: projected from one moment into another. The present for him existed frequently as a kind of featureless tower, as close to him as an epidermis, from which he manipulated searchlights over past and future. This way of living in time he had practiced ever since he could remember. It cut down discomfort and increased efficiency. If he was quicker at tasks than others, it was because he had mentally rehearsed them many times, had seen himself doing them hours, days, before he had to do them, anticipated all eventualities. In the act of doing them, he was somewhere else already, rehearsing new tasks. Or perhaps remembering previous rehearsals of the present task. Just now, for instance, as he sank the knife into his freshly made sandwich, he was not in the kitchen at all, but both on the golf course anticipating these hours before Francesca and in the restaurant sitting across from the candlelit face of his newly returned wife, listening to her news while waiting to tell her his own. He was not here at all. This ability "not to be here" was, in fact, the secret of his well-known imperviousness. He never got shaken in court for the simple reason he was no longer there. He had arrived and departed before the others ever came. That bland face they saw was only mouthing rehearsed lines while the mind behind the face was already preempting some future confrontation.

In the bath, he lay back and let the hot water redden his pale flesh, tanned only from the neck up and the elbows down. He imagined Francesca, in the air by now on the last half of her journey. She would be leafing through a fashion magazine or gazing blankly out the window at cloud formations, thinking perhaps nothing at all.

He shaved, considered his face in the mirror. He compared it to a recent cartoon in which the artist had copied Dürer's famous Four Horsemen woodcut and substituted Cameron's head for Death's. "Who Will Clean up after the Apocalypse?" the caption had read. Cameron bared his big teeth and grimaced at himself. That goddam dentist. The black gum irritated him, but the rest of his face did not. The flat cheeks, the prominent jawbones, the thin nose pointed and sharp like an accusing finger, the roughened skin beneath the year-round tan. Some men would not be overjoyed to confront such a reflection in their shaving mirror, but it had not done badly by Cameron. His formidable courtroom presence would have diminished considerably had he been born a jovial endomorph and reached manhood with his Ivory complexion intact. More than half the population was and always would be half in love with death, and not so easeful, either. A stern retributive figure riding his skinny horse of justice roughshod over their bugbears, that was what they craved. And as their chaotic guilts increased in direct proportion to the freedoms they could not handle, the bugbears would breed like pests. For the bugbears were but their guilts turned inside out, made manifest.

He was an expert on guilt, had observed with interest its cumulative patterns for years. It was a most ingenious phantom builder who needed only one or two scraps of remorse with which to construct a city of endless woe. Give it an inch of concrete shame or self-doubt and it would spin out a four-lane expressway of self-vilification. Give it the tiniest amount of silence and it would fill that silence with a cacophony of conscience-stingings and prickings. If a man's (or a woman's) guilt mechanism was in working order (and whose wasn't these days?) all you needed to do was sit back. Wait. He couldn't stand the silence, the waiting. Soon the old phantom builder would drive him to your door, his (usually overwritten) confession signed and sealed. You would take it from him, relieve him of the burden, and he would sink happily into your graces, a willing servant. On the other hand, *if you refused to take it from him,* the effect would be just the same.

Cameron patted his cheeks with a stinging after-shave. He put on clean underwear, re-fastened his watch, and shrugged into his black silk wrapper. He retrieved the sandwich from under its napkin on the kitchen counter and went into his study to read the seven letters his wife had written him during her month's vacation. As each letter had arrived, he had dutifully slit it open with the Moroccan letter opener the court stenographer had brought him from his holiday. He had skimmed the contents, just to make sure she was doing what he thought she was doing. To tell the truth, he preferred his wife's silences. He wished there were more of them. Then her ineffable beauty shone out and she was his mysterious, beautiful woman again. Still, Francesca would expect him to have read the letters and if he read them through like this, at one sitting, he would capture her chronology of the trip and impress her with his understanding of the way she saw things.

The first letter was short and disconnected. Cameron skipped the plane and bus travelogue. Some new "friend" of Kate's had met Francesca at the bus station. No more was said about this friend. Kate had changed. She had a "new taciturnity." Cameron was pretty sure this new taciturnity did not keep the two women from discussing everything thoroughly the first day.

Second letter. In which she was obviously bored to death but trying to be chatty. Too many details which meant nothing. Trees, leaves, skies, Kate's garden. The friend, it seemed, was allowed in Francesca's narrative to "help out in the garden" and make himself useful to the women in general. Cameron could see it all from what Francesca left unsaid.

Third letter. Uh-oh. Reminiscence time. Francesca was now dredging up the old, opulent days of Jonathan & Co., how she'd met Cameron that first evening. "Here I was, expecting you to be so terrifying and so I decided to terrify you first." Now why did she have to go and tell him that? He would speak to her when she returned. Not tomorrow, no, let a couple of days go by, let her have time to become sufficiently impressed by his news. Then: Francesca, you are a mysterious and beautiful woman. Why spoil the effect by telling too much. Don't explain yourself. Let people wonder.

His telephone rang.

"Hello?"

"Cameron, you are going to kill me."

"Francesca, where are you?"

She'd missed her flight, she said.

"Ah me," he sighed, suppressing his keen disappointment. She embarked on a confused saga of how she'd gone to the wrong terminal, there were so many at that airport, she'd thought it was an American Airlines flight, the one coming east had been, then when she checked her ticket it had been too late . . .

Cameron knew his wife, he knew every tone of her voice. He knew she was lying.

"Cameron? Are you furious?"

"Of course not. Why should I be? But do try hard to get the right terminal tomorrow. Can I count on your being on the same flight tomorrow?"

"Yes, of course," she said, too quickly, uncertainly.

"Where will you stay tonight?"

"Oh, I found this nice hotel very near the airport. You can even see the planes in their hangars from here."

"That's very nice." Cameron carefully did not ask the name of this hotel.

There was a pause. Cameron waited, listening with interest to the airwaves between them. He waited for her to fill up the empty space.

"Cameron, I really am sorry to ruin your Saturday. I know how you like things to go according to schedule."

"All the more eager to see you tomorrow, love. Just please don't ruin my Sunday."

"What . . . what will you do tonight?"

"Eat dinner by myself. Re-read your letters."

"Oh you make me feel terrible."

"I don't mean to. It's not your fault you missed the flight. It could happen to anyone. See you tomorrow, Francesca."

"Well, goodbye . . ." She hung on, chastened.

"Goodbye, Francesca."

After he hung up, he took the half-eaten sandwich into the kitchen and dropped it into the trash can. He fastened the top of the yellow disposal bag and took it outside to the incinerator. He returned to the kitchen and re-lined the trash can with a fresh bag. Then he wandered into the bedroom, opened Francesca's closet and studied her clothes for a while, running his fingers softly over various things. He touched a pair of jade green silk hostess pants, which she wore with a perfectly simple white Russian tunic. She was stunning in that outfit. His face went abstracted, rather dreamy, he swayed a little on his bare feet like a man who has lost his balance. He looked down where his black wrapper had come apart and studied the enormous erection. Then he got dressed quickly in clean golf clothes, grabbed his hat, his clubs, and left the apartment.

* * *

Cameron woke early on Sunday, which annoyed him, as he had planned to sleep late. Francesca's delinquency had cut a hole in his schedule and he had to fill it in. This morning, which was to have been reunion morning (he had planned a breakfast of popovers, *omelette fines herbes,* and a blueberry and mango compote he had invented himself), he was spending alone in bed. Last night, after his second nine holes, which he played badly, he had eaten in a Chinese restaurant in town, where he was known. Then he had walked and thought. He paid a visit to Crystal Gardens, that outdoor residence of the degenerate young, the source of so many headaches for the city. A philanthropist who had been bitten by the youth-and-relevance bug in his eighties had given a fifteen-acre walled garden adjoining his estate to the city on the condition that no young person who needed a place to sleep would ever be evicted. The city said they didn't want it under such conditions. Cameron said, take it. But every hippie and drug addict in town will use it as a crashing pad, they protested. Take it, Cameron said. Let them come. We'll know where they are. But the filth, the sanitation problems. So, put in a couple of toilets. Maybe even a shower under the trees. Build them a lovely outdoor prison. They'll maintain it. Cameron, do you really think . . . ? Sure. I think of all the hours it will save our boys . . .

Now Cameron often went and sat in this rapidly deteriorating walled garden which had been christened Crystal Gardens by the narcs who languidly conducted their periodic raids, making thirty or forty arrests every time. Still, the place filled with newcomers. They mingled with the longer-term residents, building little communal campfires which scorched the grass, making welfare babies at night under the trees, strumming and living their dream. It calmed Cameron to come here, dressed in his elegant clothes, and sit in full view of them on a wooden bench under a eucalyptus tree. The politics of it interested him. They liked him in a way. He would stroll a while first, before sitting down, nodding to familiar faces along the way. Some of them nodded back. He often wondered how he came across to them, what archetype he played in their drug-induced dramas. He had some pretty good ideas. Last night, a girl who had just been released from prison again waved her baby's hand at Cameron as he ambled by with his odd duck walk. She looked really glad to see him again. She knew, many of them knew, that Cameron was the one who was responsible for their indefinite lease in the Garden. He was their landlord in a sense.

Cameron reached out and took a letter from the bedside table. He had already read it many times. It was Francesca's last letter written from Kate's. After informing him of her flight times back, which he already had written carefully in his memo book, she related a nightmare she'd had about him.

"We'd just come back from the airport and you said to go up in the elevator while you parked the car. Our apartment was draped in sheets. There was an operating table set up. A surgeon with a black mask said, 'Get undressed, Francesca, we haven't much time.' There was an arrogant nurse, also in black, with big breasts, and she said to me, 'Here, quick, slip into this.' (An operating gown.) I ran out of the apartment back to the elevator just as it opened and you got out, also wearing a black mask . . ."

"I'm such a villain," murmured Cameron. He replaced the letter in its envelope. "I want her to be happy and therefore I am such a villain."

He got up and made himself breakfast, interrupted once by his secretary, who was working overtime and couldn't find something, and once by someone calling to remind him of an eight a.m. emergency session of the Crime Commission tomorrow morning. Monday morning. Son of a bitch. That meant there could be no time for the special welcome-home breakfast of popovers, omelet, and compote. Cameron was disappointed. Such ceremonies were important to him.

He sat eating his breakfast, sipping the freshly ground coffee, wiping his lips with a napkin, thinking. He was not a villain, no. Unless your definition of a villain was that of a person who spent his whole life being disappointed in people. Whose fault was it if people entered his life disguised as more than they were and, once inside, flung off their masks with relief and revealed their paltry selves? They then blamed him for not approving of them any more. They called him "inhuman," "unable to love," "sadistic." By human they usually meant mixed up, a mess of unthought-out reactions. By love they usually meant need or fear. And his sadism was simply a matter of letting them stew in their own juice while he looked on, arms folded over his chest, a curious wonderment in his eyes that they could not see, could not really see, that they had jumped into their dreary mess all by themselves.

Your standards are too rigid, Cameron, acquaintances had said to him for years.

But I don't ask anything of anyone that I wouldn't ask of myself twice over, he would reply, meaning it. He knew he had more will, more energy, more patience to wait for what he wanted, more intelligence than most people. The majority of people did not know what they wanted. They had vague feelings, but could not sit down and write out a list of what they wanted, what was good for them. Cameron knew what he wanted, what was good for him; he carried a neat list in his head, arranged in priorities. He also knew what was good for others. Now the time was coming when his milieu recognized this. He was ready. He had the energy to spare. He had not changed through the years; it was the times that had changed. He stayed the same, a fixed point, and waited for the times to return to him.

As he was washing the dishes, the telephone rang. He plucked at the rubber gloves, but they stuck to his hands. He grabbed a dishcloth and dried off his gloved hands and picked up the receiver in the bedroom.

"Cameron? Where were you?" Francesca's voice, crackling over the wire, guilty.

Cameron looked at his watch. "I was in the kitchen, I hope *you* are at the airport."

"Actually . . . I'm not."

"I see." He waited.

"Cameron? Would you mind if I stayed on in the city for another week? I thought . . . well, I thought I might shop for some clothes. Some of the new fashions are really fabulous, I've been looking at the new magazines alone in my room."

I wonder who he is, thought Cameron, massaging the yellow rubber fingers against one another.

"Cameron? Are you still there?"

"I'm here, Francesca. But what about money? You'll need money if you're going to shop."

"Oh money! Well I have all of my traveler's checks. There was certainly nothing to spend them on at Kate's. I have my credit cards."

"You won't buy many fabulous clothes for the amount of those checks, love. And the good stores won't take your cards." He knew he was making her squirm a little. "What I'll do is this: are you listening?"

"Yes," she said. Meekly.

"Tomorrow morning, first thing, I'll wire a bank draft to First National City Bank, the one at Park and Fifty-third. It will be made out in your name. You won't be able to shop before early afternoon, because of our time lag, will that inconvenience you too much?"

"Oh no, oh no! Not at all. Oh Cameron —"

"Will a week be long enough, Francesca?"

"Oh yes, I mean — Cameron, you aren't mad?"

"Why on earth should I be? I'm disappointed, of course. I have missed you. But you are your own woman and I want to help you preserve that status. I will ask two things —"

"Oh, sure. What?"

"Both for my own peace of mind. One is that you stay in a decent hotel. The other is that you promise to give me a call, sometime during the week, some promised time that I can look forward to. Let's say . . ." He thought carefully. "Thursday night."

"That's a promise: Both things." Oh she was relieved. Relieved and guilty.

"Now I must go and see what I can do about salvaging my poor Sunday," he said.

"Oh, Cameron —"

"Till Thursday, my love."

He returned to the kitchen and finished washing the dishes. He dried them. Then he sponge-mopped the floor. He stood at the edge of the room, arms hugged tight against his chest, watching the water dry in little patches. He got out the container of liquid wax and some clean cloths and worked himself scrupulously around the floor on all fours till he saw a reflection of his bland, impassive face upon his handiwork. He glanced at his watch. Not even noon! He stood up, feeling a little displaced, and wandered into the bedroom, going again to her closet. Once again he stood in its enclosure. He breathed her perfume, a perfume which he had selected for her himself, a costly, haunting scent. How he wished he could break every other bottle of this perfume in the world, so that this scent would be identified as his wife's alone! He touched her dresses, her shoes, which she always kicked off, left anywhere, and he himself replaced on the rack. Here was that white Roman toga he had bought her, she had never worn it, it was after she had stopped going to parties. She had tried it on only once, in this room. Now the fact that he alone had seen Francesca in this garment was in its favor. With a rapt expression on his face, he removed it from the garment bag. He carried its softness to the bed and sat down with it draped across his lap, musing over it.

Then, with a deep sigh, he lay back on the bed and covered himself with the garment. He breathed the scent of her perfume.

Judith Guest

from

Ordinary
People

RAZOR IN HAND, he stands before the rectangular, gold-trimmed mirror, offering up a brief prayer. *Thanks. Appreciate all you've done so far. Keep up the good work,* while, beside him, his wife brushes her hair. Her face is soft in the morning, flushed, slightly rounded, younger than her thirty-nine years. Her stomach is flat, almost as if she never had the babies. She raises her hands to the back of her neck, pinning her hair into a neat coil at the back of her head. Beautiful hair, the color of maple sugar. Or honey. Natural, too. The blue silk robe outlines her slender hips, her breasts.

"Did you call him?"

"Yeah, he's up."

She sighs. "I hate to play golf when it's cold. Why doesn't anybody in this league know enough to quit when the season's over? Leaves on all the fairways, your hands freeze — it's ridiculous."

He leans toward her; gives her a kiss on the neck. "I love you."

"I love you." She is looking at him in the mirror. "Will you talk to him this morning? About the clothes. He's got a closetful of decent things and he goes off every day looking like a bum, Cal."

"That's the style. Decency is out, chaos is in —" As her brows lift, he nods. "Okay, I'll talk to him."

"And the other thing, too."

"What other thing?"

"Stopping by Lazenbys' on the way home. Carole called again last week. It's such a little thing. . . ."

"I don't want to pressure him about that. He'll do it when he wants to. Carole understands."

She shrugs. "When people take an interest, it would seem courteous —"

"We all know he's courteous." He turns his attention to his beard. Every morning the same face, the same thoughts. A good time to take stock, though. Calvin Jarrett, forty-one, U.S. citizen, tax attorney, husband, father. Orphaned at the age of eleven. He has caught himself thinking about that lately, thinking of the Evangelical Home for Orphans and Old People, an H-shaped, red brick building on Detroit's northwest side, where he grew up. Wondering if after all these years it is still in existence. Strange that he has never bothered to check. An odd kind of orphanage: most of the kids had at least one living parent; some even had two. He had moved there when he was four, leaving the tiny apartment where he was born. His mother sent him gifts on his birthday, and at Christmas. Occasionally she visited him. Periodically she explained why he was living there, and not with her: there was no room for him in the apartment, no money; it was no neighborhood in which to bring up kids. She had a friend who knew people that were connected with the Home; just luck. The director had told him once that the Home was financed by "religious benefactors."

He was named Calvin, for his dead uncle; Jarrett had been his mother's maiden name. When she came to see him, she came alone. No one claiming to be his father had ever been in attendance; he had no memories of being any man's son. So, if anyone should ask, he can always point out that he had no example to follow.

And what is fatherhood anyway? Talking to a kid about his clothes. Not applying pressure. Looking for signs. He knows what to look for now: loss of appetite, sleeplessness, poor school performance — all negative, so far. His son eats, he sleeps, he does his homework. He says he's happy. Another duty: asking silly questions. *Are you happy?* He has to ask, though; pretends that he is kidding, just kidding; Conrad replies in kind. Pointless. Would the answer have been any different, even if he had thought to ask, before? Good manners have nothing to do with communication, he must remember that. And being a father is more than trusting to luck. That, too. Nobody's role is simple, these days. Not even a kid's. It used to mean minding your manners, respecting those who were bigger than you, treating each day as a surprise package, waiting to be opened. Not any more. So what's changed? Not enough surprises? Too many, maybe.

He has had a vision all these months, of boys, with their heads next to stereo speakers feeding music into their ears, their long legs draped over chairs and sofas. Or their arms, stretched toward a basketball hoop in the side drive (he had sunk the posts in cement himself, when Conrad was eight, Jordan, nine; just after they bought the house). Where are all these kids? Joe Lazenby, Phil Truan, Don Genthe, Dick Van Buren — they are all seniors in high school this year. Is eighteen too old to play touch football on the lawn? Basketball in the side drive? Is it girls? Studies? Since he has been home, Conrad has gone once to the movies. Alone. "Didn't anybody else want to see it?" Cal had asked. "I don't know," he said. "I didn't ask."

Responsibility. That is fatherhood. You cannot afford to miss any signs, because that is how it happens: somebody holding too much inside, somebody else missing signs. *That doctor in Evanston. Make sure he calls him. It is for his own good.* Why? Because his own vision, that of the boys hanging around, isn't coming true? It has only been a month. All the other signs seem right. Stay calm. Keep it light. Try not to lean. A balance must be struck between pressure and concern.

Back when Conrad was in the hospital, back when the visits were limited to twice a month, he could afford to take responsibility for everything: the sections of gray peeling paint in the stair wells; small gobs of dirt swept into the corners of the steps; even a scar at the side of one orderly's mouth. Now that he is home again, things are different. The responsibilities seem enormous. Staggering. His job alone, nobody else's. Motherhood is different, somehow. And what about fathering girls? He must ask Ray Hanley sometime, how it feels. Is there more, or less responsibility? He couldn't take more. *Your mother wants me to tell you, you have a closetful of decent clothes.* He will smile. "Okay. You told me." But, in a minute, he will ask, "What's wrong with what I've got on?"

Nothing. Nothing I can see. Only I don't pass up any chances to discharge these fatherly duties, this is the age of perfection, kid. Everybody try their emotional and mental and physical damnedest.

Strive, strive. Correct all defects. All those Saturday trips to the orthodontist, when they were in junior high. Both of his boys had inherited from him, that long, slightly hooked nose; from their mother, the small, determined lower jaw. On them it had required thirty-eight hundred dollars' worth of work, courtesy Peter Bachmann, D.D.S., M.S. "Hell, what's a little money?" he had raved. "Overhaul their whole damn jaws if necessary, this is the age of the perfect mouth!" But, secretly, he had been proud that he was able to afford such expenses. He was supporting his family, *his boys,* in style: whatever they needed, whatever they wanted, they got. He had arrived. He was here. Not bad for the kid from the Evangelical Home.

And now? Where is he now?

Beth sets breakfast in front of Cal: eggs, bacon, toast, milk, juice.

Conrad looks up. "Morning."

"Morning. You need a ride today?"

"No. Lazenby's picking me up at twenty after."

He treats this as a piece of good news. "Great!" Said too heartily, he sees at once. Conrad looks away, frowning.

"I've got to get dressed," Beth says. "I tee off at nine." She hands him his coffee; crosses to the doorway; motes of dust flutter nervously in her wake. Conrad is studying. The book is propped against the butter dish.

"What is it, a quiz?"

"Book report."

"What book?"

He raises the cover. Cal reads, *Jude the Obscure.*

"How is it?"

"Obscure."

He sips his coffee. "No bacon and eggs this morning?"

He shakes his head. "I only wanted cereal."

He has lost twenty-five pounds in one year. Another year before his weight will return to normal, Dr. Crawford predicted.

"You feel okay?"

"Yeah, fine. I just didn't want a big breakfast."

The bony angles need to be fleshed out.

"You ought to keep trying to put weight on," Cal says.

"I am. I will. You don't have to be heavy to swim, Dad."

Back to the book, and Cal studies the crisp, dry rectangles on the tile floor. Patterns of sunlight. Familiar and orderly. "How's it going?" he asks.

Conrad looks up. "What?"

"How's it going? School. Swimming. Everything okay?"

"Yeah, fine. Same as yesterday."

"What does that mean?"

A faint smile. "It means you ask me that every day."

"Sorry." He smiles, too. "I like things neat."

Conrad laughs. He reaches out to flip the book closed. "Okay," he says, "let's talk."

"Can't help it," Cal says. "I regard it as a challenge, people reading at the table."

"Yeah."

"So, how come Lazenby's picking you up?"

"He's a friend of mine."

"I know that. I just wondered if it meant you'd be riding with him from now on."

"I don't have a formal commitment yet. I'm gonna have my secretary talk to his, though."

"Okay, okay."

"We should have the contract drawn up by the end of the week."

"Okay."

He does a familiar thing, then; shoves his hands into the back pockets of his levis as he rocks backward in the chair. Conrad, after all. A good sign, despite the brutal haircut; the weary look about the eyes. The eyes bother him every day. He still believes in the picture he carries in his wallet of a boy with longish, dark hair and laugh lines about the mouth and eyes; no weary look there. This gaunt, thin figure that sits across from him, hair chopped bluntly at the neck, still grins; still kids, but the eyes are different. He cannot get used to it.

His old self. That is the image that must be dispelled. Another piece of advice from the all-powerful Dr. Crawford, Keeper of the Gate. "Don't expect him to be the same person he was before." But he does expect that. As does everyone. His mother, his grandmother, his grandfather — yesterday, Cal's father-in-law had called him at the office: "I've got to admit, Cal, that it shocked me. He looked so —" and Cal felt him hunting for the painless adjectives "— tired out. Run down. I would think, for the kind of money you paid, they would have at least seen to it that he ate properly, and got enough sleep. And he was so quiet. Just not like his old self at all."

And who was that? The kid who got straight A's all through grade school and junior high? Who rode his two-wheeler sixteen times around the block on his sixth birthday, because somebody bet him he couldn't? Who took four firsts in the hundred-meter free style last year? *Last year*. No, he is not much like that kid. Whoever he was.

He says his piece about the clothes, and Conrad nods absently. "Okay. I just haven't thought about it much. I will, though."

What, no argument? No raising of the eyebrows, no hint of sarcasm in the reply? What kind of a sign is this? Surely not good. Okay, now is the time. Lean, if you have to.

"Another thing," he says. "That doctor in Evanston, what's his name? Berger? Have you called him yet?"

An immediate reaction. The look on his face is tight; closed. The chair legs come down. "No. I don't have time."

"I think we ought to stick to the plan —"

"I can't. I'm swimming every night until six. He didn't say I had to call him, Dad."

"No, I know." He waits while Conrad stares at the table. "I think maybe you ought to. Maybe he could see you on the weekends."

"I don't need to see anybody. I feel fine."

A strained silence. Conrad pushes the cereal bowl, lightly; left, then right.

"I want you to call him anyway," he says. "Call him today."

"I don't finish practice until dinner —"

"Call him at school. On your lunch hour."

An obedient boy. Polite. Obedient. Well mannered. Even in the hospital, with his fingernails bitten to bloody half-moons, the dark circles, bloody bruises under his eyes; always, always his behavior was proper, full of respect.

"Thanks for coming." Each time he would say that, as Cal readied himself to leave. The shirt he is wearing today — the way his shoulder blades shove out beneath the soft skin of jersey — it is a shirt he used to wear in the hospital. Growing up is a serious business. He, Cal, would not be young again, not for anything. And not without sponsors: a mother and father, good fortune, God.

* * *

He hates fighting, and last night they had fought — over London.

"I think you're being unreasonable," she said, "not even daring to ask him about it. Why don't you just admit that it's you who doesn't want to go?"

"You ask him, then! What am I? The official interpreter here? You see him every day, don't you? Show him the travel folders, give him the pitch."

"I don't see him any more than you do," she said coolly. "What are you afraid of? It's a question. It requires a yes or a no. You certainly ask him enough other questions — How did he sleep? How does he feel? How did *I* sleep? How do *I* feel?"

"Okay," he said. "How *did* you sleep? How *do* you feel?"

"That's not *it!*" she said. "If we could all just relax a little! If things could just be normal again. I don't want you to start asking *me* the questions, I want you to just stop!"

Well, okay. Fair enough. If she knew, though, that it is not only of Conrad but of himself that he is asking questions now; basic, hopeless questions that mock him, finger him as a joker, a bumbler, a poor dope. *Who the hell are you?* as he walks down the street, and who can step in time to that music for more than thirty seconds? He ducks into a drugstore for respite, buys himself a cigar. *Who the hell are you?* follows him inside, leaning on the glass counter, waiting. Maybe everybody does it, that is the thought he hangs on to, like a drunk at a friendly lamppost. Who in the world knows who he is all the time? It is not a question to ask a guy over a sandwich at the Quik-Lunch. If you must ponder it, then do it alone at isolated periods with long intervals in between, so as not to drive yourself bats.

I'm the kind of man who — he has heard this phrase a million times, at parties, in bars, in the course of normal conversation, *I'm the kind of man who* — instinctively he listens; tries to apply any familiar terms to himself, but without success.

Arnold Bacon. There was a man who knew who he was. Years since he has thought about him. In 1967, Ray noticed his obit in the *Tribune* ". . . nationally known tax attorney dies at seventy-two. . . . Tragic loss to the profession, ABA president says. . . ."

He was seventeen years old when he first met Arnold Bacon. Seventeen, a senior in high school, his plans for the future not extending past the next afternoon, and Bacon had come up to him at, of all places, a Christmas Tea in the lounge of the Evangelical Home. "Well, young man, what are you planning to do with the rest of your life?" He had laughed politely, looking for a neat and pleasant exit to the conversation, but Bacon was serious. "I've looked at your grades," he said. "You're smart. You know the importance of a good education. You ever thought about going into law?"

He had thought about being a Soldier of Fortune, after reading *The Three Musketeers*. Or a fireman. A professional athlete. He was a good tennis player, he was well coordinated. He learned games quickly. Those vague and wistful occupations faded out of the picture after that December afternoon. He did more than think about the law. He applied and was accepted to prelaw at Wayne University; he took a part-time job clerking in Bacon's office; he graduated from Wayne and was accepted into law school at the University of Michigan, backed by Bacon's influential recommendation, he later found out from one of the deans.

A lucky accident. Bacon took him on; decided to be his mentor; told him what courses to take and which ones to stay away from; which scholarships to apply for; which professors he must not miss. He came to his aid financially whenever it was necessary. It was the closest thing to a father-son relationship

199

— it *was* a father-son relationship, he thought. Bacon had one daughter; no sons. Bacon's daughter might have made a smashing lawyer; but women lawyers were rarer, then, and suspect. And he had this reverence, this vast, eclipsing love for the law that had to be coalesced. He needed a student, an apprentice. He needed to know that he was leaving his baby protected.

Bacon had not approved of law students who married while they were in school. Diffusion of energy, he called it. And so, of course, everything had changed, after Beth. Bacon was a man of strong views. He had principles. Integrity. He knew who he was and where he stood on certain — what he considered — inviolable issues. Bacon had been Cal's first actual experience with loss.

When he was eleven, he learned the association of that word with death. The director of the Evangelical Home had called him in to tell him of his "loss." His mother had "passed away" — another term he was more familiar with, having heard it used frequently in connection with the elderly, wraithlike beings who inhabited the east wing of the Home, coming and going very quickly. He remembered the feeling of awe that possessed him that day. He was aware that an event of some magnitude had happened *to him*. Someone close to him had passed away and it was his loss, and his alone. For a short time he became a figure of some importance to his peers. And he was invited to the director's office for cocoa and sermons on *Love and Loss*, and *How a Christian Deals with Grief*. The only difference he perceived was that he no longer had any visitor or presents on his birthday, or at Christmas. Well, that wasn't true, really. He had presents, they just weren't from anyone he knew. But he did not, at the time, understand the meaning of loss. And of grief. He still had not experienced those words at all.

He had grieved over Arnold, though. Not when he died, it was too late, then; years since he had seen him. But when he discovered that it had been a business venture, after all, that had felt like grief. It *was* grief. He and Beth had, together, repaid the money. It was, as Bacon pointed out to him, a financial obligation. It took five years, but it was not a hardship. Beth had her own money; he had a good scholarship, and they hardly felt the monthly bill. But Arnold's indifference, after the marriage — that had hurt him so much. It had undermined him, taken away something that he hadn't even realized he possessed; he had regarded it so lightly, so casually.

* * *

I'm the kind of man who — hasn't the least idea what kind of man I am. There. Some definition. He is no closer than he was back in the director's office, back when he listened to the sermons, his mind wandering, not even aware, then, that he was searching.

So, how does a Christian deal with grief? There is no dealing; he knows that much. There is simply the stubborn, mindless hanging on until it is over. Until you are through it. But something has happened in the process. The old definitions, the neat, knowing pigeonholes have disappeared. Or else they no longer apply.

His eyes move again to the calendar. Wednesday, November fifth. Of course. Obvious. All the painful self-examination; the unanswered questions. At least he knows what is wrong today. Today is Jordan's birthday. Today he would have been nineteen.

* * *

The light is on in Conrad's room. He is asleep, lying on his back, his mouth open and relaxed. He sweats heavily in his sleep. His hair is damp, clinging slickly to his forehead, curling against his neck. A book lies face-down and open on the bed. *U.S. History: Constitution to Present Day.* Cal picks up the book and closes it quietly. He sets it on the night stand. Reaching for the switch on the lamp, he looks at Conrad. His left arm is shoved underneath the pillow. His right is outstretched; the hand with its strong, square fingers curved protectively over the palm is motionless. Still biting his nails. A nervous habit. So what? Lots of people do it; he himself used to do it when he was that age.

He looks, really looks, this time at the thin, vertical scar that extends up the inside of the arm, above the palm. More than two inches long, ridged, a gray-pink line. "He meant business," the intern told him in the ambulance. "Horizontal cuts, the blood clots. It takes a lot longer. You were damn lucky to catch him."

High achievers, Dr. Crawford told him, set themselves impossible standards. They have this need to perform well, to look good; they suffer excessive guilt over failure. He had groped to understand. "But what has he failed at? He's never failed at anything!"

Conrad's head moves on the pillow, and Cal snaps off the light, not allowing himself to look again at the scar, not wanting to be guilty of any more violations of privacy. *Listen*, he prays, *let the exams be easy. Don't let him feel he is failing.*

Beth is awake, waiting for him, her hair loose about her shoulders. She reaches up to put her arms around him, all tawny, smooth skin, those gray eyes with thick lashes, silent and insistent. She leads tonight, and he follows, moving swiftly down that dark river, everything floating, melting, perfect, and complete. Afterward, she slides away from him, and her hair, soft and furry against his shoulder, smells sweet and fresh, like wood fern. He buries his face in it, still hungry. "Let me hold you awhile."

But she is tired. She curls away from him; pushes him gently from her, in sleep. He rolls to his back, hands under his head, staring upward. Other Saturday nights, lying, waiting after sex, for the comforting sound of a car door slamming, and whispers of laughter under the windows. And earlier, at the beginning of the evenings, the endless jokes, the hassles over clothes *Hey, that's my sweater! The hell it is, possession is — hey, Dad, what's possession? Possession is gonna get your head broke — now give it to me!* And sounds of a struggle and fiendish, sadistic laughter *Take it, fag, it's a fag sweater, you'll look great in it* and more laughter *You oughta know!*

He will not be able to sleep tonight for hours; another side effect of drinking too much. It condemns him to wakefulness. Without expectation of anything — of a car, of whispers or laughter. Resigned, he keeps watch and continues to listen.

Josephine Humphreys

---

from
Dreams
of
Sleep

AFTER HIS father died, Will decided that North Carolina was a better place than South Carolina. North Carolina was dignified and masculine, intelligent. It had mountains, a good university town, a lonely remote shore. South Carolina after Edmund's death seemed fat and flushed, oppressive. Will stayed in Chapel Hill during his vacations instead of going home. He got out of English literature and into pre-med. He convinced Danny to do the same. "We've been kidding ourselves," he said. "How are we going to make a living on this shit? Teach poetry in junior high? Coach the chess team for extra pay? We've got to move fast, Cardozo. Think of something." The next day they changed majors. The switch meant two whole summers of classes in chemistry and biology, but Will was not eager to be anywhere else. It suited him fine to have to stay in school longer than expected.

During his junior year he had taken Alice out occasionally. She was a freshman at Hollins, and he drove up to Virginia three or four times to take her to a steak house where she ate next to nothing and then they'd sit in the dorm parlor and watch television. The idiocy of the situation did not disturb him. She was a girl he knew from home, and he was comfortable with her; it was worth the long drive. She wasn't easy to talk to, she generally sat quietly through the meal and through the TV shows and let him talk. She was aloof in a shy way, studying all the time, not particularly interested in lovemaking, what little of it he had attempted, but more than tolerant. One night he looked at her in the light from a yellow porch bulb at the restaurant, and he fell in love with her. He noticed beauty in her face. Her brownish eyes were deeply kind, her brownish hair soft and gently waved back from her temples. He had the distinct feeling that she was threatened. Right then he reached for her, scaring her with the sudden movement of his arm.

"What is it?" she said, looking around quickly. She thought he was trying to warn her of something about to fall on her. He managed to turn his gesture into an attempt to button her coat. She was cold, the coat was not lined. Her fingers were freezing, while his own were almost hot. He marveled at her metabolism. He could not live without her. Taking a dismal room at the Hotel Roanoke, he swore he would never be parted from her. Alice was fond of him, but it was partly out of concern for his academic career that she agreed, finally, to transfer to Chapel Hill. "At the end of the semester," she said. "If you promise to go back now. You've missed a whole week of classes!" (For it was *he* then who thought only love mattered, and she who argued the exigencies of practical life, like class attendance.) During the rest of the autumn he spent his afternoons finding an apartment, repainting its two rooms, caulking the tub, collecting things he thought she would like, such as a smoking-room ashtray on a pedestal and a fringed lamp shade. He moved out of the Beta house and slept alone in the apartment, staying to one side of the bed. A week before she came he bought two coffee mugs with names on them, "Alice" and "William." They sat together on the kitchen table, "Alice" facing "William," ceremonious and anonymous as the first-named lovers in a ballad. When she moved in she left behind a math scholarship at Hollins, and her father never forgave her.

She was cold all winter. He kept the gas heaters high, actually afraid of losing her to the cold. He bought an electric blanket to keep her warm. Finally spring came, and she could sit out in the sun, which she loved. She was there when he came home, cross-legged on a striped rug in the grass, reading math. The air was fresh and tinkling with the faint glassy sounds of faculty children's voices. "How do you read math?" he wanted to know. "How does it turn out? What happens after the part about derivatives?" But she couldn't explain to him what she was working on. Her white peasant blouse drooped in front to show the bony plate of her breastbone. Her hair touched her shoulders. He thought it was shocking that the plain sight of her could wrench his heart the way it did. The faraway children were an added influence. "Marry me," he said, taking the book out of her hand.

"No," she said. "It scares me." She picked up the book.

"What aspect of it scares you?"

"The loneliness." His face must have shown surprise, because she laid the book face down in the grass and looked at him. Her face changed, as if she had only just then seen something about him that might be worth having.

"But then I'm always lonely," she said. "When I'm by myself I don't notice it so much. Okay. Let's get married."

But his feelings were hurt. "Okay" wasn't what he wanted to hear. This was marriage, not a football weekend. This was *history*. He tried to point that out. "By marriage I mean the real kind. Permanent marriage."

"I should hope so," she said.

"But why are you so offhand about it?"

"I'm sorry," she said. "I'm not, really." She took a joint from her pocketbook and lit it, right out in the yard. "It's just that I always thought I'd live alone. You keep making me revise the forecasts." She smiled and held out her hand to him. "I'm glad," she said.

"And when we get married, no more grass."

"Oh, come on."

"No, I'm serious." She got it from math people; he was surprised they even knew about it, the men with their slide rules and short-sleeved shirts, the women plain and thick-ankled. Alice was the only handsome human being in the department.

"Chromosome damage I do not want," he said. "I expect fat, healthy, symmetrical children."

And marriage suited Alice, Will found. She grew even more beautiful, though she had no idea of it. Her thin face took on a glow, her eyes seemed to darken, after she married him. He watched her in fascination late at night while she worked at a table next to the bed. She worried that the light would keep him awake. No, he said; but it would, that was the whole point — he wanted to stay awake and be able to see her, the hair slipping forward, the forehead pinched up in thought, the mouth taking slow, regular drags on her cigarette. The smoke went under the fringed lamp shade and funneled back out at the top. She worked in her slip. She was both boyish and girlish. Her breasts were more nipple than round flesh. Late, near one or two, she would lean back in the chair, smoke one more cigarette, and change into a nightgown. When she finally put out the cigarette and turned off the light and came to bed, he pretended to wake up, and took her in his arms. Making love to her, he always had the feeling there was something just beyond his reach.

He changed himself for her. She loved music, liked to have something playing all the time, whether it was Mozart or Mick Jagger. She liked it going even while she worked, while they talked, while they loved. But music had always distracted him and made him nervous. He couldn't grasp the pattern of the sonatas or the lyrics of the songs. Still, he didn't want her to form any alliance that excluded him, so he pretended to listen along with her. For her sake he even grew to like a few things. He liked Tchaikovsky, a Russian, and he liked James Taylor, a North Carolinian.

All along he sensed that he was too deeply involved in this marriage. He blamed his father. Edmund's obituary had said, "Surviving are his widow, the former Marcella Stalvey, and one son." That sentence had alarmed him. It yoked the two survivors in a bereft future. So he did not go home for Christmases or summers, and when Alice stepped into the yellow light from the bug bulb he fell into an obsessive, exclusive love. It had to be that strong, had to be everything. It had to be more than it was, actually. The marriage was not made of Alice and William but was a hard bright metallic nugget located just through and beyond his wife, and he pushed toward it, crazy to get at it. That's what that was, the thing out of his reach: the marriage itself.

It was unmanly the way he fussed over her. When she got pregnant he followed her around the house to make sure she was not going to trip on something or faint and fall, and though Alice herself never got morning sickness, Will's stomach was queasy.

Then one afternoon he came home to find her in bed. She was four months along but had not slowed her pace, still stayed up late despite his objections. "I'm glad to see you're taking this seriously," he said; he grinned at her and sat on the side of the bed. "You'll need sleep."

"I'm losing it," she said.

"What?"

"I'm starting to miscarry. I've been bleeding for two hours."

He jumped for the telephone.

"I already called," she said.

"But you should be in the hospital."

"The doctor said just lie still. He said if it happens it happens." She unfolded a paperback book on her stomach.

He went about the apartment straightening up, emptying ashtrays, reshelving books, sneaking a look through the bedroom door when he could without letting her see how frantic he was. He brought her some tomato soup and Oysterettes for supper, but she wouldn't eat. Her pain was getting worse. "Please take an aspirin, at least," he pleaded.

"I can't do that. You know they have no idea what aspirin does to the fetus."

"Yes but, ah . . . honey, you're miscarrying, so it won't . . . make a difference. You know?"

She looked at him cruelly. "We don't know that. We don't know if that's what's really going to happen." Then her face turned white with the pain.

"I'm going out for some codeine. You're in bad shape."

"No!" she gasped. "Don't! Don't go." She reached out for him as he pulled on his jacket.

"I'll be back." He ran. There was a drugstore three blocks away. He ran with her colorless face before him, its blood suddenly drained by the shock of pain. It made him think of his father and how quickly death could come upon an unsuspecting heart. Of course she was not in danger, he knew that, he kept repeating it to himself as he sped down the sidewalk. What kind of doctor would say "If it happens it happens" and leave ordinary human beings to deal on their own with a terrible event?

"Alice, I'm here," he called as soon as he was back, slamming the door and running to her. She had pulled herself around in the bed so that she was half-sitting, half-lying against the headboard, trying to encircle her pain, her head and knees drawing together around it.

"Is it worse?"

Her eyes were blank. "Yes," she whispered, then screamed.

"It's nothing, don't worry! It will be over. Alice! Don't be afraid, I'm going to help you!" He ran to the bathroom and filled a tumbler with water. He had trouble with the childproof cap on the bottle; he pressed down and turned but the cap kept slipping past the grooves it was meant to catch on, so he set the plastic bottle on the floor and stomped on it. The tiny white tablets scattered across the floor. He scooped one up and ran to the bedroom. Alice swallowed the pill and gulped water.

"I feel better already." She looked at him gratefully. He knew the pill could not possibly work that fast. He knew that the sudden end of pain meant that the fetus had been expelled. Alice relaxed. He helped her to move back down into the bed.

"I think it's all right, Will," she said. "Maybe it was something else. I think the baby is going to be all right." She fell asleep.

He knew it was not all right. Now what, was the question. He could not leave it up to her. She would not be able to handle it. He stroked her long thin arm for a while. Her skin was cold from the evaporation of sweat. He covered her with a blanket. Then he gathered her up close to him, cuddling her in his arms. She mumbled. He rubbed her legs, her stomach. She was sleeping as only one can sleep who has outlasted pain — not a normal sleep but an extraordinary, deep, healing sleep. He felt between her legs for the sanitary pad and unhooked it, slid it out.

He couldn't tell much. The fetus was less than the length of his finger. It looked normal, but without lab work there was no way to tell whether it had been long dead or not. He could take it in tomorrow and have it checked. But where would he keep it till then? In his palm it was barely visible inside its dark bubble, but he could see its shape, its whiteness. He had to flush it down the toilet. There was nothing else to do with it! He was angry, and struck his head against the bathroom door, and cried. He had had no choice in this; it was worse than his father's death, when at least he had alternative courses of action to take. He felt his life begin to cloud over, as lives must at a certain stage when there is nothing to do but what has to be done.

In the morning she was happy. "No pain," she said. "It's okay."

"No," he said, cupping her face in his hands, kissing her forehead. She understood. She never asked for the details. He made sure she was hospitalized for the next two miscarriages.

It dawned on him that the loneliness of marriage, the thing Alice had so feared, starts out of the love itself, which can never deliver on its promises. He gave up certain hopes he'd had, of Alice and William as progenitors of a whole new clan, the North Carolina Reeses. Alice gave up her work. Eventually they moved back to South Carolina, to the flat tidal lowcountry, where, when Alice finally became pregnant again, Marcella brought over honey in warm milk every night, which she said would make the baby "stick"; and God knows what made the difference but nine months passed, and a girl was born, his serious Beth.

So North Carolina, which he had looked to almost as to a promised land, turned out to be only an interlude in his life, and he ended up where he began. The children were born, and though he had nothing against daughters, that's what they were, and not likely to change his life as he'd thought children might. His wife had turned vague and timid, a Phi Beta Kappa in math unwilling to drive a car! And his work, which in North Carolina had promised to be a second love when his first faltered, has become a business, simply one more ob-gyn office with air-conditioned, carpeted, silent rooms.

Coming into the kitchen he doesn't notice immediately that the woman there is his mother, not his wife. She stands at the sink, her back to him. Then she turns, and he realizes it is Marcella. He has not seen her washing dishes in years; it is like catching her at something at which she would rather not be caught.

Her eyes are bright and excited. She reminds him of a Katharine Hepburn character, beautiful but with a screw loose, not trustworthy. He doesn't trust her answers to the simplest questions, such as "What is the date?" or "Is it raining?" She is good at fooling people; but she doesn't fool him anymore.

"Where's Alice?" There is no longer a need for formalities between them, like hello, how are you. Other men become more polite toward their mothers with age, but he has gone the other way.

"Alice," she announces, "has gone out to interview a prospective baby-sitter."

"What are you talking about?"

"I gave her the name of a girl who's looking for a baby-sitting job, and she went to talk to the girl. She asked me to stay with the children until she comes back."

"And when will that be?"

"Oh, soon, I expect. The girl lives around here somewhere."

"Since when has she needed a baby-sitter? Beth is in school every day and Marcy goes twice a week."

"She needs one. Take my word for it. She needs to get out more. This girl can come afternoons."

"It was your idea, then."

"No. It was Queen's idea. Queen knows the girl, and suggested Alice might want to use her. The girl is white," Marcella hurries to explain. "But Queen says she is very nice. Queen seems to take a protective interest in her."

He goes into the living room, knowing she will follow him. She can't help it. He casts scowls at her, which she does not notice; he will have to tell her outright to go home. But when he starts to, she begins talking at the same instant, and she prevails.

"Duncan wants very much to have you and Alice over for dinner," she says.

"Fine."

"When will you come? You couldn't come the first time. You couldn't come the second time. So I want you to set the date. When are you available?"

"I don't know," he says.

215

"Then will you talk with Alice and let me know?"

"Fine."

"Don't forget to tell Alice." Marcella's fingers are incredibly long, tapering down over the back of a velvet chair. One of them traces a path through the pile of the fabric. Her hands are always moving, as if independent of her thoughts. And it is not only these insignificant movements that are made without thought; even her major actions are often not considered in advance.

Suddenly he is struck by an idea. *She* isn't sad. She is the only woman he knows who is not sad. The others, whom he tries to please and cheer, are sad; and she, whom he ignores, even insults, is happy.

* * *

In front of the television his two daughters sit, bending their torsos forward as if drawn by a magnet, up and out toward the screen where the Brady Bunch's father is kissing the Brady Bunch's mother while all of the Brady Bunch look on. They are trying to smooth out some difficulty so that the household can run happily again. Beth and Marcy don't see him. He stands behind them and watches the show. Then Marcella comes and stands behind him.

To tell the truth, he is interested in the program and wants to know what the Brady Bunch is going to do about the snakes one of them has hidden in a cage under the bed. But he can't watch with Marcella there. He turns the set off. The girls don't even look at him. Beth reaches out to turn it on again.

"Hold it," he says. "I'm home."

"So?"

"What happened today?" Usually they insist that nothing happened. They did nothing. Mommy did nothing. He imagines their days when he is at work as a series of long empty mornings making a silent, hollow childhood for them.

"Mommy threw the dolls away. I don't care, though. I didn't love them or anything. They were dumb," Beth says.

"I care," says Marcy. "I want Tiffany back. Tiffany had on her wedding dress. Now she is burnt up."

"I didn't even like Crystal and Heather. But Tiffany was Marcy's baby," Beth says. He sees their faces begin to redden toward tears, and he is helpless. He knows Marcella is watching him to see what he will do.

"You do something here," he says to Marcella. They are her grandchildren; she ought to be able to console them or do whatever it is they need.

The bed in his room is unmade. In the middle of it is a full blue enamel ashtray. Ashes have smudged the sheets. He checks the butts: Golden Lights. At least she hasn't gone back to Marlboros. He empties the ashtray and rinses it in the bathroom sink, then changes the sheets. But he must have pulled a single-bed sheet from the closet by mistake; after he gets two of the contoured corners on he sees the sheet won't reach to the other side of the bed. Alice doesn't keep the sheets in any order. They are all jumbled into the linen closet. He knows he could organize the house better than she does. He would even enjoy it more than she does. He could take care of the children, too.

Maybe, though, he should not have left them with Marcella. She is not very good with them; she can't put herself in their shoes, she doesn't have the imagination. He finds the three of them settled in a big chair, Marcella reading *Sleeping Beauty* with Marcy in her lap and Beth straddling the arm. He had forgotten the princess is not the only one who sleeps. The whole castleful is conked out — guests, servants, dogs, dead to the world. When they wake up they seem not to know that a whole lot of time has gone by.

After the story Marcella has nothing to say. The script has run out.

* * *

And could transvestites harm his daughters? They are gone as he comes around the corner, and he doesn't know which house they might have come out of and gone back into.

He could live in a safer place. He could live downtown near the Battery instead of in this ambiguous zone between rich and poor. Marcella keeps finding houses for sale in better neighborhoods, but he won't move, he has set his family here. "Courting disaster," Alice says.

He had wanted a family. Unmarried and childless he was loose in time, fatherless, mother-threatened. After he got his family, his sense of orientation and stability improved, but at times now, and increasingly often, a new, dizzying suspicion grabs him and spins him: the suspicion that the stability is false; that he will round his corner one day and there will be no house; and worse, that he will be glad to see it gone.

There is still enough light on the porch to reveal a difference in color between the deck-gray wooden floor and the white columns, banisters, and ceiling. The porch is empty, a corridor from the street to the black leafy yard. His house is entered sideways, through a door to the east.

"Bedtime!" he calls.

"Mommy isn't home," Marcy says.

"She's probably in the Piggly Wiggly," Beth says. "Sometimes she gets lost in there, she thinks she's in Harris-Teeter instead. But then the mayonnaise or something isn't in the place she thought it would be. I know where everything is in both stores."

"Good for you, girlie."

He helps them undress and step into the bathtub. They are so thin he averts his eyes. At one time he wanted lots of children, a family big enough to boom through life, absorb its own difficulties and spring back from trouble robustly. Small families are feeble. But in a big family, affliction and grief are less destructive; they get diluted. If he had not been an only child, for example, it would not have mattered so much when he refused to go into his father's business. Another son could have done it. Another son could have done all that he had failed to do.

He wanted to have the children his father had not had. But Alice's body would not yield a big family, reluctant at every stage. Three miscarriages. And the bodies of his surviving children don't promise fecundity. They are too thin. Against their knobby shoulders and ribs, his hands look large and grotesque. He washes their meek, bent necks; the soap slides in rivulets down their backs, over the shoulder blades that are like wings, over the bumps of their spines, and he rinses them and lifts them slack-limbed and dripping out onto the bathmat. They stand still and let him towel them dry, as quiet and compliant as orphans; they raise their arms into the air as he slips their nightgowns down over their heads, then tucks them into bed with the sheet and blanket gathered up under their chins. They sleep together in an old sleigh bed that used to be his mother's (when she remarried she bought a new bed, king-sized, with stereo in the headboard) and he tells them the sleigh will carry them into sleep.

* * *

A sad woman can trigger disaster, and Will doesn't want disaster. All his life he has feared it: something bad from the stars — catastrophe, cataclysm, calamity — all those ancient words for flood and earthquake. He has never had a disaster. He thought his father's death would prove to be one — it seemed one at the time — but life for everyone except his father went on. And went on in pretty much the same way it had gone before. He has had only false alarms, never a true disaster, and yet he has always feared it. Now the smell of it is in the air. Claire wants to talk.

The first false alarm, his first whiff of disaster's possibility, came when he was six, the day he began the first grade. School scared him: the thick, unwieldy crayons, the sudden and repeated alarms of bells, the unsmiling gray teacher whose upper arms shook with ominous fat, the chattering, loud children. But the real terror came when he got home. He had survived the day, he was safe, he had been a "brave boy," as his mother had told him to be, and he was laughing with relief when he reached his block and saw his house. He called his mother as soon as he was within earshot, eager to answer her questions and remake the horrible day into a pleasant one, for her. She wasn't there. He looked in every room. He had never been alone in his house before. Suddenly the brave boy was in tears and panic-stricken. He rushed to her room, to her dresser, and opened each drawer to see if she had taken her clothes. They were there, her underclothes white and folded in tissue paper. Her dresses were still hanging in the closet, thin ghosts of her. Then he knew something had happened to her, someone had taken her away. He thought of the vegetable man who came every day in a truck, an old black man who, though he seemed kindly and gentle, might be poor enough to hold his mother for ransom. When he telephoned his father's office he could hardly say the words, he had to repeat them: "Something has happened to my mother." He thought his heart would stop, its thumping was so fast and heavy inside him. Had she told him to be brave because she knew something terrible was about to happen? He was in his bed when his father came home, but he could hear the several phone calls his father made, and by the time Edmund came to his room, Will knew it was a "false alarm," as his father said, and that he had made a fool of himself.

He heard his father chastise his mother when she came home.

"The boy was terrified. He was shaking. How could you do such a thing?"

"But I forgot. I forgot he would be out early on the first day." Their voices drifted up to him as he lay stiff in his small bed, his brain already forming a resolution for life: to do without her.

"How could you forget your own child?" his father had asked her.

So that chance of catastrophe passed. She had not left, had not been abducted; she had been at the grocery store. Maybe disaster no longer comes as a fire or flood or any single stroke of ruin, but is instead a creeping, insidious thing — a decay. Things go bad, but slowly; things degenerate, rot.

* * *

The first rift between Danny and Will had come when they were twelve, and Danny found out that his great-grandfather was a Jew. Joseph Cardozo arrived in Charleston in 1781 from Portugal, built up a pharmacy business, and married the governor's daughter. She raised her children as Episcopalians, and he gave money to the Episcopal church, which in one year even listed him among its members. But to prevent misunderstanding among future generations, Joseph Cardozo in a codicil to his will renounced "all connection, real or reputed, to Christianity" and required that his heirs do the same. They did not, and forfeited a sizable inheritance.

But something came down to Danny when he was twelve. Till then Will and Danny had been best friends in the ways boys in the South can be, paired off as a couple through childhood, so that when people thought of one they thought of the other, and said the names in a breath: Will and Danny, Reese and Cardozo. But suddenly Danny drew back. He read books about Jews for a year and wrote in a notebook. It looked as if a Jew grew up inside him, and Will envied that secret self. It gave

221

Danny a strength that stayed, though it was not always visible.
The Jew in him could keep an ironic eye on things, see past
trouble; could preserve a distance and a dignity even when
things went bad — land deals and marriages, for example.

Will's own genealogy is a dull succession of generations that
has left him no spiritual legacy. As a boy, he wished for Danny's
Jewish soul. He longed for a heart like the one his friend was
getting, an unstoppable pump that would not falter. Danny
might appear to be in trouble, but he never really is, he has this
secret strength. Now, though he's lost fifty thousand dollars in a
golf-course scheme and his ex-wife is suing him and he lives
without furniture, these are minor details. The man is complete. Self-destructive to some extent, but whole enough to take
it.

The partnership offer was a rescue mission. There is no other
explanation.

They used to hunt together: ducks, quail, squirrels. They
were young doctors, married but without children, and there
was something fine about going out from their homes in the
early still-dark hours, each man knowing the other had left a
marriage bed and a woman's warm limbs for this cold dawn.
They had hunted together as boys, too, but the best hunting
came in those early years of marriage. They talked very little
then, drank some but not immoderately. They did not kill
much game. Then slowly the talk and drink increased, the killing increased, they went after bigger animals: turkey, deer, feral
hogs. Finally Will said no more deer or hogs. Then no turkey.
No squirrels. Eventually no doves or partridges. His last hunt
was a duck hunt with Danny three years ago in an abandoned
rice field on the Santee. They sat facing one another in the
blind, each with his knees apart but almost touching the
other's, their hands dropped down between their legs. It was
cold. The broken dikes impounding the wetlands looked like
ancient earthworks built in a design that could be seen only
from a spaceship; but he knew the dikes were built by slaves in

an expense of human labor greater than what it took to build the Great Wall of China. He began to feel uncomfortable. The sun still had not gotten up over the horizon but its color was already on the marsh like a slow flood tide. The rice field, which had been a gray shadow, turned white, pink, yellow, before settling into gold-green. He began to think something was essentially comical about two men with guns huddled in a thatched box waiting for ducks. Here was the same heartrending stillness that used to dazzle him, the marsh at dawn hazed and unsuspecting seconds before the shots and the panic — here it was, same as ever, and yet it was now only an old ritual of old men, played out for the sake of what it used to be.

"Carol's had it with me," Danny said. "She's gone. I deal with a lawyer from now on."

"No kidding," Will said. He saw Cardozo's eye fasten on something in the sky, over Will's left shoulder.

"Coming in over the north dike," Danny said. "Teal."

"Blue-wing."

"We weren't concentric. We had different centers. She says I'm nuts — it's in the divorce suit."

"No," Will said. Neither man looked at the other.

"Yeah. I have to fight it because it means I couldn't see the kids. If it gets into court, would you testify? Here they come." Danny shot into the flock just coming over their heads. Then Will shot. His duck fell awkwardly, not straight like a dead bird, but still flapping a wing. It flapped again in the water, drifting into the cattails. He marked its spot. He would have to wade out to get it, then twist its neck. Danny shot again.

"Would I have to say I think you're sane?" Will said.

"That's the general idea."

"I'll perjure myself, for a friend." One flying duck was circling back. *Don't be a fool, don't come this way,* Will thought. He could see the bird's confusion; not knowing where the danger was, it had veered from its path to turn back, and this course would carry it directly over the blind once more. Will shot straight up. The bird flew two feet higher into the air, then dropped straight down into the water, a yard from the blind. Shot fell down around them like rain, making blips in the water and clicks on the pine flooring of the blind. Will's eye itched, and a gnat flew into his ear with a tiny whine and tickle.

"Her proof of my insanity is that I won't give her a divorce. That I claim I still love her. I'm not facing reality." Danny sighed. "It was a surprise to me, you know? A surprise. Things go along and go along, marriage and practice and children, and then *kablam!* it's all in jeopardy, everything's on the line at once."

"That's not true. It's only the marriage."

"Maybe. We'll see." They drank some more bourbon. Six wood ducks came in on the west side, their harlequin markings caught by the sun. Two fell when they were shot, but the rest hardly wavered in their flight, just lifted a little higher and away toward the next field.

"We need a damn dog. I can't remember where the first four ducks are," Danny said.

"Let's pick them up now. The gnats are bad, and it's getting late, anyway. We won't see many more."

"You can't tell. Wait awhile," Danny said. Will's stomach was churning from the shock of straight bourbon. The sun began to heat up his head and neck, and the haze over the field lifted like a scrim, revealing the world to be much brighter and more clearly delineated one part from another than he had thought it was. The dead birds were already beginning to decompose, the microscopic tissues breaking down, the organs stopped, juices souring, as they drifted with the breeze on the water's surface, making paths through the yellow sludge of algae and duckweed. Across the field in a dead pine, a great blue heron spread its broad wings, then flew off across the dikes. Will gazed after the slow, strong wingbeat, the careful curve of neck, the long legs trailing.

Danny fired twice at some teal that were out of range. "What do you think, Will," he said.

"About what."

"All this."

"All what." But he knew, he knew. He did not want to talk about it; talk like this was self-indulgent, pointless.

"Carol. All that," Danny said.

"You'll pull through."

"Yes, but what did I do wrong? I mean here we are, you and I, we've lived almost the same life, grown up together, med school together, everything, but now I've made a mess of it and you haven't. And I didn't even know I was doing it. Christ, I didn't even know. If she had said something, I would have changed whatever it was she didn't like, you know?"

"What was it? Why'd she leave?"

"She thought I didn't love her, she said. I did love her, but she said it wasn't a deep love, it wasn't deep enough to make up for the rest, the bad parts. Does that make sense? I loved her. It wasn't enough. She took off. Now I say I want her back because I love her. She says it isn't enough to come back to. God." He was drinking his bourbon from the bottle now. There was not much left, so Will knew they would leave soon.

"So what do you think?" Danny said.

"I think she was right."

"You do? I didn't love her enough?"

"Well, did you?"

"Shit, I guess not." Danny put the bottle down and looked out over the yellow-green field, the yellow-green water. Tears filled his eyes, then ran down his face.

"Let's get out of here," he said. They untied the rowboat and set off to look for the fallen ducks, following the black wakes through the scum. They found all but one, the wounded blue-wing. Its trail led into a clump of cattails too dense to get into with the boat.

"You want to put on the waders and go after it?" Danny said.

"No." It was the first time in his life he had ever left wounded game in the field.

"Me neither. Let's go."

That night, through lawyers, Danny told Carol she was right (he was crazy, he didn't love her enough, she could have all the money and his children too), hoping this belly-up display of love would bring her back to him. Instead she accepted the terms and moved into a Harbortown Villa at Hilton Head. Now she plays tennis and poisons his children's hearts against him.

Will eats lunch in the hospital cafeteria, then drives back to his office for the afternoon appointments. Days are too long.

Now Claire is doing her nails. This is the only woman he has ever known whose fingernails look like the ones in magazines; such fingernails are possible only for unmarried, childless women. Filed to a curving point, they are painted salmon-pink, a color he doesn't much like, but he likes it on Claire's nails. He likes to see her doing them with the little set of tools: orangewood sticks with different-shaped points, cuticle scissors, dips and creams, and the slim, long-handled brush. She concentrates on the work, bending over her hands, painting each nail slowly, meticulously.

Once, a year ago, he watched her do her toenails in bed on a Saturday morning. She clipped them, her knees pulled up under her chin. He saw the white band of underpants between her thighs. Her toes lifted up to meet the clippers in her hand. Then she held out the bottle and her foot for him to paint. The nail on her little toe was so small it was only a spot of pink. He knew as he touched it, touched the soft instep, the heel, the tendon like a tight string, that he would not in his lifetime see this happiness again; it was the still zenith of his time on earth. In the room all objects — the radio, the dresser and its tilted mirror, the thin white towel hung over a chair — were as they should be, instantly complete. Nothing could have been added or removed. Rooms, mornings, women to come would be less than this.

And so it proved. Now Claire paints her fingernails at the reception desk. Her back straightens. His heart is a shambles of its own making.

"Shall I do the other hand?" he asks, coming up behind her. She squints at him, smiles, says no.

"What have we got?" He looks over her shoulder to the appointment book under her fingers. "Mrs. Jenner canceled?"

"Yes. She didn't say why."

So there are only two appointments for the afternoon.

"I have an idea," he says. "Where are the girls?"

"Cindy's on break. I sent Michelle out to get coffee filters."

"Let's cancel these two patients and spend the afternoon at your place."

"You can't cancel them. They're already here, waiting. Mrs. Donato was a twelve-thirty appointment. You're twenty minutes late."

"Just go out and tell them I'm caught up at the hospital in an emergency. Reschedule them for next week."

"No," she says.

"Why not?"

"You can't do that."

"You don't want to spend the afternoon with me?" he says.

"No, I don't. You're coming over tonight, remember?"

"Six o'clock," he says. "Okay. Claire, let me ask you something. Have you and Danny been talking about me?"

He knows from her face they have. Claire can't lie.

"What do you mean?"

"In the future, I'd appreciate it if you'd keep the details of my practice and of my private life confidential."

He steps out into the waiting room, courageous as a gladiator. "Good news, ladies," he announces. "I can't see you today because I've got to run over to the hospital for a delivery. Baby couldn't wait. If you'll see the receptionist she'll give you another appointment." They will be glad, after all, not to see him. Women dread these visits. As they should.

Claire is angry and won't look at him when he passes. So he locks himself in the back office. He didn't really want to spend the afternoon with her, anyway; he just didn't want to spend it with the patients.

He sits at the desk. He draws a picture of a stickman at a crossroads — a tatterdemalion who can neither find his way nor ask for help.

John Irving

from
The World According To Garp

from
Walt
Catches Cold

HELEN THOUGHT she was in control of what was going on; she at least had controlled how it began (opening her office door, as usual, to the slouching Michael Milton, and bidding him enter her room). Once inside, she closed the door behind him and kissed him quickly on the mouth, holding his slim neck so that he couldn't even escape for breath, and grinding her knee between his legs; he kicked over the wastebasket and dropped his notebook.

"There's nothing more to discuss," Helen said, taking a breath. She raced her tongue across his upper lip; Helen was trying to decide if she liked his mustache. She decided she liked it; or, at least, she liked it for now. "We'll go to your apartment. Nowhere else," she told him.

"It's across the river," he said.

"I know where it is," she said. "Is it clean?"

"Of course," he said. "And it's got a great view of the river."

"I don't care about the view," Helen said. "I want it clean."

"It's pretty clean," he said. "I can clean it better."

"We can only use your car," she said.

"I don't have a car," he said.

"I know you don't," Helen said. "You'll have to get one."

He was smiling now; he'd been surprised, but now he was feeling sure of himself again. "Well, I don't have to get one *now*, do I?" he asked, nuzzling his mustache against her neck; he touched her breasts. Helen unattached herself from his embrace.

"Get one whenever you want," she said. "We'll never use mine, and I won't be seen walking with you all over town, or riding on the buses. If *anyone* knows about this, it's over. Do you understand?" She sat down at her desk, and he did not feel invited to walk around her desk to touch her; he sat in the chair her students usually sat in.

"Sure, I understand," he said.

"I love my husband and will never hurt him," Helen told him. Michael Milton knew better than to smile.

"I'll get a car, right away," he said.

"And clean your apartment, or *have* it cleaned," she said.

"Absolutely," he said. Now he dared to smile, a little. "What kind of car do you want me to get?" he asked her.

"I don't care about that," she told him. "Just get one that runs; get one that isn't in the garage all the time. And don't get one with bucket seats. Get one with a long seat in front." He looked more surprised and puzzled than ever, so she explained to him: "I want to be able to lie down, comfortably, across the front seat," she said. "I'll put my head in your lap so that no one will see me sitting up beside you. Do you understand?"

"Don't worry," he said, smiling again.

"It's a small town," Helen said. "No one must know."

"It's not *that* small a town," Michael Milton said, confidently.

"Every town is a small town," Helen said, "and this one is smaller than you think. Do you want me to tell you?"

"Tell me what?" he asked her.

"You're sleeping with Margie Tallworth," Helen said. "She's in my Comp. Lit. 205; she's a junior," Helen said. "And you see another *very* young undergraduate — she's in Dirkson's English 150; I think she's a *freshman*, but I don't know if you've slept

232

with her. Not for lack of trying, if you haven't," Helen added. "To my knowledge you've not touched any of your fellow graduate students; not yet," Helen said. "But there's surely someone I've missed, or there *has* been."

Michael Milton looked both sheepish and proud at the same time, and the usual command he held over his expressions escaped him so completely that Helen didn't like the expression she saw on his face and she looked away.

"*That's* how small this town, and every town, is," Helen said. "If you have me," she told him, "you can't have any of those others. I know what young girls notice, and I know how much they're inclined to *say*."

"Yes," Michael Milton said; he appeared ready to take notes.

Helen suddenly thought of something, and she looked momentarily startled. "You *do* have a driver's license?" she asked.

"Oh yes!" Michael Milton said. They both laughed, and Helen relaxed again; but when he came around her desk to kiss her, she shook her head and waved him back.

"And you won't ever touch me here," she said. "There will be nothing intimate in this office. I don't lock my door. I don't even like to have it shut. Please open it, now," she asked him, and he did as he was told.

He got a car, a huge Buick Roadmaster, the *old* kind of station wagon — with real wooden slats on the side. It was a 1951 Buick Dynaflow, heavy and shiny with pre-Korea chrome and real oak. It weighed 5,550 pounds, or almost three tons. It held seven quarts of oil and nineteen gallons of gasoline. Its original price was $2,850 but Michael Milton picked it up for less than six hundred dollars.

"It's a straight-eight cylinder, three-twenty cubic, power steering, with a single-throat Carter carb," the salesman told Michael. "It's not too badly rusted."

In fact, it was the dull, inconspicuous color of clotted blood, more than six feet wide and seventeen feet long. The front seat was so long and deep that Helen could lie across it, almost without having to bend her knees — or without having to put her head in Michael Milton's lap, though she did this anyway.

She did not put her head in his lap because she *had* to; she liked her view of the dashboard, and being close to the old smell of the maroon leather of the big, slick seat. She put her head in his lap because she liked feeling Michael's leg stiffen and relax, his thigh shifting just slightly between the brake and the accelerator. It was a quiet lap to put your head in because the car had no clutch; the driver needed to move just one leg, and just occasionally. Michael Milton thoughtfully carried his loose change in his left front pocket, so there were only the soft wales of his corduroy slacks, which made a faint impression on the skin of Helen's cheek — and sometimes his rising erection would touch her ear, or reach up into the hair on the back of her neck.

Sometimes she imagined taking him into her mouth while they drove across town in the big car with the gaping chrome grille like the mouth of a feeding fish — *Buick Eight* in script across the teeth. But that, Helen knew, would not be safe.

The first indication that the whole thing might not be safe was when Margie Tallworth dropped Helen's Comp. Lit. 205, without so much as a note of explanation concerning what she might not have liked about the course. Helen feared it was not the course that Margie hadn't liked, and she called the young Miss Tallworth into her office to ask her for an explanation.

Margie Tallworth, a junior, knew enough about school to know that no explanation was required; up to a certain point in any semester, a student was free to drop any course without the instructor's permission. "Do I have to have a reason?" the girl asked Helen, sullenly.

"No, you don't," Helen said. "But if you *had* a reason, I just wanted to hear it."

"I don't have to have a reason," Margie Tallworth said. She held Helen's gaze longer than most students could hold it; then she got up to leave. She was pretty and small and rather well dressed for a student, Helen thought. If there was any consistency to Michael Milton's former girl friend and his present taste, it appeared only that he liked women to wear nice clothes.

"Well, I'm sorry it didn't work out," Helen said, truthfully, as Margie was leaving; she was still fishing for what the girl might actually *know*.

She knew, Helen thought, and quickly accused Michael.

"You've blown it already," she told him coldly, because she *could* speak coldly to him — over the phone. "Just *how* did you drop Margie Tallworth?"

"Very gently," Michael Milton said, smugly. "But a drop is a drop, no matter how different the ways of doing it are." Helen did not appreciate it when he attempted to instruct her — except sexually; she indulged the boy that, and he seemed to need to be dominant there. That was different for her, and she didn't really mind. He was sometimes rough, but not ever dangerous, she thought; and if she firmly resisted something, he stopped. Once she had had to tell him, "No! I don't like that, I won't do that." But she had added, "Please," because she wasn't *that* sure of him. He had stopped; he had been forceful with her, but in another way — in a way that was all right with her. It was exciting that she couldn't trust him completely. But not trusting him to be *silent* was another matter; if she knew he had talked about her, that would be that.

"I didn't tell her anything," Michael insisted. "I said, 'Margie, it's all over,' or something like that. I didn't even tell her there was another woman, and I *certainly* said nothing about you."

"But she's probably heard you talk about me, before," Helen said. "Before this started, I mean."

"She never liked your course, anyway," Michael said. "We *did* talk about that once."

"She never liked the course?" Helen said. This truly surprised her.

"Well, she's not very bright," Michael said, impatiently.

"She'd better not know," Helen said. "I mean it: you better find out."

But he found out nothing. Margie Tallworth refused to speak to him. He tried to tell her, on the phone, that it was all because an old girl friend had come back to him — she had arrived from out of town; she'd had no place to stay; one thing had led to another. But Margie Tallworth had hung up on him before he could polish the story.

Helen smoked a little more. She watched Garp anxiously for a few days — and once she felt actual guilt, when she made love to Garp; she felt guilty that she had made love to him not because she wanted to but because she wanted to reassure him, *if* he had been thinking that anything was wrong.

* * *

As for Helen, she developed a fondness for the bare, sharp shaft of the Volvo's stick shift; its bite at the end of the day, driving home from her office, felt good against the heel of her hand, and she often pressed against it until she felt it was only a hair away from the pressure necessary to break her skin. She could bring tears to her eyes, this way, and it made her feel clean again, when she arrived home — when the boys would wave and shout at her, from the window where the TV was; and when Garp would announce what dinner he had prepared for them all, when Helen walked into the kitchen.

Margie Tallworth's possible knowledge had frightened Helen, because although Helen had said to Michael — and to herself — that it would be over the instant anyone knew, Helen now knew that it would be more difficult to end than she had first imagined. She hugged Garp in his kitchen and hoped for Margie Tallworth's ignorance.

* * *

"I *can't* see you," Helen told him when she called. "It's as simple as that. It's over, just the way I said it would be if he ever found out. I won't hurt him any more than I already have."

"What about me?" Michael Milton said.

"I'm sorry," Helen told him. "But you *knew*. We both knew."

"I want to *see* you," he said. "Maybe tomorrow."

But she told him that Garp had taken the kids to a movie for the sole purpose that she finish it tonight.

"I'm coming over," he told her.

"Not here, no," she said.

"We'll go for a drive," he told her.

"I can't go out, either," she said.

"I'm coming," Michael Milton said, and he hung up.

Helen checked the time. It would be all right, she supposed, if she could get him to leave quickly. Movies were at least an hour and a half long. She decided she wouldn't let him in the house — not under any circumstances. She watched for the headlights to come up the driveway, and when the Buick stopped — just in front of the garage, like a big ship docking at a dark pier — she ran out of the house and pushed herself against the driver's-side door before Michael Milton could open it.

The rain was turning to a semisoft slush at her feet, and the icy drops were hardening as they fell — they had some sting as they struck her bare neck, when she bent over to speak to him through the rolled-down window.

He immediately kissed her. She tried to lightly peck his cheek but he turned her face and forced his tongue into her mouth. All over again she saw the corny bedroom of his apartment: the poster-sized print above his bed — Paul Klee's *Sinbad*

237

the Sailor. She supposed this was how he saw himself: a colorful adventurer, but sensitive to the beauty of Europe.

Helen pulled back from him and felt the cold rain soak her blouse.

"We can't just *stop*," he said, miserably. Helen couldn't tell if it was the rain through the open window or tears that streaked his face. To her surprise, he had shaved his mustache off, and his upper lip looked slightly like the puckered, undeveloped lip of a child — like Walt's little lip, which looked lovely on Walt, Helen thought; but it wasn't her idea of the lip for a lover.

"What did you do to your mustache?" she asked him.

"I thought you didn't like it," he said. "I did it for you."

"But I *liked* it," she said, and shivered in the freezing rain.

"Please, get in with me," he said.

She shook her head; her blouse clung to her cold skin and her long corduroy skirt felt as heavy as chain mail; her tall boots slipped in the stiffening slush.

"I won't take you anywhere," he promised. "We'll just sit here, in the car. We can't just *stop*," he repeated.

"We knew we'd have to," Helen said. "We knew it was just for a little while."

Michael Milton let his head sink against the glinting ring of the horn; but there was no sound, the big Buick was shut off. The rain began to stick to the windows — the car was slowly being encased in ice.

"Please get *in*," Michael Milton moaned. "I'm not leaving here," he added, sharply. "I'm not afraid of him. I don't have to do what he says."

"It's what *I* say, too," Helen said. "You have to go."

"I'm not going," Michael Milton said. "I know about your husband. I know everything about him."

They had never talked about Garp; Helen had forbidden it. She didn't know what Michael Milton meant.

"He's a minor writer," Michael said, boldly. Helen looked surprised; to her knowledge, Michael Milton had never read

Garp. He'd told her once that he never read living writers; he claimed to value the perspective he said one could gain only when a writer had been dead for a while. It is fortunate that Garp didn't know *this* about him — it would certainly have added to Garp's contempt for the young man. It added somewhat to Helen's disappointment with poor Michael, now.

"My husband is a very good writer," she said softly, and a shiver made her twitch so hard that her folded arms sprang open and she had to fold them closed at her breasts again.

"He's not a *major* writer," Michael declared. "Higgins said so. You certainly must be aware of how your husband is regarded in the department."

Higgins, Helen was aware, was a singularly eccentric and troublesome colleague, who managed at the same time to be dull and cloddish to the point of sleep. Helen hardly felt Higgins was representative of the department — except that like many of her more insecure colleagues, Higgins habitually gossiped to the graduate students about his fellow department members; in this desperate way, perhaps, Higgins felt he gained the students' trust.

"I was not aware that Garp *was* regarded by the department, one way or another," Helen said coolly. "Most of them don't read anything very contemporary."

"Those who do say he's minor," Michael Milton said.

This competitive and pathetic stand did not warm Helen's heart to the boy and she turned to go back inside the house.

"I won't go!" Michael Milton screamed. "I'll *confront* him about us! Right now. He can't tell us what to do."

"*I'm* telling you, Michael," Helen said.

He slumped against the horn and began to cry. She went over and touched his shoulder through the window.

I'll sit with you a minute," Helen told him. "But you *must* promise me that you'll leave. I won't have him or my children see this."

He promised.

"Give me the keys," Helen said. His look of baleful hurt —
that she didn't trust him not to drive off with her — touched
Helen all over again. She put the keys in the deep flap pocket
of her long skirt and walked around to the passenger side and
let herself in. He rolled up his window, and they sat, not touching, the windows fogging around them, the car creaking under
a coat of ice.

Then he completely broke down and told her that she had
meant more to him than all of France — and she knew what
France had meant to him, of course. She held him, then, and
wildly feared how much *time* had passed, or was passing there in
the frozen car. Even if it was not a long movie, they must still
have a good half hour, or forty-five minutes; yet Michael Milton
was nowhere near ready to leave. She kissed him, strongly, hoping this would help, but he only began to fondle her wet, cold
breasts. She felt all over as frozen to him as she had felt outside
in the hardening sleet. But she let him touch her.

"Dear Michael," she said, thinking all the while.

"How can we stop?" was all he said.

But Helen had already stopped; she was only thinking about
how to stop *him*. She shoved him up straight in the driver's
position and stretched across the long seat, pulling her skirt
back down to cover her knees, and putting her head in his lap.

"Please *remember*," she said. "Please try. This was the nicest
part for me — just letting you drive me in the car, when I knew
where we were going. Can't you be happy — can't you just
remember that, and let it go?"

He sat rigid behind the steering wheel, both hands struggling
to stay gripped to the wheel, both thighs tensed under her
head, his erection pressing against her ear.

"Please try to just let it go at that, Michael," she said softly.
And they stayed this way a moment, imagining that the old
Buick was carrying them to Michael's apartment again. But
Michael Milton could not sustain himself on imagination. He

let one hand stray to the back of Helen's neck, which he gripped very tightly; his other hand opened his fly.

"Michael!" she said, sharply.

"You said you always wanted to," he reminded her.

"It's *over*, Michael."

"Not yet, it isn't," he said. His penis grazed her forehead, bent her eyelashes, and she recognized that this was the old Michael — the Michael of the apartment, the Michael who occasionally liked to treat her with some *force*. She did not appreciate it now. But if I resist, she thought, there will be a scene. She had only to imagine *Garp* as part of the scene to convince herself that she should avoid *any* scene, at any cost.

"Don't be a bastard, don't be a prick, Michael," she said. "Don't spoil it."

"You always said you wanted to," he said. "But it wasn't safe, you said. Well, now it's safe. The car isn't even moving. There can't be any accidents now," he said.

Oddly, she realized, he had suddenly made it easier for her. She did not feel concerned anymore with letting him down gently; she felt grateful to him that he had helped her to sort her priorities so forcefully. Her priorities, she felt enormously relieved to know, were Garp and her children. Walt shouldn't be out in this weather, she thought, shivering. And Garp was more *major* to her, she knew, than all her minor colleagues and graduate students together.

Michael Milton had allowed her to see himself with what struck Helen as a necessary vulgarity. *Suck him off*, she thought bluntly, putting him into her mouth, and *then* he'll leave. She thought bitterly that men, once they had ejaculated, were rather quick to abandon their demands. And from her brief experience in Michael Milton's apartment, Helen knew that this would not take long.

Time was also a factor in her decision; there was at least twenty minutes remaining in even the shortest movie they could have gone to see. She set her mind to it as she might have done if it were the last task remaining to a messy business, which might have ended better but could also have turned out worse; she felt slightly proud that she had at least proved to herself that her family *was* her first priority. Even Garp might appreciate this, she thought; but one day, not right away.

David Leavitt

from

Family
Dancing

Aliens

A YEAR AGO today I wouldn't have dreamed I'd be where I am now: in the recreation room on the third floor of the State Hospital, watching, with my daughter, ten men who sit in a circle in the center of the room. They look almost normal from a distance — khaki pants, lumberjack shirts, white socks — but I've learned to detect the tics, the nervous disorders. The men are members of a poetry writing workshop. It is my husband Alden's turn to read. He takes a few seconds to find his cane, to hoist himself out of his chair. As he stands, his posture is hunched and awkward. The surface of his crushed left eye has clouded to marble. There is a pale pink scar under his pale yellow hair.

The woman who leads the workshop, on a volunteer basis, rubs her forehead as she listens, and fingers one of her elephant-shaped earrings. Alden's voice is a hoarse roar, only recently reconstructed.

"Goddamned God," he reads. "I'm mad as hell I can't walk or talk."

It is spring, and my youngest child, my eleven-year-old, Nina, has convinced herself that she is an alien.

Mrs. Tompkins, her teacher, called me in yesterday morning to tell me. "Nina's constructed a whole history," she whispered, removing her glasses and leaning toward me across her desk, as if someone might be listening from above. "She never pays attention in class, just sits and draws. Strange landscapes, star-charts, the interiors of spaceships. I finally asked some of the other children what was going on. They told me that Nina says she's waiting to be taken away by her real parents. She says she's a surveyor, implanted here, but that soon a ship's going to come and retrieve her."

I looked around the classroom; the walls were papered with crayon drawings of cars and rabbits, the world seen by children. Nina's are remote, fine landscapes done with Magic Markers. No purple suns with faces. No abrupt, sinister self-portraits. In the course of a year Nina suffered a violent and quick puberty, sprouted breasts larger than mine, grew tufts of hair under her arms. The little girls who were her friends shunned her. Most afternoons now she stands in the corner of the playground, her hair held back by barrettes, her forehead gleaming. Recently, Mrs. Tompkins tells me, a few girls with glasses and large vocabularies have taken to clustering around Nina at recess. They sit in the broken bark beneath the slide and listen to Nina as one might listen to a prophet. Her small eyes, exaggerated by her own glasses, must seem to them expressive of martyred beauty.

"Perhaps you should send her to a psychiatrist," Mrs. Tompkins suggested. She is a good teacher, better than most of her colleagues. "This could turn into a serious problem," she said.

"I'll consider it," I answered, but I was lying. I don't have the money. And besides, I know psychiatry; it takes things away. I don't think I could bear to see what would be left of Nina once she'd been purged of this fantasy.

Today Nina sits in the corner of the recreation room. She is quiet, but I know her eyes are taking account of everything.

The woman with the elephant-shaped earrings is talking to one of the patients about poetry *qua* poetry.

"You know," I say to her afterward, "it's amazing that a man like Alden can write poems. He was a computer programmer. All our married life he never read a book."

"His work has real power," the teacher says. "It reminds me of Michelangelo's *Bound Slaves*. Its artistry is heightened by its rawness."

She hands me a sheet of mimeographed paper — some examples of the group's work. "We all need a vehicle for self-expression," she says.

Later, sitting on the sun porch with Alden, I read through the poems. They are full of expletives and filthy remarks — the kind of remarks my brother used to make when he was hot for some girl at school. I am embarrassed. Nina, curled in an unused wheelchair, is reading *The Chronicles of Narnia* for the seventeenth time. We should go home soon, but I'm wary of the new car. I don't trust its brakes. When I bought it, I tested the seatbelts over and over again.

"Dinner?" Alden asks. Each simple word, I remember, is a labor for him. We must be patient.

"Soon," I say.

"Dinner. It's all —" He struggles to find the word; his brow is red, and the one seeing eye stares at the opposite wall.

"Crap," he says. He keeps looking at the wall. His eyes are expressionless. Once again, he breathes.

Nearby, someone's screaming, but we're used to that.

A year ago today. The day was normal. I took my son, Charles, to the dentist's. I bought a leg of lamb to freeze. There was a sale on paper towels. Early in the evening, on our way to a restaurant, Alden drove the car through a fence, and over an embankment. I remember, will always remember, the way his body fell almost gracefully through the windshield, how the glass shattered around him in a thousand glittering pieces. Ear-

lier, during the argument, he had said that seatbelts do more
harm than good, and I had buckled myself in as an act of ven-
geance. This is the only reason I'm around to talk about it.

I suffered a ruptured spleen in the accident, and twenty-two
broken bones. Alden lost half his vision, much of his mobility,
and the English language. After a week in intensive care they
took him to his hospital and left me to mine. In the course of
the six months, three weeks, and five days I spent there, eight
women passed in and out of the bed across from me. The first
was a tiny, elderly lady who spoke in hushed tones and kept the
curtain drawn between us. Sometimes children were snuck in to
visit her; they would stick their heads around the curtain rod
and gaze at me, until a hand pulled them back and a voice
loudly whispered, "Sorry!" I was heavily sedated; everything
seemed to be there one minute, gone the next. After the old
woman left, another took her place. Somewhere in the course
of those months a Texan mother arrived who was undergoing
chemotherapy, who spent her days putting on make-up, over
and over again, until, by dusk, her face was the color of bruises.

My hospital. What can you say about a place to which you
become addicted? That you hate it, yet at the same time, that
you need it. For weeks after my release I begged to be readmitted. I would wake crying, helplessly, in the night, convinced
that the world had stopped, and I had been left behind, the
only survivor. I'd call the ward I had lived on. "You'll be all
right, dear," the nurses told me. "You don't have to come back,
and besides, we've kicked you out." I wanted cups of Jell-O. I
wanted there to be a light in the hall at night. I wanted to be
told that six months hadn't gone by, that it had all been, as it
seemed, a single, endless moment.

To compensate, I started to spend as much time as I could at
Alden's hospital. The head nurse suggested that if I was going
to be there all day, I might as well do something productive.
They badly needed volunteers on the sixth floor, the floor of the
severely retarded, the unrecoverable ones. I agreed to go in the

afternoons, imagining story corner with cute three-year-olds and seventy-year-olds. The woman I worked with most closely had been pregnant three times in the course of a year. Her partner was a pale-skinned young man who drooled constantly and could not keep his head up. Of course she had abortions. None of the administrators were willing to solicit funds for birth control because that would have meant admitting there was a need for birth control. We couldn't keep the couple from copulating. They hid in the bushes and in the broom closet. They were obsessive about their lovemaking, and went to great lengths to find each other. When we locked them in separate rooms, they pawed the doors and screamed.

The final pregnancy was the worst because the woman insisted that she wanted to keep the baby, and legally she had every right. Nora, my supervisor — a crusty, ancient nurse — had no sympathy, insisted that the woman didn't even know what being pregnant meant. In the third month, sure enough, the woman started to scream and wouldn't be calmed. Something was moving inside her, something she was afraid would try to kill her. The lover was no help. Just as easily as he'd begun with her, he'd forgotten her, and taken up with a Down's syndrome dwarf who got transferred from Sonoma.

The woman agreed to the third abortion. Because it was so late in the pregnancy, the procedure was painful and complicated. Nora shook her head and said, "What's the world coming to?" Then she returned to her work.

I admire women who shake their heads and say, "What's the world coming to?" Because of them, I hope, it will always stop just short of getting there.

Lately, in my own little ways, I, too, have been keeping the earth in orbit. Today, for instance, I take Alden out to the car and let him sit in the driver's seat, which he enjoys. The hot vinyl burns his thighs. I calm him. I sit in the passenger seat, strapped in, while he slowly turns the wheel. He stares through the windshield at the other cars in the parking lot, imagining, perhaps, an endless landscape unfolding before him as he drives.

Visiting hours end. I take Alden in from the parking lot, kiss him goodbye. He shares a room these days with a young man named Joe, a Vietnam veteran prone to motorcycle accidents. Because of skin-grafting, Joe's face is six or seven different colors — beiges and taupes, mostly — but he can speak, and has recently regained the ability to smile. "Hey, pretty lady," he says as we walk in. "It's good to see a pretty lady around here."

Nina is sitting in the chair by the window, reading. She is sulky as we say goodbye to Alden, sulky as we walk out to the car. I suppose I should expect moodiness — some response to what she's seen this last year. We go to pick up Charles, who is sixteen and spends most of his time in the Olde Computer Shoppe — a scarlet, plum-shaped building which serves as a reminder of what the fifties thought the future would look like. Charles is a computer prodigy, a certified genius, nothing special in our circuit-fed community. He has some sort of deal going with the owner of the Computer Shoppe which he doesn't like to talk about. It involves that magical stuff called software. He uses the Shoppe's terminal and in exchange gives the owner a cut of his profits, which are bounteous. Checks arrive for him every day — from Puerto Rico, from Texas, from New York. He puts the money in a private bank account. He says that in a year he will have enough saved to put himself through college — a fact I can't help but appreciate.

The other day I asked him to please explain in English what it is that he does. He was sitting in my kitchen with Stuart Beckman, a fat boy with the kind of wispy mustache that indicates a willful refusal to begin shaving. Stuart is the dungeon master in the elaborate medieval wargames Charles's friends conduct on Tuesday nights. Charles is Galadrian, a lowly elfin-warrior with minimal experience points. "Well," Charles said, "let's just say it's a step toward the great computer age when we won't need dungeon masters. A machine will create for us a whole world into which we can be transported. We'll live inside the machine — for a day, a year, our whole lives — and we'll live the adventures the machine creates for us. We're at the forefront of a major breakthrough — artificial imagination. The possibilities, needless to say, are endless."

"You've invented that?" I asked, suddenly swelling with Mother Goddess pride.

"The project is embryonic, of course," Charles said. "But we're getting there. Give it fifty years. Who knows?"

Charles is angry as we drive home. He sifts furiously through an enormous roll of green print-out paper. As it unravels, the paper flies in Nina's hair, but she is oblivious to it. Her face is pressed against the window so hard that her nose and lips have flattened out.

I consider starting up a conversation, but as we pull into the driveway I, too, feel the need for silence. Our house is dark and unwelcoming tonight, as if it is suspicious of us. As soon as we are in the door, Charles disappears into his room, and the world of his mind. Nina sits at the kitchen table with me until she has finished her book. It is the last in the Narnia series, and as she closes it, her face takes on the disappointed look of some- one who was hoping something would never end. Last month she entered the local library's Read-a-Thon. Neighbors agreed to give several dollars to UNICEF for every book she read, not realizing that she would read fifty-nine.

It is hard to me to look at her. She is sullen, and she is not pretty. My mother used to say it's one thing to look ugly, another to act it. Still, it must be difficult to be betrayed by your own body. The cells divide, the hormones explode; Nina had no control over the timing, much less the effects. The first time she menstruated she cried not out of fear but because she was worried she had contracted that disease which causes chil- dren to age prematurely. We'd seen pictures of them — wiz- ened, hoary four-year-olds, their skin loose and wrinkled, their teeth already rotten. I assured her that she had no such disease, that she was merely being precocious, as usual. In a few years, I told her, her friends would catch up.

She stands awkwardly now, as if she wants to maintain a distance even from herself. Ugliness really is a betrayal. Suddenly she can trust nothing on earth; her body is no longer a part of her, but her enemy.

"Daddy was glad to see you today, Nina," I say.

"Good."

"Can I get you anything?"

She still does not look at me. "No," she says. "Nothing."

Later in the evening, my mother calls to tell me about her new cordless electric telephone. "I can walk all around the house with it," she says. "Now, for instance, I'm in the kitchen, but I'm on my way to the bathroom." Mother believes in Christmas newsletters, and the forces of fate. Tonight she is telling me about Mr. Garvey, a local politician and neighbor who was recently arrested. No one knows the details of the scandal; Mother heard somewhere that the boys involved were young, younger than Charles. "His wife just goes on, does her gardening as if nothing happened," she tells me. "Of course, we don't say anything. What could we say? She knows we avoid mentioning it. Her house is as clean as ever. I even saw *him* the other day. He was wearing a sable sweater just like your father's. He told me he was relaxing for the first time in his life, playing golf, gardening. She looks ill, if you ask me. When I was your age I would have wondered how a woman could survive something like that, but now it doesn't surprise me to see her make do. Still, it's shocking. He always seemed like such a family man."

"She must have known," I say. "It's probably been a secret between them for years."

"I don't call secrets any basis for a marriage," Mother says. "Not in her case. Not in yours, either."

Lately she's been convinced that there's some awful secret between Alden and me. I told her that we'd had a fight the night of the accident, but I didn't tell her why. Not because the truth was too monumentally terrible. The subject of our fight was trivial. Embarrassingly trivial. We were going out to dinner. I wanted to go to a Chinese place. Alden wanted to try an Italian health food restaurant that a friend of his at work had told him about. Our family has always fought a tremendous amount about restaurants. Several times, when the four of us were piled in the car, Alden would pull off the road. "I will not drive with this chaos," he'd say. The debates over where to eat usually ended in tears, and abrupt returns home. The children ran screaming to their rooms. We ended up eating tunafish.

Mother is convinced I'm having an affair. "Alden's still a man," she says to me. "With a man's needs."

We have been talking so long that the earpiece of the phone is sticking to my ear. "Mother," I say, "please don't worry. I'm hardly in shape for it."

She doesn't laugh. "I look at Mrs. Garvey, and I'm moved," she says. "Such strength of character. You should take it as a lesson. Before I hang up, I want to tell you about something I read, if you don't mind."

My mother loves to offer information, and has raised me in the tradition. We constantly repeat movie plots, offer authoritative statistics from television news specials. "What did you read, Mother?" I ask.

"There is a man who is studying the Holocaust," she says. "He makes a graph. One axis is fulfillment/despair, and the other is success/failure. That means that there are four groups of people — those who are fulfilled by success, whom we can understand, and those who are despairing even though they're successful, like so many people we know, and those who are despairing because they're failures. Then there's the fourth group — the people who are fulfilled by failure, who don't need hope to live. Do you know who those people are?"

"Who?" I ask.

"Those people," my mother says, "are the ones who survived."

There is a long, intentional silence.

"I thought you should know," she says, "that I am now standing outside, on the back porch. I can go as far as seven hundred feet from the house."

Recently I've been thinking often about something terrible I did when I was a child — something which neither I nor Mother has ever really gotten over. I did it when I was six years old. One day at school my older sister, Mary Elise, asked me to tell Mother that she was going to a friend's house for the afternoon to play with some new Barbie dolls. I was mad at Mother that day, and jealous of Mary Elise. When I got home, Mother was feeding the cat, and without even saying hello (she was mad at me for some reason, too) she ordered me to take out the garbage. I was filled with rage, both at her and my sister, whom I was convinced she favored. And then I came up with an awful idea. "Mother," I said, "I have something to tell you." She turned around. Her distracted face suddenly focused on me. I realized I had no choice but to finish what I'd started. "Mary Elise died today," I said. "She fell off the jungle gym and split her head open."

At first she just looked at me, her mouth open. Then her eyes — I remember this distinctly — went in two different directions. For a brief moment, the tenuousness of everything — the house, my life, the universe — became known to me, and I had a glimpse of how easily the fragile network could be exploded.

Mother started shaking me. She was making noises but she couldn't speak. The minute I said the dreaded words I started to cry; I couldn't find a voice to tell her the truth. She kept shaking me. Finally I managed to gasp, "I'm lying, I'm lying. It's not true." She stopped shaking me, and hoisted me up into the air.

I closed my eyes and held my breath, imagining she might hurl me down against the floor. "You monster," she whispered. "You little bastard," she whispered between clenched teeth. Her face was twisted, her eyes glistening. She hugged me very fiercely and then she threw me onto her lap and started to spank me. "You monster, you monster," she screamed between sobs. "Never scare me like that again, never scare me like that again."

By the time Mary Elise got home, we were composed. Mother had made me swear I'd never tell her what had happened, and I never have. We had an understanding, from then on, or perhaps we had a secret. It has bound us together, so that now we are much closer to each other than either of us is to Mary Elise, who married a lawyer and moved to Hawaii.

The reason I cannot forget this episode is because I have seen, for the second time, how easily apocalypse can happen. That look in Alden's eyes, the moment before the accident, was a look I'd seen before.

I hear you're from another planet," I say to Nina after we finish dinner.

She doesn't blink. "I assumed you'd find out sooner or later," she says. "But, Mother, can you understand that I didn't want to hurt you?"

I was expecting confessions and tears. Nina's sincerity surprises me. "Nina," I say, trying to affect maternal authority, "tell me what's going on."

Nina smiles. "In the Fourth Millennium," she says, "when it was least expected, the Brolian force attacked the city of Landruz, on the planet Abdur. Chaos broke loose all over. The star-worms escaped from the zoo. It soon became obvious that the community would not survive the attack. Izmul, the father of generations, raced to his space-cruiser. It was the only one in the city. Hordes crowded to get on board, to escape the catastrophe and the star-worms, but only a few hundred managed. Others clung to the outside of the ship as it took off and were blown across the planet by its engines. The space-cruiser broke through the atmosphere just as the bomb hit. A hundred people were cast out into space. The survivors made it to a small planet, Dandril, and settled there. These are my origins."

She speaks like an oracle, not like anything I might have given birth to. "Nina," I say, "*I* am your origin."

She shakes her head. "I am a surveyor. It was decided that I should be born in earthly form so that I could observe your planet and gather knowledge for the rebuilding of our world. I was generated in your womb while you slept. You can't remember the conception."

"I remember the exact night," I say. "Daddy and I were in San Luis Obispo for a convention."

Nina laughs. "It happened in your sleep," she says. "An invisible ray. You never felt it."

What can I say to this? I sit back and try to pierce through her with a stare. She isn't even looking at me. Her eyes are focused on a spot of green caught in the night outside the window.

"I've been receiving telepathic communications," Nina says. "My people will be coming any time to take me, finally, to where I belong. You've been good to this earthly shell, Mother. For that, I thank you. But you must understand and give me up. My people are shaping a new civilization on Dandril. I must go and help them."

"I understand," I say.

She looks at me quizzically. "It's good, Mother," Nina says. "Good that you've come around." She reaches toward me, and kisses my cheek. I am tempted to grab her the way a mother is supposed to grab a child — by the shoulders, by the scruff of the neck; tempted to bend her to my will, to spank her, to hug her.

But I do nothing. With the look of one who has just been informed of her own salvation, the earthly shell I call Nina walks out the screen door, to sit on the porch and wait for her origins.

Mother calls me again in the morning. "I'm in the garden," she says, "looking at the sweetpeas. Now I'm heading due west, toward where those azaleas are planted."

She is preparing the Christmas newsletter, wants information from my branch of the family. "Mother," I say, "it's March. Christmas is months away." She is unmoved. Lately, this business of recording has taken on tremendous importance in her life; more and more requires to be saved.

"I wonder what the Garveys will write this year," she says. "You know, I just wonder what there is to say about something like that. Oh my. There he is now, Mr. Garvey, talking to the paper boy. Yes, when I think of it, there have been signs all along. I'm waving to him now. He's waving back. Remember, don't you, what a great interest he took in the Shepards' son, getting him scholarships and all? What if they decided to put it all down in the newsletter? It would be embarrassing to read."

As we talk, I watch Nina, sitting in the dripping spring garden, rereading *The Lion, the Witch and the Wardrobe*. Every now and then she looks up at the sky, just to check, then returns to her book. She seems at peace.

"What should I say about your family this year?" Mother asks. I wish I knew what to tell her. Certainly nothing that could be typed onto purple paper, garnished with little pencil drawings of holly and wreaths. And yet, when I read them over, those old newsletters have a terrible, swift power, each so innocent of the celebrations and catastrophes which the next year's letter will record. Where will we be a year from today? What will have happened then? Perhaps Mother won't be around to record these events; perhaps I won't be around to read about them.

"You can talk about Charles," I say. "Talk about how he's inventing an artificial imagination."

"I must be at least seven hundred feet from the house now," Mother says. "Can you hear me?"

Her voice is crackly with static, but still audible.

"I'm going to keep walking," Mother says. "I'm going to keep walking until I'm out of range."

That night in San Luis Obispo, Alden — can you remember it? Charles was already so self-sufficient then, happily asleep in the little room off ours. We planned that night to have a child, and I remember feeling sure that it would happen. Perhaps it was the glistening blackness outside the hotel room window, or the light rain, or the heat. Perhaps it was the kind of night when spaceships land and aliens prowl, fascinated by all we take for granted.

There are some anniversaries which aren't so easy to commemorate. This one, for instance: one year since we almost died. If I could reach you, Alden, in the world behind your eyes, I'd ask you a question: Why did you turn off the road? Was it whim, the sudden temptation of destroying both of us for no reason? Or did you hope the car would bear wings and engines, take off into the atmosphere, and propel you — us — in a split second, out of the world?

I visit you after lunch. Joe doesn't bother to say hello, and though I kiss you on the forehead, you, too, choose not to speak. "Why so glum?" I ask. "Dehydrated egg bits for breakfast again?"

You reach into the drawer next to your bed, and hand me a key. I help you out, into your bathrobe, into the hall. We must be quiet. When no nurses are looking, I hurry us into a small room where sheets and hospital gowns are stored. I turn the key in the lock, switch on the light.

We make a bed of sheets on the floor. We undress; and then, Alden, I begin to make love to you — you, atop me, clumsy and quick as a teen-ager. I try to slow you down, to coach you in the subtleties of love, the way a mother teaches a child to walk. You have to relearn this language as well, after all.

Lying there, pinned under you, I think that I am grateful for gravity, grateful that a year has passed and the planet has not yet broken loose from its tottering orbit. If nothing else, we hold each other down.

You look me in the eyes and try to speak. Your lips circle the unknown word, your brow reddens and beads with sweat. "What, Alden?" I ask. "What do you want to say? Think a minute." Your lips move aimlessly. A drop of tearwater, purely of its own accord, emerges from the marbled eye, snakes along a crack in your skin.

I stare at the ruined eye. It is milky white, mottled with blue and gray streaks; there is no pupil. Like our daughter, Alden, the eye will have nothing to do with either of us. I want to tell you it looks like the planet Dandril, as I imagine it from time to time — that ugly little planet where even now, as she waits in the garden, Nina's people are coming back to life.

Alison Lurie

---

from
The War
Between
The Tates

MAY 11. BRIAN is sitting in his office at the university waiting for Wendy Gahaghan to come in so he can tell her that their affair is over. The script for this scene has been worked out in advance in his mind, the significant speeches written and rewritten. Twice already he has spoken the opening lines — but without success. Wendy had not responded as she should have responded; she is in another play, or film.

For instance, the statement "My wife has found out" did not, to Wendy, constitute a sufficient reason for ending the affair. That was a heavy scene, she admitted, but it was not her scene. And his suggestion that the relationship was bad for her education had been met with eager denials. Her interest in learning and her grades had both risen, she insisted, since they started making it together — didn't he know that? And in fact, Brian did know it.

And yet the thing has to be done. He realizes now that letting Wendy into his office had been like trying marijuana (not that he has ever tried marijuana). From the mild, pleasant stimulant of her conversation he had gone on to stronger drugs: her admiration and finally her passion. Before he becomes addicted, he has to give her up. Just thinking and worrying about it has begun to exhaust his energy to the point where he is functioning only in second gear as a teacher and is completely stalled on his current project, a study of American foreign policy in the Cold War period.

Moreover, Erica believes the thing has been done. Indeed, without actually lying, Brian has implied that the affair was almost over when she read that unfortunate letter. Actually lying, he has said that it was as brief and unimportant as such an affair could be.

He would much prefer to wait until the end of the term, but the danger that Erica may make another such discovery is too great. He might lecture Wendy for hours on discretion, she might fervently promise to be careful; but she is impulsive, given to sudden romantic gestures. Only last week, seeing him unexpectedly in the hall, she ran toward him and embraced him. Since it was late afternoon, the hall was empty; but the door to one of the other offices was open, and a colleague of Brian's was sitting in this office, observing them. "I just raised the grade on her exam," Brian had lied afterward to this man, with a phony grin. And this was a double lie: Brian has never raised the grade on a student's exam — he is against that sort of thing on principle.

How has he, Brian Tate, got into this tangle of phony grins and lies? How has he, who for years was a just, honorable, and responsible person, become involved with someone like Wendy Gahaghan?

Or let's look at it from the other end for a change. Why hasn't he become involved with some girl like Wendy long before this? Not through lack of opportunity: he can remember many occasions over the last twenty years when students — some of them much more his type than she is, a few almost as attractive as his wife Erica — had made it apparent that they would welcome a more personal relationship with him. Among his colleagues he knows many who have admittedly, or by repute, taken advantage of such welcomes. But for sixteen years he had privately scorned these colleagues. He had even rather looked down on his friend Leonard Zimmern, who had the excuse of an angry, impossible, unfaithful wife. He, Brian Tate, had no time for such hole-and-corner games. He loved Erica, and he had serious work to do.

But during the last year or two this work has changed. The wrong way of putting it: his work has not changed, and he has recognized that it never will. He is forty-six, and according to local criteria a success. His students think him interesting and well informed. His colleagues think him competent and fortunate; many of them envy him. He holds an endowed chair in the department and is the author of two scholarly studies in his field and a widely used and profitable text; he has a beautiful intelligent wife, two attractive and intelligent children, and a desirable house in Glenview Heights. They are not aware that internally, secretly, he is a dissatisfied and disappointed man. He bears the signs openly: a sharp W-shaped frown between his neat dark eyebrows, a pinched look around the mouth. But those who see these signs assume Brian is disappointed not by his own condition, but by the condition of the world.

Whenever he speaks in public, as he often does, on American foreign policy; or when an article by him appears in some journal, his students and colleagues are reminded of his success. Brian is reminded of his failure. Why, he asks himself sourly, is he speaking on foreign policy instead of helping to make it? Why does he still discuss other men's theories instead of his own?

He cannot blame his failure on ill fortune. He had been born with all the advantages: the son of a well-known professor, nephew of authors and lawmakers, grandson and great-grandson of ministers and judges; healthy, handsome, intellectually precocious, well-loved, well-educated. But after all these gifts had been bestowed, some evil fairy had flown in through the delivery-room window and whispered over his crib, "He should be a great man." All his life, that imperative has haunted him. His colleagues, born into cultural or economic slums, the ugly, clumsy sons of provincial neurotics or illiterate immigrants, might be proud of having become Corinth professors — not he.

As if symbolically, when he reached adolescence Brian did not grow as fast as his peers at Andover, nor in the end as far. When he entered Harvard (at sixteen) he was still small for his age. He would catch up, his relatives said, and he believed them; but he did not catch up. He remained, though not a very short man, considerably below the average in height: five feet five, if he stood up straight and held his neck in a certain way. Erica was nearly three inches taller. When she married him, she gave away to a Congregational church rummage sale all the high-heeled shoes which showed her spectacular long legs to such advantage, and accepted a lifetime of flat soles, because he was going to be a great man.

All these years, Erica (unlike his relatives) has never either overtly or covertly accused him of disappointing her. Only once years ago, after a New York party at which several famous persons were present, had she even admitted, laughing as she spoke and pulling a yellow flowered silk petticoat over her dark curls, that she would like Brian to be famous too. Previous to that evening, and subsequently, she had denied any such wish; but Brian was not convinced.

Erica had also insisted that same evening that she didn't hold it against him that he had not yet become famous. It was bad luck, that was all, like Muffy's allergy to house dust, and would similarly be outgrown. After all, she had added, still laughing softly, leaning on his shoulder to steady herself as she took off her white silk sandals — he was already a famous professor: hadn't he just been given the Sayle Chair of American Diplomacy at Corinth? Brian had replied that this meant very little — only that Clinton had retired and he was now the senior man in the field. But (as perhaps he had intended) she took this protest for modesty.

Erica still expected him to become a great man that evening — next year, or the year after. But Brian suspected even then, and knows now, that he will not. It is too late, for one thing: he is nearly as old as Lindsay, and five years older than Bobby Kennedy would have been. Erica knows it too, and affects not to mind; or possibly does not mind. She has said that she is glad of it, because she values their privacy and dislikes official social life of the sort she had to be involved in during the two years when Brian was head of his department. If he were to become any more prominent she would see less of him, she has explained, and more of people she doesn't care for.

Brian has done his best to become a great man. He has written many long and serious political articles; he has served without pay on committees and commissions; he has offered himself at various times and more or less subtly to the Democratic, Independent Republican and Liberal parties as an adviser on foreign policy. But his theories have attracted no real interest; his opinions have been voted down, and his offers declined.

He regretted this not only for personal reasons but because he sincerely believed, even knew, that he had much to contribute. He was one of the few people he knew, for example, who realized that political expediency and idealism are not incompatible. Yet for years he had been misunderstood, just as the public figure he admired most, George Kennan, had been misunderstood; he had been considered either a fuzzy-minded theorist or a small-minded politician.

Even within the university he has been disappointed in his ambitions. He did not want the Sayle Chair, which carried with it no reduction in teaching load or significant increase in salary; what he wanted was the chair, and the desk, in the office of the Dean of Humanities, or some similar large office. Everyone agreed he had done well during his turn as department chairman, and several of his colleagues appeared to think he would make a fine dean; but when the opportunity came none of them nominated him for the post.

Brian's most inward belief is that all these defeats and his size are connected: that his appearance is the objective correlative of a lack of real stature. Years ago, some invisible force had set a heavy hand on his head to keep him from growing any taller, as a sign to the world. And this sign had been heeded. The opinions and candidacy of a man barely five feet five, weighing a mere one hundred and thirty-five pounds, were seldom taken seriously. It was felt everywhere that he was in every sense a small man, not suited to authority over anything beyond a small department. Had he been even a few inches taller, he might have fulfilled his promise and the expectations of his relatives — obeyed the imperative spoken over his crib. Conversely, once he had fulfilled this promise, his size would not have mattered. He never spoke of this to anyone, but he thought about it — not every day, but frequently.

Throughout his adult life Brian had behaved so as to compensate for, even confute, the sign set on him by fate. He had decided in college that he could not afford to make jokes or mistakes as a larger man might, lest he be thought lightweight. For a quarter-century, therefore, he had done and said nothing which would have seemed frivolous, injudicious or immoral in a university president or a candidate for Congress.

Was it the realization that all this solemn self-regulation had been for nothing — a foolish mistake, a long joke on himself — that had made him susceptible to Wendy Gahaghan? Brian does not know. He is aware of no decision to cast off his self-discipline; certainly of no decision to cast it off for Wendy.

Even as a political scientist he finds it impossible to determine when and how the affair had begun. Possibly it dated from the day two and a half years ago when he became aware that Miss Gahaghan, a small hippie-type blonde in his graduate seminar on American Institutions, was prominent among those students who remained after class to speak to him more often than necessary, and made excuses to consult him during his office hours. This might have been viewed variously: as apple-polishing, infantile dependency or simple academic anxiety. Which, Brian did not trouble to determine, since it would presumably end with the course.

American Institutions ended, but Miss Gahaghan, who had received a grade of B-plus from Brian, continued. She audited his undergraduate lectures; she waylaid him in the department office. Apparently she had formed some sort of attachment to him. This had happened before with students, and Brian had handled it, always successfully, as he tried to handle it now. That is, he began, slowly but steadily, to turn down the thermostat of his manner from faintly warm to neutrally cool. In the past he had never had to go below about 55 degrees to chill affections sufficiently; but Miss Gahaghan was not discouraged even by lower temperatures. She continued to come to his office; and he let her continue. He did not, in fact, turn the temperature down to freezing. Why not?

Principally, he thinks, because Wendy was not a graduate student in his department, but in Social Psychology. She had taken his course more or less by accident, and discovered an enthusiasm for American history which he believed to be largely real, even if it was confused in her mind with enthusiasm for him. One of her ambitions was to go into the wilderness and live in a commune based on mutual cooperation and mystical philosophy. Her department treated such groups as examples of social pathology. From Brian she learned that they were in the mainstream of the American utopian tradition.

"All those dumb old uptight behaviorists, they think anybody who believes in love and community is a deviant," Wendy exclaimed when these facts fully dawned upon her. Brian had smiled noncommittally; though he did not admit it, he shared her descending opinion of the graduate school of Social Psychology. He believed most of the men in Wendy's department to be self-seeking fools, and their courses to be composed in equal parts of common sense and nonsense — that is, of the already obvious and the probably false.

He was pleased, but not surprised, that Wendy should consult him rather than her adviser (a cynical, nervous young man called Roger Zimmern who was a cousin of Leonard's). He liked to answer questions, to explain things. What made explaining things to Wendy especially gratifying was that she wanted nothing from him but knowledge — or so he thought in the beginning. Her reactions were naïve sometimes, overemotional often, but never bored or contrived. There was no academic reason for her to listen to what he said, or read the books he suggested. He was not responsible for her examinations, her financial support, or her M.A. thesis; he would not have to recommend her for jobs or fellowships. He never saw in her eyes as he spoke the dull-red stare of academic duty and boredom; or the hard glaze of self-concealment as a prelude to self-advancement — the yellow signal "Caution" which glowed so often in the eyes of his own graduate students. Her gaze was pure green light.

Wendy's conversation also had a certain interest. She was outspoken about her professors and courses as no student in Political Science would have been, and it amused Brian to learn about another department from the underside in this way; the more so perhaps because she did not always know how much she was revealing. He encouraged her, as he would not have done had he expected to see more of her. But he assumed that the coming summer would mean the end of the acquaintance. Wendy would have her degree; she was planning to hike around Europe and then teach high school and live in a commune she had heard of in Massachusetts.

But in September of the following year she was back in graduate school and back in Brian's office. Europe was a great trip, but you couldn't stay there long without bread; the commune was a good scene until there got to be too many freeloaders, runaway kids and old acidheads; the Green River school system was a bad, ugly trip and scene. Brian was not sorry to see Wendy again: her letters from Holland, Yugoslavia and Green

River had been amusing; he had missed her reports on the psychology department, and was glad to have them resume.

What was even more important, or soon became so, was the news Wendy brought of the "youth scene." Brian had known for some time that he and his colleagues were not living in the America they had grown up in; it was only recently though that he had realized they were also not living in present-day America, but in another country or city-state with somewhat different characteristics. The important fact about this state, which can for convenience' sake be called "University," is that the great majority of its population is aged eighteen to twenty-two. Naturally the physical appearance, interests, activities, preferences and prejudices of this majority are the norm in University. Cultural and political life is geared to their standards, and any deviation from them is a social handicap.

Brian had started life as a member of the dominant class in America, and for years had taken this position for granted. Now, in University, he finally has the experience of being among a depressed minority. Like a Chinaman in New York, he looks different; he speaks differently, using the native tongue more formally, the local slang infrequently and as if in quotation marks; he likes different foods and wears different clothes and has different recreations. Naturally he is regarded with suspicion by the natives.

Of course Brian does not have to spend all his time in University. In the evenings, on weekends and during most of the summer he can return to the real world, where other standards are in effect. The trouble is, he can see quite well that the "real world" is growing to resemble University more every year, as the youth culture becomes more dominant; and he is aware that all he has to look forward to is the prospect of joining the most depressed minority group of all, the Old.

Brian had never attempted to pass as a native of University, although he realized there were certain rewards for doing so. He did not want to become assimilated, and rather despised those of his colleagues who did. He felt no impulse at all to take drugs, curse policemen, wear beads or study Oriental religions. At the same time, as a political scientist, he felt increasingly that it was his job to know something about these developments.

Unlike his other students, Wendy Gahaghan did not conceal the nonacademic side of her life from Brian. In simple, confiding tones, she related how she and her friends smoked hash, deceived draft boards, "lifted" goods from store counters, and made casual, violent love. When something politically or culturally controversial happened in University, Wendy came and told Brian what the students thought about it, concealing nothing, as if unaware that he was the enemy. In return he tried not to be the enemy: he made an effort never to show shock or disapproval, merely a steady interest.

Gradually Brian began to look forward to Wendy's appearances, especially at times of crisis — to think of her as his Native Informant. He began to be aware that because of her visits he was pulling ahead of his colleagues in knowledge of student motives and reactions — even sometimes ahead of those who attempted to ape these reactions. They were disguised as natives, but he understood the indigenous customs and language better than they; often he could tell them what SDS or the Society to Legalize Marijuana was going to do next. Scrupulously, he declined to reveal his sources. Indeed, he often concealed the fact that he had a source, preferring for several reasons to suggest that he had many informants; or that he was only brilliantly guessing, theorizing as a political scientist, about what might happen.

The final reason Brian had not discouraged Wendy's visits, he thinks — indeed, had begun to encourage them — was that he didn't believe she could ever constitute any threat to his emotional or physical equanimity. He would have been on his guard if she had been anything like his wife at that age. But Erica had been exceptional: an honor student, elegantly dressed, extraordinarily pretty; she was president of the Arts Club, an editor of the literary magazine, and one of the most popular girls in her class — always surrounded by admirers and friends.

Wendy, by contrast, was an ordinary female graduate student. She was not plain, indeed quite attractive by conventional standards, but she was completely undistinguished — a well-rounded baby-faced ash-blonde, with pink cheeks and lank silky hair. She dressed usually in Indian style, but — like his children when they were small — confusing the Eastern and Western varieties. She wore, indiscriminately, paisley-bedspread shifts, embroidered velvet slippers, fringed cowhide vests and moccasins, strings of temple bells, saris, shell beads, sandals, and leather pants very loose in the ankle and tight in the ass. In spite of all this paraphernalia, she never looked like either sort of Indian. Rather, with her round pink freckled face and limp yellow hair, she resembled a solemn schoolchild got up for a Thanksgiving or United Nations Day pageant. Even when not in costume, she often tied a beaded or embroidered strip of cloth tightly across her brow in the shape of a headache.

"Don't you mind that thing around your head?" he had once asked her. "It looks uncomfortable. Doesn't it hurt?"

"Uh uh," Wendy replied, smiling eagerly — for at this point Brian almost never made any comment on her appearance. "It feels good. It's like — It kind of, you know, keeps my brains together."

"I see." Brian could not help smiling back, for it was true that Wendy tended to be, not so much scatter-brained (which suggests a restless movement of ideas) as mentally diffuse. Simple facts she knew very well — like the names of books she had studied and courses she had taken — became hidden in fog from time to time, causing her to stamp her foot and exclaim that she was "too stupid." Sometimes whole areas of information seemed to drift toward the misty periphery of her consciousness and fall off the edge.

Publicly Brian held this to be the result of too much marijuana and not enough sleep, and scolded her for it; but privately he suspected it was also due to lack of interest in graduate study. Wendy was intelligent enough, but her mind was not scholarly. Until very recently, girls like her, whatever their SAT scores, didn't usually go to graduate school. But nowadays, if they hadn't found someone to marry as undergraduates, they continued their education and their search, often in fields like psychology or sociology which seemed relevant to the situation.

With the slightest encouragement, Wendy would have transferred into Political Science, but Brian had no intention of giving this encouragement. He had already disregarded several hints, so he was ready when she mentioned that matter openly, on November 11 — but he was not prepared for what followed.

When Brian told her that no, he definitely did not think she should enter his department and do a thesis on utopian communities under his direction, Wendy's pale-blue eyes watered; she blinked her flaxen eyelashes. "You think I couldn't do the work," she asked or stated, her pink-smudged lower lip wobbling with the effort not to cry. "You think I'm not smart enough."

No, that wasn't it at all, Brian replied. It just seemed to him that at this stage in her graduate career . . . He went on repeating his arguments while Wendy, in a trembling voice, repeated hers. As he spoke it occurred to Brian that if Wendy wanted to, she could probably transfer into the department without his help. She was a hard-working, conscientious girl; her record in general was good. He was not on the graduate admissions committee this year; to stop her, he would have to make a written statement casting doubts upon either her sanity or her honesty. That he should even think of doing so cast doubts upon his own.

But, glancing at her again as she spoke, at her lank lemonade-blond hair parted in the middle Indian style and descending smoothly over her cheeks like the flaps of a wigwam, he realized that Wendy, like the squaw or Hindu maiden she affected to be, would never do anything he did not advise — because his approval was more important to her than her education. And at that moment, as if she had read his thoughts, Wendy said hesitantly, looking first up at him and then down at the notebooks in her lap,

"It's not so much that I can't stand my psych seminars — It's just that I want to do something you really respect — It's because, you know, I'm emotionally fixated on you, I guess you dig that." She raised her round blue eyes, but not her face, to his.

Reviewing history now, Brian realizes it was at this moment that he should have been frank. He should have met Wendy's offensive head-on; made it clear at once that he wasn't the sort of professor who encouraged, or even allowed, the emotional fixations of students. He should have recommended that Wendy either unfix her feelings or stop coming to see him. Instead he chose to pretend that nothing had happened, to treat what she had said as unimportant. He assured Wendy in a light, humorous tone that it would pass; that she was confusing appreciation of his ideas with something else. He waffled — the word was accurate, suggesting something cooked up, full of little square holes.

In effect, on November 11 of last year he had given Wendy Gahaghan permission to be in love with him, and to add this to the list of problems she came to discuss with him, two or three times a week now. The convention was maintained, on his part at least, that the attachment was a sort of mild delusion from which she would eventually recover, and which was therefore to be treated with humorous tolerance. Wendy accepted this convention to some extent. She refused to admit that she was deluded in loving Brian, or that a cure was likely; but she preserved a certain detachment from her infatuation. In his presence, at least, she took the sort of ironic, stoical attitude toward it that he had known older people to maintain toward a chronic disease.

In the weeks that followed it came to be assumed that when Brian asked, quite routinely, how she was, he was inquiring about the state of her disease, her hopeless passion for him. "Well, I thought I was a little better, until I heard you talk at the Department Colloquium last night. What you said about Cordell Hull was so beautiful, I couldn't *stand* it," she would report. Or, "I've really been trying to get over it. I was rapping with Mike Saturday night; he said what I needed was a good fuck, that was all. So we tried it . . . Uh-uh. It didn't work. I mean, it was okay: Mike's a nice guy, and he's very physical — But this morning it was like it never happened, sort of." Wendy would have gone on; but Brian, with a sense of moral scrupulousness, always changed the subject — whereas the truth was that he should never have allowed it to come up at all.

This state of things continued for about three weeks. Then two events of little apparent importance, but far-reaching effect, occurred. First, on December 3, Wendy contracted the Asian flu. For over a week she did not come to Brian's office. His first reaction was slight relief, followed in a day or so by concern. He thought back to their last meeting, and remembered her complaint that every single time she saw him she adored him more. "Well," he had replied jokingly, "in that case, perhaps you'd better see less of me." Unaware that Wendy was in the infirmary with a fever of 103 degrees, he told himself that she must have taken his advice; that this would be hard for her, but that it was probably the right decision. In the days that followed, he found these thoughts repeating themselves in his head with irritatingly increasing frequency.

The second event of slight apparent importance involved the Sayle Chair of American Diplomacy — not in the symbolic, but in the physical sense. Six years ago, when Brian inherited the Sayle Chair, he had also inherited an actual piece of furniture: an ancient, battered Windsor armchair with a high round back and a cracked leg, which had been presented to the first incumbent by some waggish students about 1928, and bore a worn label in imitation nineteenth-century penmanship: "Wm. M. Sayle Chair of American Diplomacy." This object now occupied a corner of Brian's office, which was already too small in his opinion, without serving any useful purpose. Nobody could sit on it safely; you could not even put many books on it.

Gradually, Brian had begun to feel that the Sayle Chair did not like him; doubtless it thought he was not of the stature of its previous occupants. For a while he tried hanging his raincoat over it, but this only made it ever more obtrusive. It looked like someone tall and thin and round-shouldered, probably Wm. M. Sayle, crouching in the corner with his head down. Brian would have liked to throw the chair out, but that was not feasible, for it had become a Tradition in a university which valued Tradition.

On the morning of December 12, there was a knock at Brian's door.

"Yes?"

"Hi." Wendy Gahaghan, in her fringed leather costume, entered the office.

"Well hello, stranger!" Brian forgot that Wendy had been avoiding him for her own good — his voice expressed only pleasure, and slightly injured surprise.

"I had the Asian flu," Wendy panted, out of breath from running up two flights of stairs. "I was in the infirmary, I couldn't even call you."

"I'm sorry to hear that." Under her long, untidy, damp-streaked hair (there was a cold rain outside) Wendy was paler than usual. "You look tired."

"Yeah, I just got out this morning." She smiled weakly.

"Well, sit down then, rest yourself — No, not there!" he cried, as Wendy sank into the Sayle Chair. Too late: there was a sharp crack; the seat split, the left front leg collapsed, and

Wendy collapsed with it. Her legs sprawled out, her books skidded across the gray vinyl floor.

"Ow, ooh!" she shrieked as she landed hard on her back and the chair fell forward on top of her.

"God damn." In what seemed to him slow motion, Brian got around his desk and crossed the room. He lifted the chair. "Are you all right?"

"I guess so." Wendy flexed her arms and legs. Her fringed cowhide miniskirt had been pushed up to the waist, below which she was now covered only in a transparent pale nylon membrane, faintly shiny, like the sections of an orange or pink grapefruit. "Yeh, I'm okay. Hey." She smiled weakly, but made no move to adjust her skirt or get up. "I broke your chair."

"It was cracked already," Brian said. "I told you before not to sit there." He set the chair down; it sagged lamely against the bookcase.

"Oh, wow." Wendy began to laugh. From where he stood above her, the effect was strange. Her transparent eyes rolled back; her mouth opened, showing wet pink depths; her full hips shook inside the nylon membrane. Brian felt a strong mixed emotion which he chose to interpret as impatience.

"Here, get up," he said firmly, almost angrily, holding out his hand.

Responsive to his mood, Wendy stopped laughing at once. She scrambled up off the floor, looking frightened; her hand in his felt cold and small. Brian removed the *Times* and some books from another chair and pushed it forward. Wendy sat down.

"Hey, listen, why I was laughing. I'm sorry, I didn't mean — See, I didn't know your chair was broken. I thought you just didn't want me to sit in it all this time because I wasn't worthy of it." She grinned timidly. "I thought you were saving it for, like, important people."

"That's ridiculous."

"I know it. Oh, I'm always so stupid, stupid, stupid." She hit her freckled face with her small freckled fists, half humorously, half melodramatically. "You probably must hate me now," she added.

"Of course not."

"But I ruined your famous chair."

Both Brian and Wendy looked at the Sayle Chair, which was down on one knee in the corner; its right arm hung broken at its side. It could be thrown out now, he realized. It would be thrown out.

"Looks like it," he agreed, smiling.

"I guess you'll never forgive me."

"I'll forgive you," Brian said generously. "As long as you don't break anything else."

* * *

Waiting in his office now, Brian vows to himself that the end of his affair will be better governed than the beginning. His two previous attempts to break it off had not worked because they were based on a faulty political analysis of the situation — possibly due to unconscious resistance on his part. Wendy does not care if his wife knows of the affair; among her friends such matters immediately become public anyhow. She knows also that her work has not fallen off since January; and even if it had fallen off, she wouldn't have cared.

But there is one thing which will convince her that the affair must end; one sentence Brian can speak which will make her almost as eager to end it as she had been to begin. When she comes in today, Brian can tell her that his own work is suffering; that he has been unable to write his new book, a project she regards with awe.

"Too much of my energy is going into our relationship," he will say, in a few minutes now. "There's not enough left for my work."

And what is more, this will be the literal truth. It is not only that his affair with Wendy consumes certain hours; more profoundly, it consumes the emotional and physical energy which at other times has been sublimated into the writing of political history. As his roommate had put it once back at Harvard, when Brian made a similar choice before an important exam: "Brian thinks it all comes out of the same faucet."

"I know it does," he had replied.

"You're nuts," said his roommate cheerfully. "The way I look at it, the more I screw the better I work." But time proved him wrong: he received a grade of only B-plus on the important exam, while Brian was rewarded for his abstinence with a straight A.

Gloria Naylor

———

from
Linden Hills

XAVIER DONNELL was falling in love with a black woman. It was one of the most terrifying experiences of his life. He was trying to remember when he had ever been this afraid. Why, it was worse than that summer at boy scout camp when he'd gotten his fly caught in the motor of the garbage compactor. And far worse than the report last year from the auto clinic that two of his transmission valves might be irreplaceable. At least he had been able to scream his way or buy his way out of those situations because he could pinpoint exactly where the danger lay. He had seen the iron gears chewing up the front of his shorts, smelled the oily teeth as they pulled him into the back of the machine. But when he looked at Roxanne Tilson, all he saw was a woman, no better or worse than the dozens of others who had flowed into and out of his life — soft where she should be, curved where he'd expect it, sweet behind the ears, mellow between the breasts, and pungent in that mystifying zone where the thighs joined the center of her body. She had flowed in that way but something was terribly wrong: she wasn't flowing out. Somehow she had frozen around his liver, on the walls of his stomach, and in the cavities of his intestines; and she was dripping out much too slowly. When he found that it had become cold enough inside to affect his heart and cause a chill that made it shiver when he touched her, he tried to build up a series of heated arguments to melt her away: she's too fat, too loud, too slow, and he always hated being kept waiting for anyone, especially a woman. But those fiery complaints didn't help when he kneaded the full flesh on her thighs and stomach, or when the waiting became anticipation of the first, piercing note of her "sorry" that would engulf him in a symphony for the rest of the evening. Those damn shivers would return, leap on him unexpectedly over a plate of fettuccine or in a darkened theater, to remind him that something was happening inside that was beyond his control. Something that kept drawing him much too quickly into a center that held his first memory of love and fear: the dark, mellow texture of her female being. White chocolate, he'd think, burying his nose into her soft neck and nibbling upward toward the dimpled chin, seeking the hidden essence of cocoa that was embedded in the deep-yellow cream of her skin, that he could taste on his tongue, smell on his hands and arms. The colors and tints from the thighs that brought him into the world, the breasts that kept him alive and warm. The mindless plunge and search for the eternal circle that would let him die over and over in the cavity that gave him life.

But Xavier had come a long way from the womb. At thirty-one, he knew he'd come a long way, period. Graduating from the University of Nowhere, through a mixture of patience, hard work, and premeditated luck he had managed to move up in a place like General Motors, where it was so easy to get lost among the myriad Ivy League and ivory-skinned credentials of men who were just as sharp and hardworking as he was. While his rise had been meteoric and his cashmere suits managed to withstand the change of altitude, that tenth-floor office with its shag carpet and oak panels housed a fragile god. Because Xavier was forced to see his exploits as much more than those of some superman, he had to join the rest of General Motors and worship the rise of a Super Nigger. So he found himself as only a high priest perched in a temple and burdened with the care of this image. And like all fragile gods, it demanded constant attention and surveillance for any telltale cracks in the clay feet, a softening around the knees, a dulling of the luster.

He was holding down two full-time jobs, and he had to carry one home with him all the time. He took it on vacations and to the gym and to visits with his grandmother. It went to bars and ball games and to bed with him. There wasn't a moment of his life that Xavier could afford to forget his duties as high priest, because if the image ever crumbled, his own fate wasn't too far behind. He didn't dare question the validity of this worship, or even the power of this hollow god, because one reality was clear: that was all they had given him to serve; and somehow in serving, he had become. So he feared this rapid descent into the essence of Roxanne while knowing no other way to be complete. Could his god survive in the arms and between the thighs of the first flesh that knew his true mortality? Or would it crack under the echoes of those eyes that put ice packs on his bruised genitals when he was sent home early from boy scout camp?

Xavier needed time to think this present situation out — lots of time — but he didn't trust himself. His insides were out of control and he knew that if he didn't take some sort of drastic action, he would ask Roxanne Tilson to marry him. And the only thing that frightened him more than that was the thought that she would say yes. He had tried everything to discourage her so she'd take the matter out of his hands. He didn't call when promised, he broke dates, confused himself and her with excessive warmth and then excessive coldness. He'd even committed the unforgivable sin in a black woman's canon by openly dating white women and seeming to enjoy it. Surely, that was enough to have her discount him as a piece of garbage, a lost soul. But after taking that empty-headed receptionist to Winston's wedding and making a complete fool of himself, hoping Roxanne would hear about it and jump to all sorts of conclusions, the phone remained silent all morning. That really pissed him off. Here he was all day yesterday thinking about her, and in a few weak moments even wishing that she was the one beside him; and now today she was on his mind, wearing him out well beyond the true importance she held in his life — and no call. It was impossible that she hadn't heard; half the neighborhood had been at that reception. No, she was just waiting him out like she always did. The woman was definitely manipulative, never complaining or asking where he'd been from week to week. Pushy and conniving is all it was. Pushing herself into his head so he'd have to start caring about why she didn't care.

He knew he just had to do something, and as a last resort, he called his friend Maxwell. He admired Maxwell's total control of any situation. They were the only two black men on the tenth floor at GM, and Maxwell's office was even closer to the executive director's than his. Xavier had watched him closely at board meetings, regional conferences, and even in the executive washroom, for the fine seam that held him together, but it was invisible. He knew that might be easy enough to cover up in a boardroom but never in the bathroom. Maxwell could sit in his huge, glass-enclosed office without a hair or paper clip out of place. Xavier had been proud when Maxwell befriended him because it showed that he had proven himself. He became Xavier's mentor in office and latrine politics, and Xavier valued his advice, which all boiled down to a constant maxim: "Keep it all inside and when it just has to come out, *you* decide where and how much." So he had to be extremely careful when he made that phone call. How could you retain the respect of a man who was able to sever a sprig of parsley from its stem as easily as some people cut the meat from around a T-bone, if you were in a panic over some woman? No, just drop by for a quick drink, a chance to shoot the breeze about the latest Mailer essay in *Penthouse*, and just maybe he could find the courage to bring up what might be one of the most important issues of his life.

* * *

Maxwell Smyth turned off the engine of his Stingray with a smooth forty-five-degree turn of his wrist, waited exactly three seconds, and pulled out the ignition key. When he swung his long legs over the low door frame, his silk scarf was arranged around his neck so that the wind could disarray the gold fringe just enough to let it stray casually on the brown and tan tweed of his open jacket, which complemented his light wool pants and matching brown turtleneck. He neither shivered nor hurried in the December air. His tropical gait in the frigid wind was as awe-inspiring as a magician breathing under water. But Maxwell's powers lay in the micro-thin weave of his thermal long-johns and in his knowledge that slow, deep breaths raise the body temperature without noticeably altering the rhythm of the chest. To even the most careful observer, this man seemed to have made the very elements disappear, while it was no more than the psychological sleight-of-hand that he used to make his blackness disappear.

Maxwell had discovered long ago that he doubled the odds of finishing first if he didn't carry the weight of that milligram of pigment in his skin. There was no feasible reason why it should have slowed him down since in mass it weighed so little, and even that was consistently distributed over his six-foot frame. But the handicap had been set centuries before it was his turn at the gate. And since he knew no tract of ground but the planet earth and no competition but the human race, he had to use the rules as written and find a way to turn a consequence into an inconsequence in his struggle to reach the finish line as a man.

He lucked onto the magic formula for this very early in life by being blessed with an uncommon spelling of a very common name. He remembered the slate-blue eyes of his first grade teacher flying back to his small dark face when she handed him a name tag reading MAXWELL SMITH and he told her no — S-M-Y-T-H, and this time the eyes actually focused him into existence. Whether it was impatience, embarrassment, or faint amusement, it was still recognition. For that moment, he counted because he had upset an assumption. And Maxwell Smyth learned to drag that moment out by not aiding the clumsy attempts of receptionists, clerks, and arrogant booking agents as they grappled with reordering their ingrained expectations of his name and his being. He relished the feelings of power and control as his blackness momentarily diminished in front of their faces — an ordinary name had turned into the extraordinary and taken its owner with it in the transformation.

The trick was now to juggle other feats that would continually minimize his handicap to nothing more than a nervous tic. In college he found that his blackness began to disappear behind his straight A average, and his reputation for never sweating or getting cold. He trained himself to survive on three hours of sleep while never appearing tired during classes, heading the student government, editing the school newspaper and the yearbook. Always immaculate and controlled, he kept them all wondering how it was done, so there was little time to think about who was doing it. His twenty-one-hour days even gave him time to socialize, and although most of his friends were white, that wasn't a conscious choice on his part. Maxwell neither courted nor shunned the other black students; he liked to think of himself as gravitating toward humans who shared his *inner* temperament, and anyone — black or otherwise — who he thought wanted to be around him because of something as inconsequential as the pigment of his skin he dismissed as shallow. So the black women he wanted to date found him strange and the white women strangely comforting.

He tackled General Motors in the same way he had the campus of Dartmouth, quietly disappearing behind his extraordinary record as regional sales representative, business manager, vice president for consumer affairs, and finally assistant to the executive director. But the stakes were a lot higher there, with no room for error; any break in his stride, any telltale mannerism or slip of the tongue might shatter the illusion he was standing behind. Because Maxwell knew they would never have dreamed of allowing a black man next to the executive director, it had to be the best man. And this delicate balancing of reality demanded perfect control over his work and his subordinates. He allowed nothing to happen at the office that didn't put him at the best advantage or that he couldn't manipulate to make it seem so. He weighed the decision of whether or not to smile at his secretary with the same gravity as that with which he considered the advisability of a new line of sedans.

There was never any danger of his breaking down; sanity lies in consistency. And Maxwell retained his mental health by exercising the same type of control over every aspect of his being. Since he couldn't manipulate the weather outside his home, he adjusted his body accordingly; but once inside his carefully appointed duplex, an elaborate series of humidifiers and thermostats enabled him to determine the exact conditions under which he would eat, sleep, or sit. He found the erratic rhythms and temperatures that normally accompany sex a problem, so he rarely slept with a woman. He didn't consider it a great deprivation because before he was even thirty, an erection had become almost as difficult to achieve as an orgasm, and hence he would save himself the trouble until he was married and just had to. In short, his entire life became a race against the natural — and he was winning.

The pinnacle of his success lay in his French-tiled blue and white bathroom. It was one of the most beautiful rooms in his home, with Italian marble fixtures: an imported toilet and matching bidet that sat on a plush white carpet. Lemonweed and wintergreen flourished in the windows and in tiered chrome planters that hooked on the shower rod. Over the towel racks he'd installed a hidden speaker that was connected to his stereo system. The only thing his bathroom lacked was toilet paper, which he kept in the closet and brought out for rare guests since he never needed it. Through a careful selection of solids and liquids, he was able to control not only the moment but the exact nature of the matter that had to bring him daily to the blue and white tiled room. His stomach and intestines were purified by large quantities of spring water and camomile tea. He found variety in clear juices — apple, strained cranberry, and, on rare occasions, small sips of Chardonnay, preferably from the vineyards of Pouilly, where no yeast was added to the fermentation. He learned that the very tips of broccoli florets, asparagus, and even parsley moved less noticeably through his system than the stems. Young animal flesh — baby scallops, calves' liver, and breasts of squab were the purest to digest. This was supplemented with dried kelp from the waters around New Zealand, ground bone meal, and wheat germ. He would have put a forkful of cabbage, a slice of onion, or a single bean into his mouth with the same enthusiasm as a tablespoon of cyanide. Because when Maxwell sat each morning, on his Italian marble — his head erect, his ankles disappearing into the thick carpet, and his fingers drumming the tempo of a violin quartet on his knees with his eyes closed, before moving straight to the bidet, where he was sprayed with perfumed and sudsy water, and then on to the shower — except for the fact that he was totally naked, those first five minutes could have taken place on the seat of a theater or concert hall, with absolutely no clues to tip off even the nearest party about his true nature.

After the success of this daily ritual, Maxwell was more than ready for any challenge at General Motors. And when he made his way into the lobby, up in the elevators, and past the file clerks, stenographers, and small offices of his subordinates, he drew the inevitable mixture of awe, envy, and hatred that is the lot of exceptional achievers. And, of course, he was misunderstood. He would have found the comments that he was trying to be white totally bizarre. Being white was the furthest thing from his mind, since he spent every waking moment trying to be no color at all. The charges of "ball-buster" or "slave-driver" were only levied because he required from his staff what he was willing to give himself. But he might have been faintly pleased had he overheard a frequent whisper in the typing pool, "Ya know, Smyth acts like his - - - - don't smell" — because it didn't. And having conquered the last frontier, there was nothing that stood between Maxwell and the ultimate finish line but time. When the executive chair became vacant, the board of trustees wouldn't think twice about giving the best man the job. And that's the only kind of man he was.

Xavier heard the first set of chimes and decided to let the bell ring again before he answered. But Maxwell had no intention of ringing twice. After one depression of exactly two seconds, he stood there calmly waiting for the door to be opened. He knew he was expected, made sure he had been heard, and so the only logical sequence would now be admittance into the house. Xavier sat nervously in the lengthening silence, finally realizing that Maxwell wasn't going to ring again. If he opened it now, he needed some excuse for not answering immediately, but if he waited much longer he gambled on Maxwell's leaving. It was a play of wills on each side of the oak door, and Maxwell won out.

"Hey, sorry I took so long. I was upstairs when you first rang and I was waiting for the second ring to be sure that it was the bell."

"No sweat, mon ami." Maxwell's scarf glided off and was held out to Xavier. "What's shakin'?"

His greeting told Xavier that he considered this a very intimate visit because he was willing to engage in French and ghetto dialect, the two pet passions he reserved for close friends. He walked toward the couch, intently surveying the room. The few times Maxwell had been there before he had glanced around, seeming to sniff the air in case some new addition or omission might call for him to realign his opinion of Xavier.

"Can I fix you a drink?"

"If you have Chardonnay — with just a *kiss* of a chill."

Xavier shrugged his shoulders. "Well, it's cold."

He poured himself a double shot of bourbon and Maxwell allowed him to talk about the weather, car repairs, and the company's annual meeting for what he deemed an appropriate amount of time, and then choosing a place in the conversation where he knew Xavier would least expect it — "So what really brings me here, mon copain? I know about the cold; I've just driven through it with my rebuilt carburetor after interrupting the outline for my brilliant presentation for the spring convention, but what I still don't know is *why?*" He leaned back on the velvet cushions and smiled, enjoying the flicker of consternation in Xavier's eyes. He had heard the suppressed panic in his voice over the phone and a true curiosity had brought him out of his house to see what could be so important that Xavier had to try so hard to make it sound trivial.

"Well, I thought it might be nice to have you over. Except for a few hurried lunches at work, we never really get a chance to relax and just be friends."

Maxwell knew that Xavier fully understood that sparing the time to lunch with a subordinate at work was an act of friendship, so he remained silent and waited for a real answer to his question.

Xavier took a deep swallow of his bourbon. "And, uh, I wanted a little feedback on some longer-range plans. The thought had occurred to me that I might want to start to think about thinking about marrying Roxanne Tilson."

"Sacré Dieu, blood. Why?"

Xavier panicked; that wasn't what he had really meant to say and now he didn't have a ready answer that would retain Maxwell's respect. How many times had he heard him say that love was for teenagers and fools? He sought desperately for a reply, wishing that he smoked. "I know this may sound bizarre" — he took another swallow of his drink — "but there are times when she reminds me of Eleanor Roosevelt."

Maxwell frowned and thought a moment. "Well, my cleaning lady bears a striking resemblance to Indira Gandhi, but that's no reason for me to drag her down to City Hall. Are you sure that's the only reason?"

"There's nothing to be sure or unsure about." Xavier got up and went over to the bar. "It was just an idea I thought about playing with, that's all. And she was just one of the many women who came to mind. To be honest, she's not even a serious contender. I mean, the real issue is whether or not this is the time for me to settle down. But I'm not too sure that I should rush into anything, you know?"

"Oh, I know perfectly well what you mean. A decision like that is loaded with disaster — even if you could find a 'serious contender,' as you put it. And I don't hold out much hope for your doing that."

"Really?"

Maxwell shook his head and sighed, turning his wineglass gently between his fingers. "Now, let's be reasonable. I know that, for whatever reasons, you're only into black women. I'm not knocking it, mind you. But you're going to have to face some hard, cold facts: there just aren't enough decent ones to choose from. They're either out there on welfare and waiting to bring you a string of somebody else's kids to support, or they've become so prominent that they're brainwashed into thinking that you aren't good enough for them. The few who just might be up to your standards, who've distinguished themselves in the world, are into white men. Name me one black woman who's making a name for herself in the arts or entertainment and I'll name you two who have white husbands. Don't we see it every day in the magazines and newspapers, or right downtown? The best and the brightest are going that way, so what's left for you? The Roxanne Tilsons of this world."

Xavier winced. "I don't really see anything wrong with her," he mumbled.

"Well now, of course she's been to the right schools — Wellesley, wasn't it? And you're from the same neighborhood — even though she's up there on the border, it's still Linden Hills."

"Of course." Xavier's voice was slightly impatient. "How could I have even looked at her if that wasn't the case?"

"And she's pretty enough, although there's a bit too much avoirdupois."

"I wouldn't call her fat." Xavier narrowed his eyes. "She's full."

"Yes, she's full *now*, but you know that most black women have a tendency to let themselves go. Look in any spa or gym and they're outnumbered ten to one. And believe me, it's not Roxanne's fault. It's an old throwback to the jungle days when they had to store up food like camels because the women did most of the hauling. So what they do now is starve themselves until they get you and then gain ten pounds before the reception's over. And from then on in . . . ." Maxwell shook his head slowly and shuddered. "But the real question is not whether you can find one who'll fit into your Porsche, but who'll fit, period."

Xavier stared off into space and thought, But we read the same books, like the same music. We both want to travel. He found himself wishing that Maxwell would shut up and go home. He hadn't called him here to listen to all this. He had done nothing but cause him to think of all the reasons why he should run out tomorrow and buy an engagement ring, but somehow he didn't want that. And what he needed desperately to know was why.

"Look, Maxwell, I find that just a little hard to buy. They're out there in all shapes and sizes once I'm ready. But maybe I'm just not ready now, you know?"

"Oh, you're ready. Ready and raring to go. But the sad thing is that there isn't a mother's daughter out there ready for you. And you want to know why?" Maxwell sat on the edge of the sofa. "Because Roxanne Tilson is only the clone of a whole mass that are coming out of these colleges with their hot little fists clenched around those diplomas and they aren't ready to hear nothing from nobody, least of all you. When they've done that four- or six-year stint at the Yales, Stanfords, or Brandeises, they no longer think they're women, but walking miracles. They're ready to ask a hell of a lot from the world then and a hell of a lot from you. They're hungry and they're climbers, Xavier, with an advanced degree in expectations. Hook up with one of them and whatever you're doing isn't good enough, and you're doing damned good as it is."

Maxwell's knuckles tightened around the stem of his glass. "I'm going to make a confession." He leaned toward Xavier. "I once thought about marrying a woman like Roxanne and she wasn't half so attractive, but she had a Ph.D. from Princeton and I was much younger then and could have forced myself to overlook a lot of other things. But when it came right down to the line, I realized that she just didn't understand me. She just didn't appreciate the problems I was going through. And if a woman can't do that, at least she should be quiet and stay out of your way. Remember, a man only lives two places — at work and at home. You and I both know the sacrifices we made and are still making to walk that tightrope out there; it takes every ounce of strength we've got. So, can you afford to be drained when you come in here?" He stabbed his finger toward the ground. "Can you afford to be reminded — in five-syllable vocabularies no less — that the rope's a lot thinner than you think and it's a lot farther to the ground?" Maxwell's voice had risen a quarter of an octave, which was his equivalent of hysteria, and it stunned Xavier.

"But if you feel that way about it," Xavier almost whispered, "I don't understand why you were willing to weather all that flack when you promoted Mabel Thompson."

"Of course I promoted her." Maxwell leaned back and smiled, taking a split second to regulate his breathing. "Any fool could see from her résumé that she was overqualified for that lousy job in the bookkeeping department. I brought her into my office and now I have one of the most efficient cost analysts in the eastern division. While all those other clowns were busy looking at her color and sex, I looked at her personnel file. And I knew that any woman who managed to support herself and two younger brothers while getting through accounting school with straight A's would have to be a tiger. But you know what happens when you try to bed down with one? You get your balls clawed off. And that's the bottom line, isn't it?"

Yes, that was the bottom line. Xavier could never see himself with any woman who wasn't determined to go somewhere with her life. But he knew that the road was a lot more cluttered for a black woman and a successful journey meant sharpening her spirits to grind away all the garbage that stood in her way. And just maybe when that switch was turned on, it couldn't tell the difference between his living flesh and anything else. If he needed anything more than Roxanne, he needed those constant reminders hung on him healthy and intact that he could still hang on.

"Mabel probably needed those claws to survive." Xavier frowned into his bourbon.

"I'm sure she did. And I thank her, and my twenty percent reduction in marketing costs thanks her. But let somebody else marry her."

Xavier sighed and watched his ice cubes melt away into the amber fluid. He knew that if he watched them long enough, the frozen crystals would lose their shape and edges, become indistinguishable from the mahogany sea that was keeping them afloat. We read the same books, like the same . . . Just concentrate on the brown liquid that's dissolving the ice. He didn't have to get up and find a stirrer, or even rotate the glass. Just sit there and soon, very soon, there would be nothing but a mouthful of watery bourbon that could be gotten rid of in a single swallow with no harm to his throat or stomach, and definitely no chance of heartburn.

"I understand what you're saying, Maxwell. But that doesn't leave much for me, and I've no intention of spending the rest of my life alone."

Reynolds Price

---

from
Kate Vaiden

THE MIRACLE IS, you can last through time. You pray to die when you pass a calendar — all those separate days stacked before you, each one the same length and built from steel. But then you butt on through them somehow, or they through you. However many days I doubted I'd make it, I got through the rest of spring, summer, and fall on Holt and Caroline's quiet baffled trust, Noony's rough concern, the news of the Normandy invasion in June, and a good many more long rides with Fob, my own wits, and possibly the hand of God (also possibly not; He can leave for long stretches, I seem to have found).

At first I spent a lot of time in my room, stretched out on the walnut bed Dan had bought me — the one with the carving of my young face up at the head. I'd stare at the ceiling, reach back and feel the face with my fingers, and try to guess how the human that had got through my life till now could walk on forward through the seen and unseen for maybe one more year, not to mention forty (I've had forty more).

Hours could pass doing no more than that, and I know it sounds like a fatal case of purple self-pity at a time when in Europe and Asia people younger than me were tortured and torn with no bed beneath them, no roof, no food. Back then though what I felt was more like pure curiosity than actual pain. The question seemed to be *What was this girl* for *and would she be missed, if she vanished or died?* (I'd noticed how nobody ever really missed me, but subsequent years have shown the same thing, and it's yet to kill a soul.)

I didn't ever say the question out loud. I also barely touched on it in prayers. I've said several times how — in Norfolk, after Christmas at least — I felt *led on*, planned for and protected. In my room in Macon, I felt like a creature on the flattest widest plain with nothing but skyline, a trillion ways to go, and the choice up to me — no volunteer guide.

I also hauled out my Indian bead-loom and made a beautiful belt for Douglas. Don't ask me *why him?* Till Halloween week I never had so much as a postcard from Douglas. Walter wrote to me faithfully (and tried to send money, which I sent back with thanks); and every time he'd add "No word of our friend." I didn't tell that to anybody — I knew they'd laugh. But somehow, to me too, Douglas still seemed a friend. I couldn't wish harm on his memory or his whereabouts. I even kept thinking that the baby, as he grew, was a shared thing Douglas was helping to make by remote control (and before you yell at my ignorance, wait and see what he did). Once the belt was finished, I of course had to keep it. I had no idea if Douglas was alive, much less where he lived. I thought about making it half-again longer and giving it to Fob, but I knew he wouldn't wear it and would joke about Tonto or fancy-boys.

Fob stood by me though. Even after he could see I was pregnant, he'd stop at the house every two or three days and take me out for a long country-ride or to one of his farms where all we'd see was a sunbaked tenant who didn't know me from Adam's back-teeth. Fob never asked me a single painful question, and he never tried to show me off in public where people could watch.

I *was* a sight. Through early summer I was still thin enough to walk downtown to the store or post office (downtown was mostly men; you seldom saw women). Occasionally old men would stop and ask was I Frances's child and hadn't I been up living in Norfolk? I'd smile and answer and that would satisfy them. In a place that small, which people seldom left, you were always being confused with your mother or a dead third-cousin — whoever you looked like, and you looked like half the town. I welcomed the confusion; you could hide behind it. By July though, I was big as a carload of green watermelons, and swaybacked from it. So I kept to the house and porch and back yard.

After the day I stepped off the train, I never attempted church again. Church was too full of women who'd known you forever and were still clearheaded enough to know you were *Kate*, not *Frances*, and that *Kate* wasn't married; so who'd set her working on this huge child? Church anyway is an optional thing I can take or leave. When God or whoever wants touch with me, I find myself sending prayers up the line. Many times He and I go our ways in silence.

Macon was not a social town; but in that many months, we had a few visitors — neighbors and kin. At first I'd go to my room and avoid them, but finally Caroline said "You're welcome all over this house. Our friends have survived worse shocks than you." After that I'd show up more times than not. And nobody said a hurtful word, not in my presence anyhow. Still I could see how hard they strained not to look below my face or to mention Norfolk. Sometimes when they'd left I'd go to my mirror and check *was I there?* and laugh at the answer (*yes, or the Macy's balloon of me*).

But mainly I realized how strange it was. Here was plainly a well-raised healthy white girl with no signs of being a moron or crook; and a baby was hatching due-south of her chest that nobody understood, spoke of, or stopped (I'd personally known of two abortions in my years in Macon, both paid for and suffered in Richmond, Virginia).

Even Dr. Hunter in Warrenton, that Holt took me to once a

month, might as well have treated me for housemaid's knee. He was bound to have noticed I didn't wear a ring; but maybe he thought I'd married in haste and had a teenaged husband fighting overseas, missing or dead (maybe I did, though no teenager — maybe Douglas had enlisted). Sometimes I'd want to yell "Let's just *discuss* it. It's a fair-to-good story," but I never quite did. I already saw it was probably a mercy — I'd turned to clear glass. You could see right through me.

Another mercy was, I didn't have girlfriends to pass by and stare. In the Macon town-limits there were literally none, not white anyhow. All eligible candidates lived in the country and rode the schoolbus. To see them, I'd have had to haunt the schoolgrounds. I'd have rather haunted Hell.

Speaking of which, Swift finally showed up. They'd moved, as I said, after I went to Norfolk. And though they'd gone less than twenty miles, their visits were scarce (*Swift's* visits — his wife Elba never showed her face; she resented his people). Holt and Caroline had mentioned him occasionally early in the summer. He'd got a new job, new glasses for his weak eyes, but still seemed to grieve at being too blind to fight in the war. Nobody spoke of inviting him home. Still one Sunday afternoon in July he showed up.

I was on the sideporch by myself and recognized his car in time to go hide. But for some cold reason, I held my ground. I'd been reading Willa Cather, *Sapphira and the Slave Girl*; I kept on at it as he climbed the steps toward me. Then something told me "You speak the first word or live to regret it." So over the open book I said "I seem to remember you from somewhere, stranger. But your eyes have changed." I went back to reading (he did look better, less startled and shifty).

He paused on the top step and said "We were kin in a previous life."

"Were we friends?" I said.

"Good friends."

I said "Then I don't remember."

Swift smiled much better than he'd ever done before. "Keep trying; you will. I thought the world of you."

I'd stayed in the chair, so I suddenly wondered if he'd noticed my belly (by then I was wearing those awful smocks that were all the maternity clothes yet invented). I decided, on the spot, to hold nothing back. I said "I'm in no position right now to forget old friends."

Swift waited, then nodded. "I heard you weren't."

"Heard from who?"

Swift said "The air — it's a general fact."

He and Elba had never had children, though we knew she'd tried. I said "A little new blood in the family might not be amiss."

"Might not," Swift said. "You're the one picked to bleed it."

Whatever he meant, I hadn't meant that. My mind wiped clean and my mouth shut down. Pain and death hadn't been real dangers till he laid them out on the steps like fabric.

He went in the house and talked to his mother; and when he left half an hour later, he just said "Write me when the going gets rough."

It never truly did. I had a lot of boredom. And I went through the miseries of the last two months when you waddle like a duck in a fast getaway and are so off-balance that tying your shoes or rolling over in bed at night are problems like spanning the Rockies with a bridge or hauling Lake Erie cross-country in your arms, not spilling a drop. But my mind held up, a lucky kind of blindness.

I just didn't try to see far ahead — where I'd be in one year, not to mention forty. There'd be this baby (a boy, I still knew). I'd be fed by my family and could then feed him. Ravens would likely supply the rest. What was the rest? Time, years of time. I didn't think of asking for love or touch.

He came a week early, November 16th. And though he'd

been rambunctious in the ninth month, he slid into life as calm and easy as an underwater swimmer with breath to spare. Holt and I stayed up for the late news — MacArthur was back in the Philippines, and the Japs were sorry. Then Holt went with me back to my room and built me a fire to take off the chill (it was not really cold). When he said "Good night," he pointed to the little bell on my table. Despite the metal shortage, he'd found it at a country store and set it beside me in case I was needy but speechless some night. I said "Never fear."

Once Holt was gone, I stretched out fully clothed on top of my bed; something told me not to strip. I read half an hour in *The Reader's Digest* — how to keep your chin high in all grades of weather. Then I pulled my quilt up and dozed awhile with the light still on. At ten to one I came to slowly. It seemed like a low wave had just passed through me.

Nowadays of course girls all but get master's degrees in pregnancy and labor. Back then you never heard anything but jokes on the pain involved ("like peeing a baby-grand piano, bench and all"), the dangers of mishaps; the only advice was "Bear-down and pray." Still I knew right off that the big thing had started. The wave was not pain; but when I reached downward, my skirt was wet. First I listened for any sign of life in the house — pure black silence. Then I opened my bedside-table drawer and found the letter I'd got two weeks before. I've long since lost it, but it said something like

Dear Kate,

That train ride got lonesome fast. But I made it to Raleigh and tried three jobs before finding one that I think is the ticket. Not much money but a cheerful boss and a good place to stay. I wonder if you've got any news for me? Like I said, I'll stand still to hear it any time. And I'll do my part if you say what it is.

Love anyhow from
Douglas

That had come Halloween, delivered by Noony, so I knew it was a secret from Caroline and Holt; and I kept it that way. I also knew it was maybe a tunnel towards better times. Douglas gave an address on Person Street, but I didn't rush to use it. I thought I would wait and have the child; then if it was strong with a full set of features, I'd let Douglas know the fact and the name.

When I'd hid it deeper in the drawer, I composed myself and called "Caroline." She didn't seem to hear, so I rang the bell.

In less than a minute, she was there — Holt behind her. She said "Lord, you're dressed."

I smiled, not to scare her. "I never undressed and now my bed's wet."

Caroline said to Holt "You stand here and wait." Then she came over, raised the quilt, and checked slowly. She looked back to Holt and said "It's not blood."

"What does that mean?" he said.

"It means we all get dressed and head out. Kate's having this child."

I knew she was right. I felt warm and more or less safe in their presence. Before I stood up, I'm glad to say, I thanked them both.

Holt said "You're welcome."

I had changed my clothes and packed a bag (and Holt and Caroline had come back to get me) when I looked to the bedroom door and saw my mother's straight back six years ago — following Swift to the graves, the creek, her own quick death. It froze me long enough for Caroline to frown, but I didn't speak of it.

Dr. Hunter's clinic was a twenty-mile drive. We were all so quiet; and my pains were so light, it gave me time to settle finally on the baby's name. I'd started out months before with names from books, movies, or the war — Balfour, Anthony, Cordell, or Coventry. But in the last week, I came round to thinking that a name ought to be a kind of private owning up

— own-up for the baby, who he is and why, unless it's so bad it brands him for life. As we passed the Warrenton jail that night and turned toward the clinic, I said "In case anything goes wrong, this baby's name is Daniel Lee Vaiden — called *Lee*, not *Daniel*."

Caroline didn't speak but Holt said "What if it comes here a girl?"

"It won't," I said.

Holt laughed. "You hope."

Caroline said "Just drive. She's right."

I was — nine pounds-eight ounces worth, named Daniel Lee Vaiden with my own voice the instant I saw him. That was when he was maybe four minutes old. Back then in America "natural childbirth" was reserved for people too poor to buy ether. White girls like me, with grownups behind them, got anesthesia for every yell. What surprised me was, how little it hurt — more like passing a streamlined spinet than a full-sized grand. Even Caroline, who'd stood hails of pain, had warned me to pray it wouldn't last long. *Long?* — the nurse had no more than got me undressed, hitched in the stirrups, and slightly dazed when Dr. Hunter walked in sleepy in street clothes and started to scrub.

It took him awhile and he tried to chat with me till finally I felt a hard wave coming. I said to him "Man, you're missing this baby" (I've mentioned I was dazed, a big whiff of gas). Then I thought "Oh, I'm wrong; my bowels are moving" — I know I blushed. They weren't. The baby was three-fourths born, and the nurse had to catch him so he didn't hit the floor. By the time they'd spanked him, washed out his eyes, and showed him to me, I'd waked up enough to say his name, though I didn't try to hold him.

The nurse said "Danny Boy, poor little Dan."

I heard the *poor* and decided to ignore it; but I did say "*Lee*, he'll be called *Lee*."

By then she was already taking him off to the crib in my room and Caroline.

Dr. Hunter said "Kate, how old are you?"

I said "A hundred seventeen last June the third." And I felt every minute of it that morning.

He'd finished his scrubbing and put on his gloves, so he walked toward the table to close me down. First though he met my eyes and waited. Then he said "Old as that, you may not have more babies ahead. Be glad now you got you a beauty." He smiled like he meant it, like it all was true.

It was, especially the beauty part. I stayed in the clinic exactly ten days. Since breast-feeding hadn't come back into style and doctors assumed you'd lose your organs if you stood up and walked before the eighth day, Lee was mostly in other people's hands. I saw him for maybe thirty minutes a day. He still looked more like a parboiled old-man midget than a boy, but he would stare at me — I remember that. What he saw I can't guess. He wouldn't smile or frown, but he'd choose a spot between my eyes and watch it like a sunflower eating the light. Being an only child myself, I thought that was normal till Caroline said, "He's a scholar, this child. He's *studying* us." That made him seem, more than ever, like something else I could hurt.

But the beauty showed when we got him home. He seemed to know he was there and safe when we turned in the drive. I was on the front seat with him in my lap, the longest I'd ever held him. And when Holt drove the car right up to the steps, I raised Lee high and said "You live here." The sun was strong and the trees were bare, but could he have seen a low white house with eyes that young? He laughed anyhow.

Holt saw him first and said "*He* knows."

Then I looked. Ten days old, he was grinning wide and flushed as a rose. I held him sideways for Caroline to see.

309

She said "It's wind. He's too young to smile." But she smiled back at him.

And he kept that up. Not the grin (he waited weeks longer for that) but the kind good-nature, the grateful ease he met life with. He'd cry at bottle time; and once every few days, he'd have a bad dream. But when he was full and belched and dry, you could count on as friendly a pet as any feist. So everybody liked him and the word got out.

Fob was the first to visit of course. He brought Lee a present of old gold-money he'd kept when Roosevelt confiscated gold — three ten-dollar coins with Liberty's head. I thanked Fob and offered him Lee to hold.

He said "I'd break him. I'll wait till he walks." But then he said "You give him his horn?"

I said "What horn? He's got a good yell."

Fob said "Gaston's foxhorn. We'll be hunting him soon."

I hadn't understood and hadn't really thought of the foxhorn in months. How did Fob know about it? Before I went to Norfolk, I'd hid it far back on my wardrobe shelf; and once I was home, I couldn't bear to see it. I wondered now if Fob thought Gaston was the father, but even Fob couldn't be that dumb (Gaston had been dead sixteen months). Still it made me wish I could change Lee's name — *Gaston Lee Vaiden* or just *Gaston Vaiden*. I knew it would be a name I could love, the name I'd hoped to give children to. But I also knew, in a place small as Macon, it would start brushfires I couldn't control, not to mention the boy.

Considering how I was soon to behave, I have to wonder if I ever really loved him. I'd shown most other human instincts till then. Why did mothering fail me? In the months I knew him, I can honestly say I enjoyed his company. Nobody gets a long-term kick out of dirty diapers and spit-up milk, but Lee Vaiden more than made up for his faults. I've mentioned his peaceful knowing nature; but I've seen other good babies, though they're scarce.

What Lee offered extra was quick good-looks. By three weeks old he's lost his boiled skin and straight dark hair. From then on he seemed like a big pearl growing in front of my face — a hundred colors of brown, pink, blue and eyes that just got deeper by the day and gladder to see me whenever I stopped.

But awhile before Christmas I saw I'd slacked off in tending to him. He had a bout of colic when I had a cold, and Caroline moved his crib to the hall outside her room so I could rest. We never moved it back. She didn't volunteer to and I didn't ask. I'd tend him all day, bathe, feed him, enjoy him. Then about sundown I'd start feeling like he was Caroline and Holt's — and Noony's (she liked him more than I would have guessed). They were glad to take over, in perfect silence.

Maybe it was lonesomeness, the reason I failed. I didn't have anybody my age near me. I'd got used to fun at Walter's and Tim's. Most of all though — and worst of all — I'd started to worry that no man would want me, no decent man with a regular job. A teenaged mother with a needy bastard-baby and no big skills, no big nest egg or moviestar looks. From my room in Macon, it looked like a long one-lane road ahead with a boy to raise, like a cast-iron sidecar hitched to my bike. Holt and Caroline were in their sixties. They couldn't last forever and anyhow I couldn't ask them to support us once I was on my feet. Walter was nowhere I meant to revisit permanently. I'd walked out on Tim. Also I was hungry, not for food or love.

There's no true way for me to say it — what I felt as that hard winter came down. With Gaston and Douglas I'd used my body more ways than any white girl my age I'd read about or known. And for all the harm I'd caused the world, nothing convinced me my body was wrong and ought to be curbed. It was all I absolutely knew I had; everything else in sight could vanish — parents, kin, love — and in my case already had, more than once. My own strong head and limbs had lasted and kept me happy maybe half the time (a more-than-fair average).

311

I couldn't just maim that much of myself by bolting doors on the wide green world and camping-down forever in a house with no man near me under sixty years old.

So on December 21st I wrote to Douglas Lee. I told him the child was born and strong and was named for him. I said I was sorry I'd left the train with no explanation, that I'd been confused. I said I bore him no grudge whatever and didn't want money; but if he was curious to see me or Lee, I'd meet him anywhere in reason. I'd planned to ask Noony to mail the letter.

But once it was sealed, I had the courage to walk downtown on my own — first time since the baby. I was almost there before I thought "Somebody will say something spiteful to me." But I forged on anyway and nobody did. Miss Lula Harris, when I bought my stamp, said "Noony keeps me posted; that boy sounds *pretty*. Bring him down here to see me." I almost fainted but told her I would, the first warm day.

It stayed cold through the whole next week. And Christmas was calmer than I'd ever known it. Christmas Eve we sat up late to hear the late news on the radio. The Allies had rallied in the Battle of the Bulge, and it looked again like we might beat the Germans (people now forget that was ever in question). Then we dressed the little fat cedar-tree Holt had brought in; and I laid out Lee's first Santa Claus presents — dresses, caps, and a Dopey-doll from Disney's *Snow White*. Caroline brought in hot spiced tea. Before we drank it, I made a short speech. I begged their pardon for what I'd caused and thanked their patience and their generous hearts.

Caroline smiled. "It has been a year."

Holt said "If soldier boys stand it, so can we."

Then we went to bed. But I lay wide awake for hours longer, thinking of last year's Christmas Eve (my vision in the fire with Walter and Douglas) and hunting the cold black dark of my room for any new sight or sign of guidance. I might as well have been Helen Keller in a barrel. So I told God in that case I couldn't be responsible for my next mistakes — not all of them anyhow, being so hungry. Then I slept till dawn.

It was New Year's Eve before Douglas answered, and Noony delivered the letter in the kitchen where I was feeding Lee with Caroline and Holt. The envelope didn't show his name and address (his letters never did, like spy reports); but of course I knew his hand. I stuck it in the pocket of my robe right away, though I knew Caroline would rather die than ask about it.

Still Holt said "Who's the mystery correspondent?"

I couldn't lie to him. I said "I very much suspect it's Lee's father."

"Where's he living now?" Holt smiled but was genuinely ignorant. I'd never explained why Douglas left Norfolk or where he'd gone.

Caroline stood up and left the room fast. She wouldn't hush Holt, but she wouldn't stay to hear.

We stayed quiet long enough to honor her wish. Then I said "Raleigh, the last I heard."

Holt said, "Without Walter?"

"To the best of my knowledge."

"Who supports him then?"

"He can work," I said. "He's got a good mind."

"An orphan's mind."

I said "What's that?"

"A bottomless well," Holt said. "—dry well."

"You forget I'm an orphan?"

That stopped him a second, and over at the sink Noony gave a deep grunt. But then he said "You never lacked love, Kate — not for one hour."

Holt had been more than good to me, and I took his claim seriously. I tried to remember some strong exception while I went on feeding Lee in my arms.

Finally Holt said "Was I wrong?"

So I said "No sir." To be fair, I hadn't come up with an hour when the whole world actually turned its back. At the worst, he and Caroline had always been here, ready to serve.

Noony said "Ask *me*. I'll fill up your day. I got my bill of complaints wrote out."

Holt decided to laugh. Then he asked for the baby.

I went to my room, took a short sponge-bath, dressed warmly, and sat by the window with the letter.

He said my news was more of a shock than he'd planned it to be. It had made him sure he couldn't launch one more orphan on the world, even half an orphan. He was still far from settled and still had debts, but would I bring the baby to Raleigh and let him see it and he and I talk about all our futures and what seemed right? He stressed that he wanted to see me with the baby. He enclosed five dollars, not as small a sum as it sounds today.

Something in it scared me, something hid between the lines. I halfway suspected he had plans for Lee — kidnapping him, killing him, God knew what. I guessed I was almost certainly wrong, but anyhow I wrote to him then and there. I said, in light of the weather and Lee's age, I didn't feel safe on the train right yet; we could wait till spring or the February thaw. It didn't hurt all that much to say.

Ten days passed and Douglas didn't answer. But late that Saturday when Noony had come back to fix our supper, she found me changing Lee in the hall (Holt was gone; Caroline was in the kitchen). She touched Lee's navel and said "Your daddy back in town."

He grinned and stretched out.

I went blue-cold.

Noony looked me square in the eye and frowned and whispered the rest. "Mr. Douglas at my house, waiting for you. Come in by train and asked some nigger at the depot for me; found me too. I'd have known him anywhere — this child got his color. He said he got to see you, Kate; come running right now."

I didn't think long. I finished with Lee, then said to Noony "I'm going. Tell Caroline the truth or a lie." When I'd got my coat from the rack by the door and buttoned it tight, I said "Is he wild?" I guess I had to mean was he drunk? (I'd barely seen him drink.)

Noony said "Wild as a horse in fire." She folded an extra blanket over Lee. Then she said "You ever mean to see us again?"

"I hope so," I said. I couldn't guarantee it.

The big surprise was, Douglas was calm as water in a glass — standing water in clean cutglass; he looked that fine. Even in the dark of Noony's house, he burned his own light. He was in Emlen's chair. And when I walked in, it shocked me so bad I said "That chair belongs to a ghost." But I laughed.

Douglas said "It's welcome to sit on my lap."

"It's an old man," I said.

Douglas said "Then I've had my share of that." He stood in place and watched me awhile. Then he came on forward and kissed me once.

My skin had forgot how good that felt. I said "Go on and sit down; I was joking." I went to my old cot and sat at the foot. Douglas still watched me (he could outstare an owl). So I said "I thought you hated this place."

"I do," he said, "but I had to see you."

"Shall I thank you or run hell-for-leather to the Law?" In the long cold silence (Noony's stove was out), I laughed again.

Douglas said "I've asked you to marry me. Remember that?"

I said, "Eighty years ago, on Mars or Venus — it seems even farther."

He finally smiled. "I'll repeat it. Kate, marry me."

I know it sounds crazy; but for one weird instant I couldn't understand him, couldn't think what his words meant. Eventually I said what first came to mind. "How would we live?"

Douglas laughed. "Your fortune. No, it wouldn't be Norfolk; but we'd make it someway. I've got new friends."

I said "You and I tend to lose friends, Douglas. Who've you got now?"

"Whitfield Eller, a blind piano-tuner. Don't laugh yet. He's saved four cents of every nickel he's made, think I'm his main light, and can play sweet music till morning breaks."

"You working for him?"

"Lord no," Douglas said, "— couldn't stand the monotony. He lives near my rooming house. I've chauffeured him some; he owns a car."

I said "I hope he won't drive a lot once I get there."

He said "Then you're coming?" He stood up again and started toward me.

My right hand stopped him, flat in the air. I said "The bank is shut today." I hated myself; my meanness had said it. But I knew it was a test.

Douglas passed it cold. "To hell with the bank. Save it for the baby." He came on over to the cot and sat by me.

I said "We're sitting in a field of gold."

He touched the back of my neck. "How's that?"

"The ghost — old Emlen Patrick, Noony's husband — buried his money in jars outside. Holt says it's still here."

Douglas said "Good for Noony" and pressed me downward.

When our faces were touching, I said "It's cold and it's time to feed Lee."

Douglas said "I can remedy the first complaint."

I said "All right" and he did, on Noony's narrow cot — room enough for what I knew I'd missed, a clean man wanting and using my services. Noony's clock ticked through it like a tin drumstick.

When Douglas had finished but stayed on with me, I started to count the seconds. At ninety I said "When you want us to leave?"

He waited so long I thought he had dozed. But his eyes were open, and he finally said "If *us* means you and me, the six-thirty train."

I shook my head. "It means us *three* and I won't tear Lee out of Caroline's arms — not tonight. I've hurt her enough."

He said "I figured Lee was more mine than hers."

That stopped the sweetness he'd sent all through me. I said "You ought to have said that last summer."

Douglas rolled to his back, then propped on his elbows, and faced the door. At first I thought he'd heard a noise, and I wondered if Holt might have come to get me. But we spent a long silence, and then Douglas said "I was with you, Kate, on a real train — remember? — headed somewhere real, where people can live. It was you that quit."

No denying that. I could mention how wild he'd seemed that day, and what Walter told me, but it was me that quit. I sat upright on the side of the cot and assembled my clothes.

When I bent to tie my shoes, Douglas said "You're quitting again."

Every other time I'd quit, I always knew it. Nobody else had ever just said it out flat before me, the truth. I was quitting the one person still in reach who was asking for me. I opened my mouth to say "Let's go"; but I thought "Lee'd ask for me, if he could." My eyes didn't water; my throat didn't close, but I knew I was right. And I thought of Noony — how she'd taken me in, and now Douglas Lee, and how much mischief I'd cause her by running. I stood up and said "What's so grand about me that you need me this minute?"

Douglas stayed on the cot, more than half-bare. In the chilly house he seemed at ease. He said "Your voice."

"My *voice*?" I hadn't expected a quick short answer; and

nobody ever claimed my voice was special, though people understood it.

"You could talk your way through granite rock."

Years later, having balked at a million more rocks, I knew he was wrong. Still at seventeen, in a drafty shack with nowhere else to turn but the place that had driven my father wild and killed my mother, it sounded true. I could taste the pledge of a whole fresh life — the life people want with a warm companion and chances to mend the world by giving it well-trained courteous healthy children. I turned back to Douglas and said "Would you want me now, without the baby?"

He said "I just proved that."

"We'd leave now and then come back for Lee?"

Douglas nodded. "Fine. You and I settle in; then you come get Lee."

"How soon?" I said.

"When the spirit moves you — a few days, a month, the first good weather."

"Can we stop by the house now and say what we're doing?"

Douglas said "I wouldn't pour cold cat-piss down Holt Porter's throat if his heart was on fire. Anyhow they'll know. By now Noony's told them."

I said "If she has, she's lost her job."

"She'll live." He grinned. "She can dig for gold."

I took a long moment to study his eyes. Was there any plain reason why he'd come this far, to a town he hated, to harm or deceive me? Apparently not — the eyes never flinched. I thought "One growing boy is *grown*." And I said "All right."

At the depot I took a blank telegraph-form and wrote to Holt and Caroline. I said Lee's father had a good job in Raleigh and had come to get me. I'd write again in the next day or so and let them know when I'd come for Lee.

Black Pap Somerville was out on the platform to catch the mail. I gave him a dime I'd borrowed from Douglas to take the message straight to the house. They'd have it by supper.

It was long-since dark and frozen as the Pole. When I raised my foot to board the train, I saw a face hung in the air before me, real as mine. It should have been Lee's, I know — that trustful. But it was my mother one more bad time — young and ready and lovely, screaming. I stepped back and looked at Douglas behind me. There were no lights anywhere near us; but I saw him, pale from the cold.

He nodded. "Go on."

I shook my head. "I'm going to Lee — just a few more days. We'll come to you soon. Let's do this right."

His face was so blank I thought me might strike me. But he suddenly smiled. "You're hell on train trips."

I laughed. "It saves money."

The conductor, beside me, was saying "All aboard." No other humans but us were in sight.

So I told him "This gentleman's going, not me." I stepped aside.

And — not touching me — Douglas moved on forward, skipped the mounting stool, and climbed the steps. Then he turned back toward me.

The conductor blew his whistle and signaled the engine; then he boarded too.

I wanted to speak, something like *I'm sorry. But soon — I promise.*

The engine lurched though and Douglas staggered, then saved his balance.

I've always thought his mouth said "Promise," but I didn't hear his voice.

One more lurch and his face was gone.

I went to find Pap and reclaim my note. He offered me the dime, but I couldn't take it. I said "Celebrate."

Pap said "Tell me *what*."

I said "World peace. The war's ending soon."

Pap said "Don't believe it." He'd been in the trenches for months, 'and gassed; and he'd never accepted the armistice.

Caroline and Holt had finished supper and were back in the kitchen. She was scraping plates for Noony to wash, and he had Lee asleep in his arms. When I opened the door, nobody moved but Noony. She looked back and said "You nearly too late."

"For what?" I said.

"Your something-to-eat."

I said "I'll probably live awhile longer."

Caroline faced me and went to the warming oven for my plate. She set it on the table at her own clean place — chicken pie, carrots, and little boiled onions. Then she said "Noony, it looks good as new" and beckoned me toward it.

Holt said "Damned nearly *better* than new."

Lee gave a low sigh from the almost endless dream he lived in.

I thought "They were gambling on me" and it burned. I said "That was Douglas Lee just now. He's gone back to Raleigh, but he wants his son. Lee and I'll be moving on with him soon."

Not one of them said so much as a word or met my eyes.

I wondered if I'd actually made the sounds, but I didn't try again. I sat down and ate like a harmless famished girl. And in a few minutes, we were talking together like a peaceful family that's never known any pain harsher than toothache.

Later I asked Holt to help move Lee's crib back to my room; and Caroline joined us, with no objections. Lee woke up and watched through it all, very solemn. When we had him settled in his old place, down at the foot of my bed, he took another long rolling look around; then shut his eyes and slept.

Caroline said "There may have been better children in history, but I never knew them." Neither she nor Holt though said one more word to acknowledge my announcement of moving to Raleigh.

So all night long I kept waking up between good dreams of life with Douglas and asking myself again if I'd said my plan out loud and if I meant to keep it.

By morning Lee had answered the second question. When Caroline came in at daylight to help me with his feeding, she said he felt hot. By seven he was hotter still and coughing. By ten when Dr. Hunter came, he was trapped in long spells of coughs and cries. The doctor said it was just a chest cold, but it turned out to be a severe strep-throat. And even with medicines invented for the war, it was nearly a month before we could see he was out of danger. Then he reacted to sulfa drugs with a body rash that got so raw we had to pin his sleeves to the sheet to keep him from gouging great holes in his skin.

Lee stayed in my room, and I stayed right with him till I was the one he trusted most. Some nights Caroline would sit up with me when he couldn't sleep. But that one month was my real motherhood, and I can't say I look back on it with anything but regret and pity. *Regret* that the germs must have come from me and *pity* that he had to suffer in a world I'd brought him into, unasked. To be fair, I can also say I admired him. He was my kind of person, a scrapper and cheerful when he had little cause.

* * *

Once we knew how sick Lee was, I'd written to Douglas to say we'd be delayed in our trip. I also said we still meant to come; did he still want us? He wrote straight back with much concern — keep him posted on Lee; was Dr. Hunter good enough? And yes, by all means, he wanted us there. Enclosed was a money order, fifty dollars. I hadn't imagined he was that far ahead, but I cashed it the same day and paid doctor bills.

We exchanged letters two or three more times thereafter. I'd tell our slim news — Lee's inch-worm progress — and Douglas would report on his business trips. By then he was fulltime chauffeur for the blind man. They'd work out in eastward circles from Raleigh, tuning pianos as far off as Smithfield and mending church organs. He seemed fascinated at being the eyes for two grown men (himself and the tuner). It made me think what he'd been for Walter — not the eyes but the *sight*, the thing Walter saw wherever he looked. Douglas also mentioned that his only contact with Norfolk had been the draft board. He'd sent them his new address and the news that he was the main help to a helpless person. Their reply made him think he wouldn't be needed in the war after all.

Hard as it was, locked in with a sick baby and no real company, I began to notice that Douglas was fading again — in my memory and my hopes. I'd spent so few private minutes beside him. And he was somebody who needed to be *present* before you; otherwise he'd melt off toward the edges of your mind. My mind anyhow. I knew what problems would be solved if I married him. I knew the new troubles that would certainly follow. I could feel and smell his body still on me. But he faded as I say.

And by the time Lee's throat was strong and his skin mostly clear, I was drifting in a lazy dream of freedom. I'd stay in Macon, finish high school by mail; then Lee and I would live our lives somewhere down the highway with rooms and jobs and men who wouldn't give a damn about history. I seemed that easy. It seemed crazy too. But so did the whole weight of my short life (which felt about as short as U.S. 1 from Maine to Miami).

Anne Tyler

---

from
Celestial
Navigation

Summer and Fall, 1961: Jeremy

THESE ARE SOME of the things that Jeremy Pauling dreaded: using the telephone, answering the doorbell, opening mail, leaving his house, making purchases. Also wearing new clothes, standing in open spaces, meeting the eyes of a stranger, eating in the presence of others, turning on electrical appliances. Some days he woke to find the weather sunny and his health adequate and his work progressing beautifully; yet there would be a nagging hole of uneasiness deep inside him, some flaw in the center of his well-being, steadily corroding around the edges and widening until he could not manage to lift his head from the pillow. Then he would have to go over every possibility. Was it something he had to do? Somewhere to go? Someone to see? Until the answer came: oh yes! today he had to call the gas company about the oven. A two-minute chore, nothing to worry about. He knew that. He *knew*. Yet he lay on his bed feeling flattened and defeated, and it seemed to him that life was a series of hurdles that he had been tripping over for decades, with the end nowhere in sight.

On the Fourth of July, in a magazine article about famous Americans, he read that a man could develop character by doing one thing he disliked every day of his life. Did that mean that all these hurdles might have some value? Jeremy copied the quotation on an index card and tacked it to the windowsill beside his bed. It was his hope that the card would remove half of every pain by pointing out its purpose, like a mother telling her child, "This is good for you. Believe me." But in fact all it did was depress him, for it made him conscious of the number of times each day that he had to steel himself for something. Why, nine tenths of his life consisted of doing things he disliked! Even getting up in the morning! He had already overcome a dread before he was even dressed! If that quotation was right, shouldn't he have the strongest character imaginable? Yet he didn't. He had become aware lately that other people seemed to possess an inner core of hardness that they took for granted. They hardly seemed to notice it was there; they had come by it naturally. Jeremy had been born without it.

If he tried to conquer the very worst of his dreads — set out on a walk, for instance, ignoring the strings that stretched so painfully between home and the center of his back — his legs first became extremely heavy, so that every movement was a great aching effort, and then his heart started pounding and his breath grew shallow and he felt nauseated. If he succeeded, in spite of everything, in finishing what he had set out to do he had no feeling of accomplishment but only a trembling weakness, like someone recently brushed by danger, and an echo of the nausea and a deep sense of despair. He took no steps forward. It was never easier the second time. Yet all through July, the hottest and most difficult month of the year, he kept attempting things he would not have considered a few weeks ago. He went at them like a blind man, smiling fixedly ahead of him, sweating and grim-faced, pretending not to notice that inwardly, nothing changed at all. He drew from wells of strength that he did not even own. And the reason, of course, was Mary Tell.

Did she know how much courage went into his daily good morning? How even to meet her eyes meant a suicidal leap into unknown waters? "Good, good morning, Mrs. Tell," he said.

Mary Tell smiled, serene and gracious, never guessing. He held tight to the doorframe and kept his knees locked so that she would not see how they trembled. Face to face with her, he felt that he was somehow growing smaller. He had to keep tilting his chin up. And why did he have this sensation of transparency? Mary Tell's smile encompassed the room — the dusty furniture, the wax fruit on the sideboard, and Jeremy Pauling, all equally, none given precedence. Her eyes were very long and deep. The fact that there was no sparkle to them gave her a self-contained look. It was impossible that she would ever need anyone, especially not Jeremy.

Yet at night, as he lay in bed, he went over and over that moment when she had put her arms around him. She had needed him then, hadn't she? Like an old-time heroine in one of the Victorian novels his mother used to read to him, she had come in desperation, with no one else to turn to — and out of shock he had responded only scantily and too late. He tied his top sheet into knots, wishing the moment back so that he could do the right things. He tried to recall the smallest details. He took apart each of her movements, each pressure of her fingers upon his ribcage, each stirring of breath against his throat. He turned over all possible meanings and sub-meanings. He wondered if he had made some magical gesture that caused her to think of him in a time of trouble, and what gesture was it? what trouble was it? What made women cry in modern times, in real life?

But most of all, he wondered if it might ever happen again.

Flat on his back in the dark, sleepless after his inactive days, he spent hours constructing reasons for her to turn to him. He imagined fires and floods. He invented a sudden fever for her little girl. Mary Tell would panic and come pound on his door, carrying an antique silver candlestick. He would be a rock of strength for her. He would go for the doctor without a thought, no matter how many blocks from home it took him. He would keep watch beside the sickbed, a straight line of confidence for her to lean against. Her hair would just brush his cheek. What color was her hair? What color were her eyes? Away from her, he never could remember. He saw her in black-and-white, like a steel engraving, with fine cross-hatching shading her face and some vague rich cloak tumbling from her shoulders. Her clearest feature was her forehead — a pale oval. In the novels his mother read to him, a wide ivory brow stood for purity and tranquillity.

Oh, if only he had a horse to carry her away on!

Mrs. Jarrett said, "That poor Mrs. Tell, she doesn't get out much. Her friend hardly comes at all any more, have you noticed?"

Jeremy, watching television with the boarders, revived Mary Tell from a swoon and held a glass of brandy to her lips. He didn't answer.

"I had been hoping he was *more* than a friend," Mrs. Jarrett said.

"Who is this we're speaking of?" asked Miss Vinton.

"The gentleman Mrs. Tell was seeing. Remember? Now he hardly comes at all. Have you noticed him lately, Mr. Pauling?"

Jeremy said, "Well . . ."

After a while they gave up waiting for the rest of his answer.

Nowadays his collages filled him with impatience. He became conscious of the way his eyes tightened and ached when he looked at them too long. He started wishing for more texture, things standing out for themselves. He had an urge to make something solid. Not a sculpture, exactly. He shied away from anything that loomed so. But maybe if he stacked his scraps, let them rise in layers until they formed a standing shape. He pictured irregular cones, their edges ridged like stone formations on canyon floors. He imagined the zipping sound a fingernail would make running down their sides. But when he tried stacking his scraps they turned into pads, mounded and sloping. He took them away again. He went to stand by the window, but his impatience grew and extended even to his physical position: his moon face gazing out from behind the tiny clouded panes, his hands limp by his sides, fingers curled, his feet so still and purposeless, pointing nowhere in particular.

How did people set about courtships? All he had to go on were those novels. When he thought of courting Mary Tell he imagined taking her for a drive in a shiny black carriage. Or dancing across a polished ballroom — and he didn't even know which arm went around his partner's waist. Yet it seemed as if some edginess were pushing him forward, compelling him to take steps he would never ordinarily think of. He pictured a high cliff he was running toward with his arms outflung, longing for the fall, not even braced to defend himself against the moment of impact. Then maybe the edginess would leave him, and he could relax again.

He returned to the collage. He slid colors ceaselessly across the paper, like a man consulting a Ouija board. Imaginary voices murmured in his ear. Scraps of conversation floated past. He was used to that when he was working. Some phrases had recurred for most of his life, although they had no significance for him. "At least he is a *gentle* man," one voice was sure to say. He had no idea why. Of *course* he was a gentle man. Yet the voice had kept insisting, year after year. Now that he was trying to concentrate, pushing away the thought of courting Mary Tell in an opera box, he absently spoke the words in a whisper. "At least he is a —" Then he caught himself and straightened his shoulders. Other voices crowded in. "If in any case and notwithstanding the present circumstances —" "I don't know how to, don't know how to, don't know how to —" "If in any case —"

Mary Tell sat beside him smelling of handmade lace and fine soap, lifting her mother-of-pearl opera glasses, but her dress was out of Jane Austen's time and the opera she was watching had not been shown for a century.

Monday morning Jeremy got up early, dressed very carefully, and went to Mr. and Mrs. Dowd's grocery store, where he bought a pound of chocolates. They were left over from Valentine's Day — a heart-shaped box, a little dusty, but Mrs. Dowd wiped it off for him with a dishrag. *"Somebody's* found himself a sweetheart," she said. Jeremy was still knotted up from the ordeal of making a purchase, and he only gave a flicker of a smile and kept his eyes lowered. He returned home by way of the alley, so that he arrived in his backyard. There wild chicory flowers were waving among a tangle of sooty weeds, and he squatted and began gathering a bouquet. This was something he had thought out the night before. He had rehearsed it so thoroughly that now it seemed he was picking each flower for the second time. In a shady spot by the steps he found glossy leaves that he inserted between the chicory, making a pattern of blue and green. Then he rose, hugging the candy box to his chest, and went into the house. Through the kitchen, through the dining room, straight to Mary Tell's bedroom, where he instantly knocked. If he gave himself time to think, he would fail. He would run away, scattering flowers and chocolates behind him.

When she opened the door she was wearing a bathrobe and she carried a hairbrush. He noticed that the hairbrush was a wooden one with natural bristles, which gave him a sense of satisfaction. How fitting it was! He could have said from the beginning that she would never be the type to use a nylon hairbrush. But this thought was chosen at random, to take his mind off his embarrassment. He had expected to find her dressed. He had chosen the day and the hour so carefully, knowing that she would be in now and the other boarders out or upstairs; and here she stood in her bathrobe — a pink one, seersucker. Though at least her hair was up. He hadn't wakened her. The brush was apparently meant for Darcy, who sat crosslegged on the bed in a pair of striped pajamas. "Hi, Mr. Pauling!" she called out. Jeremy couldn't manage a smile. "These are for, I brought these for the room," he said. He thrust the bouquet under Mary Tell's chin. It was terrible to see how his hands were shaking; all the flowers nodded and whispered. "I found them by the trashcans."

"Oh! Thank you," she said. She looked at them a moment and then took them. Too late, he thought of the vase. Last night he had decided on his mother's pewter pitcher from the corner cupboard in the dining room, but this morning it had slipped his mind. "Wait," he said. "I'll get a —" but she said, "Don't bother, I'm sure we have something here. My, what a beautiful shade of blue."

They're *your* blue, Mary-blue, he wanted to tell her. The blue from a madonna's robe. He had thought of that last night, but he had known all along that he would never dare to say it. Instead he looked over at Darcy, whose eyes — more chicory flowers — surveyed him steadily. "How come you brought them to *us?*" she asked.

"Why, I just thought —"

"Never mind, Mr. Pauling," said Mary Tell. "I know why you're here."

Jeremy stood very still, breathing raggedly.

"You just have to understand," she said. "Financially, things are a little difficult right now. Very soon I should be able to pay you, but —"

"Pay me?" he said. Did she think she had to *buy* the flowers?

"Pay you your money. I know that Saturday has come and gone but you see, with Darcy not in school yet I have to find work I can do at home. Till then I was hoping you wouldn't care if the rent was a little —"

"The rent, oh," Jeremy said. "Oh, that's all right."

"It is?"

"Why, of course."

He kept his eyes on the flowers. It was important to see them safely into the water. And then what? Was he supposed to leave? Yes, almost certainly, in view of the fact that she was wearing a bathrobe. Yet that would make the visit so short, and he wanted to be sure he did everything he was supposed to. He raised his eyes to hers, hoping for a clue. The brilliance of her smile took him by surprise. "Mr. Pauling, I just don't know how to thank you," she said.

"Oh, why —"

"You've really been very kind."

"Well, but I believe they should be put in water," he said.

Then she looked down at the flowers and gave a little laugh, and he laughed too. He had not expected that things would go so well the very first time. He watched her fetch a glass of stale water from the nightstand and set the bouquet in without disarranging a single flower, without upsetting his design. When she was finished she turned and smiled at him, apparently waiting for something. He drew in a deep breath. "Now I wish," he said, "that you would call me Jeremy."

"Oh!" she said. "Well, all right."

He shifted his weight to the other foot.

"And you can call me Mary," she said after a minute.

"You can call *me* Darcy," Darcy said from the bed.

That gave them something new to laugh about, only he laughed hardest and had trouble stopping. Mary by then had returned to her smile. It became a little strained and started fading at the corners, and from that he understood that it must be time for him to go. He was glad that he had managed to catch the signal. He held out his hand and said, "Well, goodbye for now, Mrs. — Mary," and she said, "Goodbye, Jeremy." Her hand was harder than his, and surprisingly broad across the knuckles. While he was still holding it he said, "Um, may I come back sometime?" — the final hurdle of the visit. "Well, of course," she said, and smiled again as she closed the door.

Although he had not had breakfast yet he returned to his studio, because it would have been awkward to run into her again in the kitchen. He went up the stairs on the balls of his feet, feeling weightless with relief. Not even the discovery that he still carried the chocolates — a warped cardboard heart plastered to his chest — could spoil his day. He only blushed, and then smiled too widely and sat down on his bed. He could always take them to her on another visit, couldn't he? There were going to be lots of other visits. But while he was planning them he absently opened the box, and he took first one chocolate and then another and then a whole handful. They had begun to melt, and they stuck to the paper doily that covered them and left imprints on his palm, but they tasted wonderful and the sweetness seeped into every corner of him and soothed his stretched, strained nerves.

He knew how these thing worked. First you set up the courtship; he had just done that. Then there were certain requirements to be met — holding hands, a kiss — before he could propose. On television there were a lot of frills as well, people running through meadows together and pretending to be children at zoos and fairs and amusement parks, but he knew better than to try for anything like that. He wasn't the type. *She* wasn't the type. And after all, he had done very well so far, hadn't he? He had completed the first step without any problems, and now he felt more confident about what was left.

Only it turned out not to be so easy. For the next morning, when he had made a pot of percolated coffee and knocked at her room, she opened the door only halfway and it seemed as if some veil fell immediately across her face. "Yes?" she said.

Today she was dressed. (He had deliberately waited fifteen minutes later than yesterday.) Even Darcy was dressed. Then why did she seem so unwelcoming? "I just made some coffee I wondered if you'd like some," he said all in a rush.

"No, thank you, I don't drink coffee."

That possibility had not occurred to him. "Tea, then?" he said.

"No, thank you."

"Well, maybe you'd just like to have a glass of milk with me."

"I don't think so. I have a lot to do today."

He couldn't leave. He had promised himself he would see this through. "Please," he said, "I don't understand. Have I done something to offend you?"

Mary sighed and looked over her shoulder at Darcy, who was peacefully stacking dominoes on the rug. Then she stepped out of her room and shut the door behind her. She said, "Come into the parlor a minute, Mr. Pauling."

Yesterday she had called him Jeremy. He felt like someone deaf or blind, prevented by some handicap from picking up clues that were no doubt clear to everybody else. "Is it something I've said?" he asked, stumbling after her. "You see, I just have no inkling . . ."

She led him to the couch, where he sat down while she remained standing. Then he realized his mistake and jumped up again. "Oh, excuse me," he said.

"Mr. Pauling," said Mary, "I realize that I'm behind on my rent."

"Oh. Well, I thought we —"

"We had a talk about that yesterday. You said you wouldn't pressure me for it. But I never suspected that there were strings attached."

"Strings?" said Jeremy.

"Isn't that what this is all about?"

"I don't understand."

Mary looked at him. He had been trying to catch her eye, but now that he had it he seemed unable to face her. He was not used to dealing with angry women. He had never pictured Mary angry at all. He said, "This is so puzzling. I don't see —"

"Yesterday," said Mary, "as soon as it was clear I'd missed paying my rent, you came calling in my room and brought me flowers. Well, I didn't think anything of it at the time but then later I — and today! You come knocking again! Do you feel that now you have some hold over me? Because all I owe you is *money*, Mr. Pauling, and I will be happy to borrow elsewhere and pay you this minute and be out of your house tomorrow. Is that clear?"

"Oh, my goodness," Jeremy said. He lowered himself to the couch again. Horror curled over him like an icy film, followed by a rush of heat. He felt his face grow pink. "Oh, Mary. Mrs. Tell," he said. "I *never* meant to — why, I was just —" Now a picture came to him of exactly how he had looked to Mary Tell the day before. He heard the tentative mumble of his knuckles on her door, he saw his sickly, hopeful smile, beseeching her for everything as he stuck his bouquet under her chin. This was something he was never going to be able to put out of his mind; he knew it. He was going to go over and over it on a thousand sleepless nights, all of them spent alone, for a woman like Mary Tell would never in a million years give a thought to a man like him. He should have guessed that. He felt himself beginning to tremble, the final indignity. "Mr. Pauling?" Mary said.

"But I'm a *good* man," he said. "What I mean to say — why, I never even knew you owed me! *I* don't keep track of that money, the others just put it in the cookie jar."

"Cookie jar?"

If he spoke any more she would notice his voice was shaking.

"In the cookie jar, Mr. Pauling?"

"The cookie jar in the kitchen. Then I take it out to buy groceries whenever —" He gulped, a sound she must have heard three feet away. She came closer and bent over him, but he kept his head ducked. It was the worst moment he had ever lived through. He didn't see how it could possibly go on for so long. Couldn't she leave now? But no, he felt the sofa indenting as she settled down beside him. He saw the edge of her blue skirt, such a calm, soft blue that he felt a flood of pain for those few days when he had loved her and had some hope of her loving him back. "Jeremy," she said. "I feel just terrible about this. Won't you say you forgive me? I wasn't thinking straight. I'm going through a bad time just now and I must have —

Jeremy?" She leaned closer and took one of his hands. "Look at me a minute," she said.

Why not? It didn't mean a thing to him any more. He raised his eyes and found the perfect oval of her face level with his. The inner corners of her eyebrows were furrowed with concern. "Won't you accept my apology?" she said. He had to nod. Then he even smiled, because it had finally dawned on him what was happening: They had been discussing an issue as old-fashioned as Mary Tell herself, and here they were side by side holding hands in this second stage of their courtship.

Mornings now he woke feeling hopeful, and getting up was easier. He started being careful of his appearance. He began wearing a pen-and-pencil set in his shirt pocket — a sign of competence, he thought. He practiced smiling with his mouth shut, hiding a dark turmoil of bad teeth. In the bathroom mirror the thought of Mary hung like a mist between himself and his reflection. Her long cool fingers reached into his chest. He carried her image downstairs with him, treading gently as if it might break up and scatter like snowflakes in a paperweight. When the other boarders greeted him he sometimes failed to answer, but that had happened before and none of them thought anything of it.

Then why did this vision of Mary Tell always turn out to be wrong? Oh, not wrong in any concrete way. He had got her nose right, and the set of her head and the shape of her mouth. But when she entered the kitchen, tying an apron around her waist and smiling at Darcy's chatter, there was some slight difference in her which both disappointed and awed him. Her skin had a denser look and the planes of her face were flatter. Her manner of moving was more purposeful. In his mind she glided; in real life she stepped squarely on her heels. Every night he forgot that and every morning he had to learn it all over again.

In the beginning she used to make bacon and eggs for breakfast, but now their diet had changed. She and Darcy filled up on cold cereal. "We *always* have this," Darcy said. "I know, honey," said Mary, and then she told Jeremy, "Yesterday I heard of a job addressing envelopes. Do you think they'd let me do it at home? I'm going to see them today and ask, and if they say yes we'll never eat cornflakes again." But that job fell through, and so did the next one and the one after that, and they continued to eat cornflakes while Jeremy sat at the table with them trying to think up topics of conversation. He kept a glass of orange juice in front of him, although he never drank it. (It was impossible to swallow with Mary watching.) He rehearsed a hundred sentences offering help, what little he could manage: "Could I lend you some of the cookie jar money? Well, then, eggs? Just eggs?" But he never said any of them out loud. He was afraid to. Rinsing off their little stack of dishes Mary *bustled* so, as if she were daring him to feel sorry for her. Then she said, "All right, Miss Slowpoke, ready to go?" and she and Darcy would set off on their walk. Which was another change: in the beginning Mary waited for her friend to call before she went out. Now she went immediately after breakfast, and the few times the telephone rang it was never for her.

"Going on your walk?" Jeremy would say. "Well now. Have a good time." They passed through the house calling goodbyes, singing out greetings to Mr. Somerset, letting two doors slam behind them, ringing the air like a bell, and then all of a sudden the house would fall silent and the rooms would seem vacant and dead. The only sound was the creak of an old dry beam somewhere. A distant auto horn. Mr. Somerset's papery slippers shambling across the dining room floor.

Jeremy was like a man marooned on an island. Why had that taken him so many years to realize? He was surrounded on four sides by streets so flat and wide that he imagined he could drown in air just walking across them. Yet look, a four-year-old managed it without a thought! Oh, if it weren't for this handicap he could invite Mary Tell to a movie and then bring her home and kiss her outside her door as he had seen done on TV, and that would be the end of all his planning and worrying. It would be so simple! Instead, here it was August now and he had not taken one step toward kissing her and it began to look as if he never would.

Then one morning the telephone rang and no one was in the hall to answer it but Jeremy. Even before he picked up the receiver a knot of anxiety had settled low in his stomach. "Hello? Hello?" he said, and was answered by a voice he had not heard in weeks, but he recognized it instantly. "Mary Tell, please," said the cigarette-ad man.

"Oh! Well, I'll see," Jeremy said.

Then he went into the dining room and knocked on her door. "Someone wants you on the telephone," he called.

She took a minute to appear. She was already dressed, carrying her apron in her hand, and she looked startled. "Someone wants *me?*" she said. "Who is it?"

"Why, I believe it's your friend, the young man."

From behind her Darcy said, "Can I talk? If it's John can I talk?"

"No, you may *not*," Mary said. Jeremy had never heard her speak so sharply to Darcy. She said, "Keep her a minute, will you, Jeremy?" and walked off to the telephone. "Why can't *I* talk?" Darcy asked Jeremy.

"Oh, well . . ." said Jeremy. The knot in his stomach had grown larger. He backed into the dining room and sat down on a chair, limply, with his hands on his knees. "How are you today, Darcy?" he asked. Even to himself, his voice sounded foolish. He made himself smile at her. "When are you coming to my studio again? You haven't been all week."

But he was listening, meanwhile, to Mary out in the hall. She said, "No, no, I understand. You don't have to call *ever*, John. It's not as if you're obligated."

"But she always let me talk to him before," Darcy said.

"Maybe another day," said Jeremy. He tried a different smile. Mary said, "Look. I'm fine. *No* I don't need money."

"Shall we cut out paper dolls?" Jeremy asked Darcy.

"Not right now, Jeremy."

"You don't owe me anything, I'm managing fine. I'm fine. I still have some of what you lent me," Mary said. And then, "What's it to you how much is left? It was a *loan*, you don't have any business asking that. I'm planning to pay you back. I want to. As soon as I find a job I will."

"If I go and shout into the phone John will talk to me," Darcy said. "He likes me. I know he does."

"No, no, Darcy —"

But she was off, skating on her stocking feet into the hallway with Jeremy at her heels. From this close they could hear Mary's friend arguing or protesting or explaining, a thin violent squawk. "— for *Darcy's* sake," he said, and Darcy gave a little leap. "Hello *John!*" she shouted. "Hello *John!*" Mary held up the flat of her hand, but kept her face turned into the receiver. "All right," she said. "You win."

"Can you hear me, John?"

"Uh, Darcy," Jeremy said.

"All right," said Mary, "but it's a loan, and I want you to know that. I don't want any — Darcy! Look, John, it's hard to talk right now —"

Darcy was tugging at her mother's skirt, and Jeremy was stooped over trying to loosen her fingers. The squawk continued on the telephone, another form of tugging. Mary's skirt had the same cool, grainy feeling that her hands had had, that time on the couch. Why, after all, she was only a collection of textures. Her muscles slanted over her bones exactly as in his anatomical drawing class; her lips were yet another texture, otherwise no different than her fingers had been or this clutch of skirt in Darcy's scampering hands. "No, I mean this," Mary said. "I want you to mail it. *Don't* bring it. You are under no — John?"

She put the receiver down very slowly. "Oh, Mom, *I* wanted to talk," Darcy said. Then Jeremy straightened and looked into

Mary's face. Her expression was cheerful and she was even smiling slightly, but tears were running down her cheeks. "I'm sorry —" she said. She started back toward the bedroom, with Jeremy and Darcy stumbling over each other trying to follow. "You must think I make a habit of this," she said in her doorway. She turned, and Jeremy was so close behind her that before he thought, he had found the strength to lean forward on tiptoe and kiss the corner of her mouth. Then he took a step back, and she looked his way for a moment before her eyes seemed to focus on him. "Thank you, Jeremy," she said. "You are a very sweet man."

She wiped the tears away with the back of her hand, giving a little laugh at herself as if they embarrassed her. She shook out her apron and said, "Come along, Miss Chatterbox, let's get you some breakfast, shall we?" Then they went off toward the kitchen, leaving Jeremy smiling so hard that he could barely see. He thought he might just inflate and float away like a balloon at a birthday party.

In magazine cartoons, a suitor proposing marriage always knelt on the floor at his sweetheart's feet. Now, was that an accurate reflection of the way things were done? He suspected not. Nevertheless he kept picturing himself looking up at Mary from a kneeling position, finding her even more frightening at this angle — her sandals the largest part of her, her waist at eye level, the never-before-seen underside of her bosom and the white triangle of skin beneath her jaw. "I don't have much money," he should tell her (the speech owed to her father, he believed, but he had no idea who her father was). "I wouldn't be able to support you in very good style but at least it would be a *little* easier, I do have my pieces and a little from my mother and sometimes I win a contest and I always seem to have enough for groceries." He prepared himself for the way the hem of her dress would loom, and for the difficulty of judging her expression from so far beneath it. Yet every night he went to bed with nothing resolved, feeling thin and strained as if this balloon of hope he had become had been kept too fully inflated for too long a time. He dreamed of losing things — unnamed objects in small boxes, the roof of his house, pieces of art that he would never be able to re-create. He woke feeling anxious, and over and over again read the index card tacked to the windowsill beside him.

In his imagination this proposal always took place outdoors somewhere, although of course that would be too public. Could he be thinking of a park? The nearest park was several blocks from home. He pushed away the outdoor images and in the mornings, while he sat with his orange juice and she poured cornflakes, he tried to think of some natural way to lead in to what was on his mind. He couldn't. Mary talked about her daughter and the weather and library books, nothing more personal. "Now Darcy is shooting out of all her clothes. I've never seen a child grow the way she does. I thought as soon as I got a job I would buy some material and borrow Mrs. Jarrett's sewing machine, but sewing has never been my strong point and I'm not at all sure that I —" How could he bring love into a conversation like that? She gave him no openings. He sometimes thought that she might be sending him some silent warning, telling him not to ask even the simplest things that occurred to him: Where do you come from? Why are you here? Who was your husband? What are your plans?

"At home Darcy used to *beg* for cornflakes," Mary said once. "I've never seen a child so contrary."

"Where was that?" Jeremy asked her.

"What?"

"Where was your home?"

"Oh, well — and now she wants bacon and eggs, wouldn't you know? I believe she just thinks up these things to devil me."

Jeremy didn't press her. He contented himself with the surface that she presented to the world, and it was only inside him that the questions continued. What happened to your husband? Why did you cry with that man John? What is his significance?

Will you marry me?

Now each morning that he failed to propose he saw them to the door, tagging after them in the hope that somewhere along the way — in the dining room, the hall, the vestibule — he might gather his courage. He took to going out on the steps and waving after them. "Goodbye! Goodbye! Have a nice walk!" Turning back afterward was worse than being left in the kitchen. He always felt oppressed by the sudden dark coolness as he stepped inside. He started accompanying them farther — to the second house, to the third. Maybe, given time, he could follow Mary all the way off his island. Gradually: wasn't that the key? Oh, if there were any god he believed in, it was gradualness! If people would only let him go at things his own way, step by step, never requiring these sudden leaps that seem to happen in the outside world! But every day he was overtaken by some magnetic force that seemed to affect only him. It dragged him back with a tug at his spine; it caused him to slow and then to halt, damp with exhaustion. "Goodbye! Goodbye! Have a nice walk!" Mary and Darcy waved and grew smaller. They separated cheerfully at the approach of total strangers, they talked aloud without fear of being heard, they crossed the wide street against the light. Dogs with enormous grinning mouths sniffed at Mary's skirt and she never even noticed. Oh, he had undertaken too much. He could never keep up with a woman like that. He turned and trudged homeward, stumbling over cracks in the sidewalk and muttering words of encouragement to himself, and before he started the day's work he had to lie on the couch in his studio a while catching his breath and trying to still the twitching of his leg muscles.

It seemed to him that his sisters were always calling him on the telephone nowadays. "What are you doing, Jeremy, why haven't we heard from you? Are you getting out more? Are you eating right?" They no longer phoned only on Sundays but occasionally on weekday evenings as well, on Saturdays and in the middle of lunch. Then one morning they called so early that he was still in the kitchen with Mary and Darcy. "Jeremy, honey, this is Laura," he heard, and although he had always felt close to Laura he was conscious now of a sudden impatience tightening his fingers on the receiver. In the kitchen Darcy said something and Mary laughed. There was no telling what he was missing. "Is there something — what seems to be the matter?" he asked her.

"Matter? I was just worried about you, dear. You haven't answered our last letter."

"But I don't believe I received any letter this week," he told her. Then, too late, he remembered the flowered envelope that he had absently stuck in his shirt pocket on the way upstairs the other day. It was probably in the bathroom hamper. "He says he didn't *get* any letter," Laura told Amanda. To Jeremy she said, "Honestly, they can fly to Europe but they can't get a simple note from Richmond to Baltimore. Well, I knew there was *some* explanation. Now here is Amanda to say a few words. Amanda?"

"How do you seem to be getting along, Jeremy," Amanda's voice said very close to his ear.

"Oh, fine, thank you."

"I *told* Laura there was no need to call but she said she had a funny feeling, she gets them more and more these days. Any fool should know you can't trust the U.S. mail."

Jeremy stood up straighter. It always occurred to him, when talking on the telephone, that to people at the other end of the line he was invisible. Except for the thin thread of his voice he did not even exist. "Jeremy!" Amanda said sharply, and he said, "Yes, I'm here" — reassuring both himself and her.

"Labor Day is coming up, Jeremy."

"Oh, yes, is it?"

"Maybe you could make the trip to see us."

"Well, Amanda . . ."

"Now I don't want to go over three minutes here but I'm sending you a train schedule. Let's not hear any excuses, Jeremy. Why, you'll just *love* travel, once you catch on to it. And you don't want to spend your life just sitting home now, do you. Mother wouldn't have approved of that at all, she would have wanted you to get out and enjoy yourself."

He knew that his sisters were all that was left of the world he had grown up with, his only remaining connection with his parents, but sometimes when Amanda spoke of their mother it seemed she meant someone he didn't even know in passing — someone stern and rigid, not his own sweet-faced mother with her soft, sad smile. "Well, you see," he said, "I do try to —"

"I have to run, Jeremy. Do please answer our letters, you know how Laura worries."

"All right, Amanda."

He laid the receiver carefully in its cradle. There was a damp mark where his hand had been. He went back to the kitchen and found Mary just sponging Darcy's face, with breakfast finished. He had missed everything. His chances were over until tomorrow. "I'm going to the grocery," Mary told him. "Do you want anything?"

His despair was so enormous that it gave him courage. He said, "Oh, why, several things. Perhaps I should come along."

Mary only nodded. She was frowning at a stain on Darcy's collar. "Oh, Darcy, look at you, it's your last clean dress," she said.

"I don't care about an old stain."

"Well, I do. Come along then."

Words kept rearranging themselves in Jeremy's head. May I have the honor —? Could you possibly consider —? Is it asking too much for you to marry me? But once they were descending the front steps the only conversation he could think of was an exaggerated squint toward the sun, implying a remark about the weather. Mary didn't look up. She was reading her grocery list. "I'm going to get a gumball," Darcy said. "Am I going to get a gumball, Mom? I'm going to get a penny for the gumball machine."

"I wasn't aware they had a gumball machine," said Jeremy.

"Oh yes," Darcy said. "Perry's does."

Would you think me forward if I —?

Perry's? Why, Perry's was two blocks away; it was where his mother used to go for soupbones. And no sooner had it hit him than sure enough, they came to Dowd's grocery and passed it by, with neither Mary nor Darcy giving it a glance. Jeremy did. He gazed longingly at the crates of oranges and peaches and pears slanted toward him behind the fly-specked plate glass window. The tissue paper they nestled in seemed a particularly beautiful shade of green. He thought with love of Mrs. Dowd's gnarled old hands spreading the tissue just enough, rescuing a runaway peach and setting it back in place with a little grand-motherly pat. Mary and Darcy walked on. "Wait!" he said. "I mean — have you ever tried Dowd's?"

"They're more expensive," Mary said. She went on studying her list. Darcy took Jeremy's hand in both of hers and swung on it — a clamp on his index finger, another on his little finger. What could he do? He set one foot in front of the other, dog-gedly, barely managing each step. For Mary Tell's sake he was slaying dragons, and yet to keep her respect it was necessary that she never even guess it. He wiped his face on his sleeve. They came to the end of the block, where a red light stopped them. Cars whizzed back and forth, but what he was most afraid of was the street itself. Then the light turned green. "Wait!" he said again. Mary looked up, in the act of putting her grocery list in her purse.

"Could we — I mean I don't believe I —"

"Hurry," Darcy said, "we'll miss the light."

He stepped off the curb. All the comfort he had was Darcy's grip on his hand, but now Mary said, "Darcy, don't *swing* on people. How often have I told you that?" One of Darcy's hands fell away; only his index finger was secure. He reached out blindly and found Mary's arm, the crook of her elbow, which he hung onto as he had seen men do on the late show. Did she notice that it was she supporting him and not the other way around? "I certainly wish the price of tomatoes would go down," Mary said.

Then they had reached the other sidewalk. The air on this block was different. He could have told it with his eyes shut. It was hotter, more exposed, and old Mrs. Carraway's wind chimes were not tinkling. What was that flat-faced cement building? He didn't like the look of it. He noticed that the rowhouses ran only in twos and threes, which gave the block a broken-up look. A mean-eyed woman watched him from her front stoop. He saw a commercial printer's whose black and gold sign must have been here years ago, when he was a boy walking to school. Its sudden emergence in his memory made him feel strange. He lowered his eyes again. Pretend this is only a corridor leading off from the vestibule. Pretend it is just an unusually long room. It will all be over in a while.

Then they reached Perry's. "*Here* we are," said Mary. He looked up to find a window full of dead things stacked in pyramids — tinned vegetables, Nabisco boxes, paper towels. No fruit. "I'll wait outside," he said.

"Outside?"

"I'll just — I do my shopping at Dowd's."

Mary seemed about to ask him a question, but then Darcy said, "Can I have my penny now?"

"What penny?" Mary said.

"You said you would give me a penny for the gumball machine. You *said* you would. You said —"

"Oh, for mercy's sake," said Mary, opening her pocketbook. "Here." Then she went in, and Jeremy chose a place outside the door. First he watched the street, but the unfamiliar buildings opposite made him feel worse. He looked behind him, toward the glass door, and saw Darcy just coming out with a gumball. "Look. Pink," she said. "My favorite color."

"Is that right?" said Jeremy. He was glad to see her. He turned outward again, so that he was facing the street. Darcy stood beside him. "They have charms and things too," she said. "You can see them in the machine but they never come out. Do you think I might get one someday?"

"Perhaps so," Jeremy said.

"Or are they just to fool people. You think that's what it is? You think they're just trying to get your pennies from you?"

Jeremy had a terrible thought. He felt that he might become marooned beside Perry's Grocery. How would he ever get home again? He imagined himself dipping the toe of one shoe into the street, then drawing it out and turning away, unable to cross. "I'm sorry, I just can't," he would have to say. He thought of the time he had climbed the crape myrtle tree in his back yard when he was three. He had climbed only to the first fork but then had found it impossible to get back down. Every time he tried, his hair stood on end and the soles of his feet started tingling. "Let him stay," his father said. "*He'll* come down." Then at night, when he still hadn't managed it, his father took three long strides to the tree and lifted him off roughly, one arm around his waist, causing Jeremy to scream in that single dizzying moment before his feet touched solid ground again. Now Mary would take him in hand, nudge him out, coax him into one step after another. "Come on, you can do it, you'll see, when you get to the other side you'll look back and laugh at how easy it was." Only he wouldn't. He would have to back away, and now he was too big to be carried bodily. He imagined spending the rest of his life on this new island, exposed for all the world to see, propped against the wall like a target. "Would you like half of my gumball, Jeremy?" Darcy asked him.

"No, thank you, Darcy," he said.

"I don't have a knife, but I could *bite* it in half."

Dread rose in him like a flood in a basement, starting in his feet and rapidly filling his legs, his stomach, his chest, seeping out to his fingertips. Its cold flat surface lay level across the top of his throat. He swallowed and felt it tip and right itself. Nausea came swooping over him, and he buckled at the knees and slid downward until he was seated flat on the sidewalk with his feet sticking out in front of him. "*Jeremy,* you silly," Darcy said, but when he couldn't smile at her or even raise his eyes he said, "Jeremy? Jeremy?" She went screaming into the grocery store; her voice pierced all the cotton that seemed to be wrapped around his head. "Mom, come quick, Jeremy's all squashed down on the sidewalk!" Then he was surrounded by anxious feet nosing in upon him — Darcy's sneakers, Mary's sandals, and a pair of stubby loafers almost covered by a long bloody apron. "It's the heat," the apron said. Mary said, "Jeremy? Are you ill?"

"Sick," he whispered.

She set a rustling paper bag beside him, bent to lay a hand on his forehead and then straightened up. Her sandals were the largest thing about her. The hem of her skirt was so close he could see the stitches, he saw the underside of her bosom and the triangle below her jaw. "Will you marry me?" he asked her.

She laughed. "No, but I'll see you home and into bed," she said. "Can you stand? You need some air." And she raised his head herself, and then propped him while he got to his feet. She said, "Walk a ways, now. It'll clear your head. Here, take this." From her grocery bag she brought out a navy blue box, and while he swayed against her she tore the wrapper off and handed him a cinnamon graham cracker. "Sometimes it helps to eat a little something," she said.

"No, no."

"Try it, Jeremy."

He only clutched it in his hand. He felt that opening his mouth would cause his last remaining strength to pour out of him. Inch by inch he headed homeward, shaky but upright, leaning on Mary's arm. The bloody apron receded behind them. Darcy danced ahead. They came closer to the street while Jeremy prayed continuously to the traffic light: oh, please turn red, turn red, let me at least have time to get my bearings. But it stayed an evil green, and Mary led him without a pause off the curb, across a desert of cement, up the other side. They were home. They were on his own block. He straightened and let out a long slow breath. Mary said, "You're just like Darcy, whenever you don't eat breakfast you get sick to your stomach. Isn't that what happened?"

"I meant it seriously, I asked you to marry me," Jeremy said.

"But you both say no, you couldn't eat a thing, you don't want a . . ."

She stopped walking. She turned and stared at him across a silence that grew painful, while Jeremy waited with his head down. "Oh, Jeremy," she said finally. "Why, thank you, Jeremy. But you see, I *can't* get married."

"You can't?"

"My husband won't give me a divorce."

"Oh, I see," Jeremy said.

"But it was sweet of you to ask, and I want you to know how flattered I am."

"That's all right," Jeremy said.

He stood there a minute more, and then they both began walking again. Up ahead, Darcy leaped and skipped and twirled. Her hair made him think of something metallic falling through the air, catching the sunlight and ducking it and catching it once more. He fixed his eyes on it and stumbled along. When they were within sight of home he lifted his cracker without thinking and took a bite. Mary was right; it helped. His head cleared. His stomach righted itself. He felt cinnamon flowering out of his mouth, taking away the tinny taste, leaving his breath as pure as a child's. Like a child he let himself be led home while all his attention was directed toward the cracker. Crunching sounds filled his head and tiny sharp crumbs sprinkled his shirt front. He felt limp and exhausted, and something like relief was turning his bones so watery that he could have lain down right there and gone to sleep on the sidewalk.

Now he no longer came downstairs while Mary was making breakfast. He lay in bed late and rose by degrees, often sitting against his pillow for as much as an hour and staring vacantly out his window. The index card lost its tack and fell behind his bed; he let it lie. He sat in a sagging position, smoothing his sheet over and over across his chest, and if he wanted a change of scenery he raised his eyes from the screened lower portion of the window, which was open, to the closed upper portion where two sets of cloudy panes dulled the morning sunlight. Maybe someday he would wash them. The floors had a frame of dirt spreading out from the baseboards, thinning only where his traffic pattern had worn the dust away. There were little chips of paper everywhere, some so old that they seemed to have become embedded in the wood. If the light was right he could look out toward his studio and find a long glinting red hair snagged on one of the floorboards. It had belonged to a student from two years ago, whose name he had forgotten. He neither swept the hair away nor made any special effort to keep it. It was just there, something he registered in the mornings without considering the possibility that there was anything he might do about it.

When he had finally struggled out of bed there was the bathroom to face — a chilly place even in summer, with all its fixtures crazed and rust-stained and the swinging naked light-bulb pointing out every pore of his skin in the watery mirror. He shaved for hours. He cut one small path across his cheek and then stood looking into his own eyes until it occurred to him to lift his razor again. Even before the mirror he did not bother rearranging his expression. His muscles sagged and the soft skin of his throat pouched outward. He noticed, and disliked what he saw, but only in the detached way that he might dislike a painting or some scene that he witnessed on the street. Then when he was tired of shaving he left, often without rinsing off the last traces of soap, so that his skin felt itchy and dry. He wrapped himself in a bathrobe and put on his crocheted slippers and shuffled into his studio, where he sat on a stool for a long time looking at his latest piece. Too many browns. Not enough distinctions. More and more now he was adding in actual objects — thumbtacks and washers and bits of string and wood, separating the blur of colored papers. Brian hadn't seen these yet. Jeremy didn't care whether he saw them or not. He pulled off a piece of twine that was in the wrong corner, leaving a worm of dried white paste behind. He dropped it to the floor and then noticed, beside one leg of his stool, the tin top off a box of cough lozenges, and by the time he had figured where to paste that he had forgotten about dressing. He snipped things apart and fitted things together. He rummaged through the clutter in a bureau drawer, meanwhile holding his bathrobe together by its frayed sash. Till Mrs. Jarrett's clopping heels mounted laboriously to the second floor and she called up to the third, "Mr. Pauling? I don't see your dishes here, have you not had breakfast? We're getting worried about you. *Please* come." If he were too absorbed he merely shuffled his feet on the floor, showing he hadn't died in his sleep. Other times he sighed and laid his scissors down and went to his bedroom for clothes. Most of his clothes seemed to be falling apart nowadays. He kept having to throw away shirts with long rips and trousers with the zippers broken and shorts with the elastic gone, but he didn't bother sending to Sears for more. He tossed them in the wastebasket almost gladly. Later he would listen with a sense of satisfaction while the garbage men came clanging trashcans and bore his belongings away with them. It felt good to be done with things. He thought of the New Year's Eves he had sat up for — the relief that came from putting away another year and brushing off his hands and knowing that there were twelve months less to get through. Or of all his life — the hundreds of memories he had closed the files on, the years assigned to him that he had dutifully endured, waiting to reach the bottom of the pile.

His breakfast was other people's lunch. Mrs. Jarrett ate in the dining room with everything just right, dishes set on one of his mother's linen placemats and a matching napkin in her lap. Mr. Somerset wolfed a lacy fried egg straight from the skillet. Miss Vinton, home from the bookstore on her lunch hour, read publishers' brochures while she ate health bread at the kitchen table. "There's a new Klee in, Mr. Pauling," she might say, without looking up. "I put it on the sideboard."

"Oh, why, thank you, Miss Vinton."

He ate whatever took the least trouble — a box of day-old doughnuts or a can of cold soup. After every mouthful he wiped his hands carefully on the knees of his trousers before turning a page of the Klee. It would have to go back with Miss Vinton, spic and span, before her boss noticed it was missing. The cover of the book was a glossy white, promising him something new and untouched and wonderful. At the beginning there was a long jumble of words, a résumé of Paul Klee's life, which Jeremy skipped. What did he care about that? He plunged into the pictures; he drank them up, he felt how dry and porous he was, thirsty for things to look at. At every page he wanted to pause and spend hours, even when he had seen the pictures before in other books, but he felt a pull also to turn to the next one quickly so that he would be sure to finish in time. Sometimes he said, "Miss Vinton, I wonder if I might —?" "Oh, why surely, Mr. Pauling," she said, refolding the bread wrapper. "I can always take it back tomorrow. Mr. Mack won't notice." She had never once hurried him or shown any concern over his handling of the books, although Jeremy knew that Mr. Mack was unreasonably strict about such things. And for all of August, when Jeremy's life seemed duller and sadder than he had ever noticed before, she managed to bring a new book for him almost every day, as if she guessed that he needed comfort. Klee, a collection of impressionists, Miró, Renoir. A book of American primitives whose dollhouse landscapes and lack of perspective filled him with a kind of homesickness. If only he could just step inside them! If only he lived in a place where a man could go any distance and yet never grow smaller! Miss Vinton brought him Braque, a man he disliked. He sat through her lunch hour testing the anxiety that each picture called forth in him, the discomfort caused by some clumsiness in the shapes. Years before, when he was in high school, an art teacher explaining cubism had made Jeremy's class copy one of Braque's paintings line for line. Jeremy had felt sick all the while he was doing it. It seemed that he might melt away to nothing, letting himself get absorbed into another man's picture that way. Now he found the picture again — a still life involving a musical instrument — and stared at it until he couldn't stand it any more and had to turn the page. "Would you care to keep it till tomorrow?" asked Miss Vinton, rising to rinse her dishes. "You seem to like him."

"What? No, no," Jeremy said, "please, I don't want it, take it back with you." Then he was ashamed of his rudeness, and he blushed and looked up at her. In the summertime, stripped of her lavender cardigan, her bony freckled arms gave her a vulnerable look. White strings stood out along the inside of her wrist when she turned the faucet off. "But I'm grateful to you for bringing the book," Jeremy said. "I'm sorry, I didn't mean —"

"Oh, *that's* all right, I never much liked him myself."

She turned, cheerful as ever, to hang up her dishtowel and take her purse from the table. Meanwhile Mrs. Jarrett ate fruit cup in the dining room, the ladylike clink of her spoon sounding at perfectly spaced intervals. Mr. Somerset put his skillet down silently and gravely, making certain that it sat in the exact center of the circle of the burner, ready to be used at another meal. Was there anyone gentler than old people? Could he ever feel as much at rest as he did sitting in this triangle of muted gray voices?

Then here came the second shift, as if in answer — Darcy slamming the door and pounding down the hallway with a

bucket full of dandelions, Mary laughing and calling out warn-
ings and threats and promises, and maybe if it were a weekend
Howard's high-pitched whistle and the squeak of his sneakers.
"Where's the milk I left here?" "Who wants a dandelion?"
"You're going to bump *into* someone, Darcy!" — which Darcy
would almost surely do, as if she had to depend on someone else
to break her speed for her. *Flunf!* into Miss Vinton's middle.
"Oh, Darcy, say you're sorry." "No harm done," said Miss Vinton, and Darcy spun on through the kitchen, ending up with
her arms around Howard. "Howard, make me flapjacks,
Howard." "Let him be, Darcy." "Oh, now," Howard said to
Mary, "you're just jealous because I won't make *you* flapjacks."
Then the kitchen splintered into bits of laughter, and Miss Vinton smiled and left while Mr. Somerset turned slowly from the
stove, dazed by the laughter, baffled by frivolity. "What?" he
said. Mary folded Darcy into the circle of her arms and said,
"Milk or apple juice, young lady?" "Both," said Darcy. "Or
wait. Is apple juice what I want?" She turned toward Jeremy as
if she expected him to answer, but Jeremy was looking at Mary.
He saw the curve of her cheek against Darcy's tow hair; he
noticed how her nearly unarched eyebrows calmed and rested
him.

Why hadn't he been granted the one thing in life he ever
hoped for?

At the beginning of September, Darcy started kindergarten
and Mary found a job. It was something she could do at home:
making argyle socks on a knitting machine. In the morning
while Darcy was at school Mary worked alone in her room, but
Darcy returned at lunchtime and was in and out all the rest of
the day, leaving the door open behind her, and the sock
machine soon became part of the household. It consisted of a
circle of vertical needles, which first had to be threaded one by
one. Threading was the time-consuming part. Then Mary
cranked a large handle a prescribed number of times, after

which she paused to rethread in another color. Jeremy, passing her doorway, had a glimpse of her huddled in a C-shape and frowning at metal eyes that seemed far too close together. She reminded him of old photographs of life in a sweatshop. But when the threading was done she could straighten up and stand back, and the cranking was so easy that sometimes she let Darcy do it while she herself counted the strokes. Numbers rang out and floated through the house — "Thirty-six! Thirty-seven!" After the tense silence of the threading, her voice and the circular rattle of machinery seemed like an outburst of joy. Wherever he was, Jeremy would raise his head to listen, and he noticed that the whole house appeared to relax at those times and the other boarders grew suddenly talkative, as if they too had held tense during the threading.

At the end of her first week of work, Mary packed the completed socks in a cardboard carton. She left Darcy with Mrs. Jarrett and caught a bus to the factory, where she was supposed to deliver them. "Why can't I come too?" Darcy asked. "Because it wouldn't be any fun," Mrs. Jarrett told her. "The place where Mommy is going is the factory section, all nasty and dirty." Jeremy felt something shrink in him. As if her absence were one long threading period, he held himself rigid in a parlor chair, scarcely breathing, silently turning the pages of a book of old masters that his mother had given him. "Goodness, don't you have anything to do?" Mrs. Jarrett asked once. "I thought Saturday your students came." Jeremy looked up, still turning pages. He had lost his last student a month ago and no others had called yet, but before he could put all this into words his thoughts trailed off again and he forgot to answer.

Mary returned just before lunch, bringing a new carton of yarn. When Darcy heard she came running out of the kitchen with Mrs. Jarrett close behind, and Jeremy stood up holding his book to his stomach. He thought that now the shrunken feeling would leave him, but it didn't. Mary's face was gray and her shoulders sagged. "How's our career woman?" Mrs. Jarrett asked, clapping her hands together.

"Oh well, I'm all right."

"You seem a little tired."

"I had to wait in line a while," Mary said. "There are a lot of other people doing this work."

"Is that right? And just think, I never even heard of it before. Did you meet anybody interesting?"

"Oh, trash mostly. Just, you know. Just trash." She set her carton on the coffee table and sat down. "I didn't make as much money as I thought I would," she said.

"Now be sure they pay you what they owe, you hear?"

Jeremy, back in his armchair now, kept nodding his head to show that he agreed. He felt as tired and sad as Mary. He wanted to offer her something — a cup of coffee? She didn't drink coffee. In his mother's old books a rich gentleman would come now to rescue Mary from life in the sweatshop, but Jeremy was the only gentleman present and he wasn't rich and he didn't believe that Mary had even noticed he was in the room. She spoke solely to Mrs. Jarrett. She said, "Oh, they paid me what they owed. But I had made a few mistakes, and also I'm still slow. Some of these people just whip them out by the dozen, but I don't. I don't know why. I thought I was going so *fast*. I thought I could make up the rent and the grocery and Darcy's school clothes, all in just a few hours a day."

"Now, now," said Mrs. Jarret. "Give yourself time."

Jeremy went on nodding. He kept his eyes fixed on the label at the end of the yarn box — a rectangle of glaring yellow, a color he had always disliked. The brightness of it made his eyes ache. He imagined himself winning twenty-five thousand dollars from some soap company and offering it to her, watching her brow slowly smooth and lighten as she looked down and saw what he had put into her hands. "No, no," he would tell her, "no strings. You don't even have to be my friend, just please don't thread those needles any more . . ." Yet if she had that much money, wouldn't she leave him?

Well, but hadn't she left him already? Had she ever really been there?

"Now can we have our ice cream?" Darcy said.

She had been promised a treat. Mary had told her she would come home rich. Mrs. Jarrett said, "Not yet, Darcy, let Mommy rest a while," but Mary said, "No, I'm all right. Let's go." She picked up her pocketbook and they went out the front door. This time there were no slams, no voices calling back and forth outside. The house felt the same when they were out as when they were in, bleak and dark and tired. Mrs. Jarrett settled with a sigh onto the creaking springs of the couch. Jeremy turned a page and smoothed the edges of a Rubens. "It's a shame, it's just a shame," Mrs. Jarrett said. "Do you think they'll have to go on welfare?"

The word stabbed him. He looked up, open-mouthed.

"And she's bright as a button. I don't care what you say. A high school diploma isn't everything."

"Welfare?" Jeremy said.

But Mrs. Jarrett was talking to her needlework.

"I said, 'What you want is a husband, my dear.' 'I do, don't I,' she said, and just laughed, didn't take me seriously, but I meant what I said. Now I don't know what happened there, widowed or divorced or what, but she is a *young woman* still and on top of that she has that child. Have you noticed how out of hand that child has gotten? She used to be a real little lady. She needs a father, and you can tell it by the number of times that she says a thing over again. Shows she isn't listened to enough, her mother has worries on her mind and can't pay attention. Not that I blame her, of course, I realize what a —"

Jeremy blinked down at the Rubens, a fat naked blond lady laughing. He felt that Mrs. Jarrett's words were twining around him like vines, rooting in the sad darkness inside him. The fat lady reminded him of a student he had once had, a girl named

Sally Ann something who had wanted to learn portrait painting. She weighed two hundred pounds; she had told him so herself. She seemed proud of it. Once she asked him, "Would you like a nude model? I could do it." And then she had come very close and laid a hand on his arm, smiling at him but looking, for some reason, only at his mouth. "No, no," he had said. He was unprepared. He backed off, shaking his head, and stumbled over a tin can full of brushes. "No, that's all right, I don't paint at all, really." But afterwards he had lain awake regretting his answer, and Sally Ann, whom he had not liked, gained importance in his mind and he began to see that there could be something compelling about a person who was dimpled all over. Only the next time she came to the studio he found that he still disliked her, and he kept himself at a distance even though she never offered again to be his model. Then what happened? Did she stop coming? He couldn't remember. He stared down at the Rubens, who laughed directly at him with her eyelids lowered, and he felt some sort of wasted feeling, as if he were a very old man realizing for the first time how little was left to him.

". . . and then my very own sister was married four times," said Mrs. Jarrett. "Well, some claimed that was carrying things too far, but I don't know. I don't know that I blame her at all, to tell the truth. We do need someone to lean on. I imagine I'll spend the rest of my life feeling naked on my street side every time I take a walk, and I am sixty-four now and been a widow longer than a wife."

Jeremy sank lower in his chair, letting the book fall shut, and closed his eyes. He kept them closed for so long that Mrs. Jarrett thought he had gone to sleep. Anyway, she suspected he had not been listening.

In the middle of the night he woke with the feeling that he had just heard his name called, but he found it was a dream. He couldn't get to sleep again. First he was cold, and he had to kneel in his bed and tug the window shut. Then he discovered he had a headache. He felt his way to the bathroom, found an aspirin tin, and washed two tablets down with a mouthful of lukewarm water from the faucet. In the mirror his silhouette was gilt-edged with moonlight. He studied how his shoulders sloped. He reminded himself of a low hill. There seemed to be no good reason to move any more, even to go back to bed. He stood rooted at the sink. Then far below him he heard a whirring sound, so faint he might have imagined it. He cocked his head, trying to place its source. With his hands stretched before him like a sleepwalker he guided himself out of the bathroom and into his studio, toward the open rear window, where the sound became louder. Even there he took a minute to identify it: the cranking of Mary's sock machine. He placed both hands on the windowsill and lowered his head, forming a clear image of her in some long flowing flannel nightgown, a shawl around her shoulders, working away by the light of a smoky lantern. Then he turned and went back to his bedroom.

Still in the dark, he opened drawers and slid hangers down his closet rod and rummaged through his shoebag. He found the one dress shirt he possessed, easily recognizable in its crackling cellophane envelope from the laundry. It was limp and sleazy and the collar was frayed, but he thought it would do. He knotted a tie, fumbling a little, trying to remember the complicated set of motions learned from Mr. Somerset's predecessor many years before. Then his suit — a three-piecer, ordered by mail back in the fifties but it still fit fairly well. Socks that might or might not match — he couldn't tell for sure and it seemed important not to turn on the light. Pinchy black shoes, also mail-order. A handkerchief tucked in his breast pocket the way his mother had taught him. Then back in front of the bathroom mirror he combed his hair, puffing up the little moonlit cloud skimming his scalp. He set the comb down on the edge of the sink and walked very slowly out of the room and toward the stairs. Every step made him sicker, but he didn't let himself feel it.

All the doors on the second floor were closed and dark. The only sound was a ragged snore from Mr. Somerset's room. On the first floor, street lights shining in picked up the shapes of the furniture but not its colors. Everything was a different shade of velvety gray, like what he had imagined a color-blind man must see. Jeremy had often tried to picture color-blindness — the worst affliction he could imagine next to blindness itself — and now, as if this were the only reason he had dressed up and come downstairs, he stood for a while letting his eyes blur and swim. Then the whirring sound started up again. He straightened his shoulders and passed through the parlor and into the dining room, where a knife blade of light shone beneath Mary's door. His first knock was not heard, but at the second knock the machine stopped. There was a moment of silence. Then, "Is someone there?" she asked.

"It's me, it's Jeremy."

"Jeremy?"

"I'm sorry to bother you at this —"

The doorknob rattled, so loudly and so close to him that he started. Light flooded the dining room and screwed his eyes up, and Mary stood before him in her blue dress with her hair still knotted as if this were daytime. "Was I disturbing you?" she asked him. "I thought while Darcy was sleeping I might turn out a few extra pairs."

"No, no."

Darcy lay sprawled in the double bed, taking up more than her share of it. She was shielded from the light by a blue paper Woolworth's bag that Mary had fitted over the lamp bulb. Now that Jeremy's eyes were adjusting he saw that the room was actually dim. He couldn't imagine how anyone would be able to thread a needle here. "I should have thought," he said. "You don't have to keep the machine in your bedroom, you can set it up anywhere. No one will mind. I didn't guess that you would be doing this while Darcy was asleep, you see —"

He whispered, taking care not to wake Darcy, but Mary spoke in a normal tone. "Why, that's very nice of you, Jeremy," she said, "but I don't believe it bothers her. She's a very sound sleeper." They both looked at Darcy, who seemed pale and waxy, with her eyes sealed and her arms and legs still for once. "Thank you for thinking of it, though," Mary said, turning back and giving him a bright, social smile. She thought that was what he had come for — to offer her space. She expected him to go now. "Maybe I'll quit for tonight anyway," she said. "I do feel a little tired."

"But nobody *knows* you're still married," Jeremy said suddenly.

She stopped smiling.

"They think you're widowed, or divorced. *They* don't know you're not free to remarry."

"Jeremy, really I —"

"Please listen. That's all I'm asking, if you say no I won't ever trouble you again. Listen. You see how well you fit in here. Sometimes we have had new boarders come in one day and leave the next, they just don't seem to like it. But you didn't do that. You've stayed a whole season with us."

"Yes, but you see I really didn't —"

"You fit in here. Everybody wants you to stay. And you know it has a lot of advantages, kitchen privileges and Mrs. Jarrett babysits. As far as money goes, why, I do make a little money from time to time, not very much I know but enough so that you could stop knitting argyles, and besides Darcy needs a father, they say she's getting out of hand without one —"

"*Who* says that?" Mary asked, so loudly that Darcy stirred and murmured.

"Mrs. Jarrett does."

"Well, I'm very surprised at her."

"So this is what I was considering," Jeremy said. "Couldn't we just *pretend* to be married?"

Mary stared at him.

"Oh, no, please don't be angry," he told her, stumbling to get the words out. "I know how it sounds. But you see, to me it *would* be marriage. It isn't as if there were any other way we could do it. We could go out one morning all dressed up and then come in and tell the others we'd been married at City Hall. That's all we'd have to do. Then we would be married in the eyes of everyone we know, and I would take care of you and you would start another life instead of going along on tag ends the way you are now, you could give all your time to Darcy and have more children if you wanted and never have to leave them to go out and work in sweatshops —"

"Jeremy, dear," Mary said, "I'm sure you are saying all this with the best of intentions —"

"I am," he said sadly. He understood now that she would refuse, but still he had to go on. "I am proposing, not propositioning. I mean only the deepest respect," he told her, and he looked up to find her nearly smiling, no longer so severe but kind-faced and amused, gently shaking her head. "Besides," he said, beginning to mumble, "I love you."

"Thank you, Jeremy. I do appreciate it."

"What hope do you have for a better life, if you keep on saying no to everything new?"

But he was speaking mainly to himself now, offering himself consolation, and he had already turned to go. He saw the dining room lit into color from Mary's doorway, a clump of dusty strawflowers turning orange on the table. Then her face appeared in his mind as it had looked at the moment of his turning — the smile fading, the eyes suddenly darker and more thoughtful. He turned back again. Mary took a breath, and he knew from the sudden shock and panic flooding through him that she was about to say yes.

John Updike

———

from

Marry Me

from

The Wait

JERRY WAS A designer and animator
of television commercials, and the State Department had hired
his company to create a series of thirty-second spots plugging
freedom in underdeveloped countries, and he was the inter-
mediary for the project. From their first trip Sally remembered
the section of the State Department that could find him. "He's
not a regular employee," she explained. "He's just in town for
two days."

"We've found him, Miss. Who shall I say is calling, please?"

"Sally Mathias."

"Miss Sally Mathias, Mr. Conant."

Some electric noises shuffled. His voice laughed harshly. "Hi
there, you crazy Miss Mathias."

"Am I crazy? I think I am. Sometimes I look at myself and
think, very calmly, *You nut.*"

"Where are you, at home?"

"Sweetie, can't you tell? I'm here. I'm at the airport."

"My God, you really did come, didn't you? This is wild."

"You're mad at me."

He laughed, postponing reassuring her. And when he spoke,
it was all in questions. "How can I be mad at you when I love
you? What are your plans?

"Should I have come? I'll do whatever you want me to. Do you want me to go back?"

She felt him calculating. She saw a Puerto Rican child Peter's age standing apparently abandoned on the waxed floor outside the phone booth. The child's dark eyes rolled, his little pointed chin buckled, he began to cry. "Can you kill some time?" Jerry asked at last. "I'll call the hotel and say my wife has decided to come down with me. Take a taxi in, go to the Smithsonian or something for a couple of hours, and I'll meet you along Fourteenth Street, at New York Avenue, around five-thirty." The door of the booth beside Sally's opened, and a brown man in a flowered shirt angrily led the child away.

"Suppose we miss each other?"

"Listen. I'd know you in Hell." It frightened her that when Jerry said "Hell" he meant a real place. "If you feel lost, go into Lafayette Square — you know, the park behind the White House. Stand under the horse's front hoofs."

"Hey? Jerry? Don't hate me."

"Oh, God. Wouldn't it be nice if I could? Just tell me what you're wearing."

"A black linen suit."

"The one you wore at the Collinses' party? Great. There are some terrific old trains on the ground floor. Don't miss Lindbergh's plane. See you five-thirtyish."

"Jerry? I love you."

"Love you."

He thinks it would be nice to hate me, she thought, and went out and caught a taxi. The driver asked her which Smithsonian she wanted, the old or the new, and she said the old. But at the door of the brownstone castle, she turned away. To her the past was a dingy pedestal erected so she could be alive in this moment. She turned away and walked along the Mall in the sunshine. The subsiding afternoon, the pavement dappled with shadows and seeds, the Popsicle hawkers, the tinted-windowed tourist buses stuffed with glaring Americans, the flocks of children, the fairy ring of fluttering red, white, and blue flags planted around the base of the great obelisk, the little Indian women wearing saris and Brahmin dots and nostril pearls and carrying both parasols and briefcases were for Sally all fragments of a fair; in the distance the Capitol dome, cleaner than its gray wings, had the glazed lustre of a piece of marzipan. The sunshine, imprinted everywhere with official images, seemed money to her as she walked past the Natural History Building, up Twelfth Street, through the dank arcades of the Post Office Department, along Pennsylvania Avenue to the fence of the White House. She felt airy, free. The federal buildings, fantastically carved and frosted, floated around her walk; their unreality and grandeur permeated her mood. Through the gaps between guards and greenery, she looked in at the White House; it was made of brilliant fake stuff, like meringue. She thought of the wall-eyed young Irishman who reigned here, wondered if he were good in bed, and didn't see how he could be, he was President. She turned up Fourteenth Street, strolling to her fate.

Sally carried a toothbrush in her pocketbook, and that was her luggage; she had inherited from her father a love of travelling light. Free, cool in her black linen, she felt like an elegant young widow returning from her husband's June funeral; he had been an old man, greedy and unkind. In truth, Richard, heavier than ten years ago, was still handsome enough, though his head seemed to weigh more on his shoulders and his quick gestures had been slowed and blurred by what he called, with a clipped, resentful intonation, his "responsibilities." When their marriage was young, they had lived in Manhattan, and in their poverty had walked miles as amusement. She felt Richard's ghost at her shoulder, remembered the novel rhythm of walking with, of *having*, a man. She had hated schools, prim places of Eastern exile. Richard had rescued her from Barnard and made her a woman. Where had it gone, her gratitude? Was she wicked? She couldn't believe it, feeling still so full of sky from the airplane ride, sidewalk mica glinting under her, her nostrils pricked by the peppery odor of tar. The crosswalk stripes had been tugged and displaced by the melting summer heat. On the wide pavements her stride kept overtaking the saunter of Southerners. Church chimes, the chimes of lemon-yellow St. John's, sounded the hour. It was five. She walked west along I Street. Government clerks in flapping lightweight suits squinted through her, toward the wife and Martini waiting in Maryland. A multitude of women had been released. Like a rolling golden ornament the sun rode the glassy buildings on her left, and its rays warmed her face into self-awareness. She realized she was pouting as she searched the faces for Jerry's face.

How he would grin! Despite his scruples and premonitions he would grin to see her; he always did, and she alone could bring out that smile in him. Though only a few months older than she, and remarkably innocent for a man of thirty, he made her feel like a daughter whose every defiance testified to a cherished vitality. Sally felt carved on her face a deep smile answering his imagined one.

Danger flicked from the other faces. She seemed to see a man she knew, about to turn the corner of the BOAC building, across from Farragut's gesturing statue — a young Wall Street scion Richard had had to the house. His name was Wigglesworth, preceded by two initials she could not remember. His face, expressionless, rounded the corner and vanished. Surely she was mistaken; there are millions of men and only a few types, only a few men who aren't types. But in fear of being recognized she lowered her gaze, so as Jerry had predicted, it was he who found her, though this was not Hell.

"Sally!" he was on the sunless side of I Street, hatless, his arm lifted as if for a taxi. In a business suit, he looked disconcertingly like everyone else, and as he waited at the intersection for the electric permission to walk, her stomach dipped as if she had been snapped awake two hundred miles from home. She asked herself, Who is this man? The sign said WALK. At the head of the pack, he trotted toward her; her heart thrashed. She hung helplessly on the curb while the distance between them diminished and her body, her whole hollowed body, remembered his twitchily posing hands, his hook nose that never took a tan but burned all summer long, his sad eyes of no certain color, his crooked jubilant teeth. He grinned proudly but nervously, stood uncertain a moment, then touched her elbow and kissed her cheek. "God, you looked great," he said, "rolling along with that farm-girl gait, your big feet wobbling away in heels."

Her heart relaxed. No one else saw her this way. She came from Seattle and this made her in Jerry's eyes a farm-girl. It was true, she had always felt uneasy in the East. There was a kind of Eastern woman, Ruth for example, who never bothered with make-up or conspicuously flirted and beside whom Sally felt clumsy. Richard noticed this and tried to analyze her insecurity. Jerry noticed and called her his girl in calico. Not since before her father died, on a trip to San Francisco, had she felt, what she supposed all children are supposed to feel, that it was somehow wonderful of her to be, in every detail, herself.

"How on earth did you get away?"

"I just said good-bye and got in the Saab and drove to the airport."

"You know, it's marvellous to meet a woman who can really *use* the twentieth century." This was another fancy of his, that there was something comic and inappropriate in their living now, in this century. While making love he sometimes called her his squaw. He took pleasure, she felt, in delicately emphasizing, in never letting her forget, the incongruities that hemmed them in. His tenderness itself proclaimed that their love was illicit and doomed.

"Hey," he said, calling to her across the silence. "I don't want you to take risks for me. I want to take them for you."

But you won't, she thought, looping her arm through his arm and bowing her head in concentration on his walking rhythm.

369

"Don't worry about it," she said. "I'm here."

He said nothing.

"You're mad at me. I shouldn't have come."

"I'm never mad with you. But how did you manage?"

"I managed."

His body was mainly big bones and nerves; she felt she was holding on to a corner of a kite that was struggling to get high into the wind.

He tugged her along. He asked, "Is Richard going to be away tonight?"

"No."

He halted.

"Jesus, Sally. What happened? Did you just break out? Can you get back?"

His voice rose sharply, asking this last question. Her answer sounded in her own ears scratchy and faint. "Don't worry about it, darling. I'm here with you, and everything else seems very far away."

"Talk to me. Don't try to shame me. Tell me what happened."

She told him, reliving it all, frightening herself: the beach, her panic, the children, Josie, the airplane, her walk, her plan to call home in an hour saying she was in Manhattan and that the Saab had broken down, refusing to start, and the Fitches had invited her to stay the night, since the art-appreciation course she was taking at the Metropolitan Museum met tomorrow morning.

"Sweetie, it won't swing," he told her. "Let's try to be sane. If I put you on the plane now, you can still get back by eight."

"Is that what you want?"

"No. You know I want you with me always."

And, for all the evidence to the contrary, she felt this as true. She was his wife. This strange fact, unknown to the world but known to them, made whatever looked wrong right, whatever seemed foolish wise. She, Sally, was Jerry's woman, and what had been precious in the first illicit trip was that in those two days she had felt this truth growing, had felt him relax. The first night, he had not slept. Several times she had been twitched awake by his body sliding from the bed, getting a drink of water, adjusting the air conditioner, rummaging in his suitcase.

"What are you looking for?"

"My pajamas."

"Are you cold?"

"A little. Go to sleep."

"I can't. You're unhappy."

"I'm very happy. I love you."

"But I don't keep you warm."

"You *are* a little cooler than Ruth, somehow."

"Really?"

Her voice must have shown that this unexpected comparison had hurt her, for he tried to retract. "No, I don't know. Forget it. Please go to sleep."

"I'll go back tomorrow. I won't stay tomorrow night if I give you insomnia."

"Don't be so touchy. You don't give me insomnia. The Lord gives me insomnia."

"Because you're sleeping with me."

"Listen. I love insomnia. It's a proof that I'm alive."

"Please come back to bed, Jerry." She had held on to his body, trying to drag the kite down from the sky, and herself fell asleep suspended between the earth and the dawn growing in the brick airshaft beyond their blinds. The second night, though still twitchy, he slept better, and on this, the third night, three months later, when spring had relaxed into summer, his breathing slowed and became mechanical while her heart was still lightly racing. She thought herself flattered by his trust. But early in the morning, having slept on a vague sense of loss, she awoke to a sharp deserted feeling. The room was different from the first one. The walls, though it was the

371

same hotel, were yellow instead of white, and instead of the
flowered prints there were two pallid Holbein portraits. It was
brightening enough beyond the blinds for her to see the faces,
so dim they seemed real presences — small-mouthed, fastidious.
How many adulterous and drunken couplings had they been
compelled to witness? A street-sweeper passed swishing on the
avenue below. Their first room had given on an airshaft; this
one overlooked, from five stories up, a square. Somewhere
below them in the maze of the capital a collection truck whined
and a trash can clattered. She thought of her milkman crossing
her porch to set his bottles, clinking, inside an abandoned
house. Jerry lay diagonally, the sheet bunched around his
throat, his feet exposed. She nudged him awake and made him
passionate. In the heart of intimacy, he drowsily called to her
"Ruth." It took him a second to realize his mistake. "Oh, I'm
sorry. I don't seem to know who you are."

"I'm Miss Sally Mathias, a crazy woman."

"Of course you are. And you're very beautiful."

"But a little cool, comparatively."

"You've never forgotten that, have you?"

"No." It fascinated her; at home, stepping into a bath, she
would quickly lay fingers on her skin as if to surprise there the
tepidity he had mentioned, and once, shaking Ruth's hand
good-bye after a dinner party, she had held on curiously, trying
to grasp the subtle caloric advantage this cool-looking woman
had over her. She had noticed how Jerry's skinny body often
seemed feverish. When they first began to make love, she had
felt through his motions the habitual responses his wife must
make; while locked in this strange man's embrace she struggled
jealously against the outline of the other woman. On her part
she bore the impress of Richard's sexual style, so that in the
beginning four contending persons seemed involved on the sofa
or in the sand, and a confused, half-Lesbian excitement would
enclose her. Now these blurs were burned away. On the brightening edge of the long June day that followed the third night

they had ever spent together, Jerry and Sally made love lucidly, like Adam and Eve when the human world was of two halves purely. She watched his face, and involuntarily cried out, pierced by the discovery. "Jerry, your eyes are so sad!"

The crooked teeth of his grin seemed Satanic. "How can they be sad when I'm so happy?"

"They're *so* sad, Jerry."

"You shouldn't watch people's eyes when they make love."

"I always do."

"Then I'll close mine."

* * *

Jerry closed his eyes and it hurt her. She loved to watch love, to witness the nibbling, the mixing of ivory and fur, the solemn softening of the eyes. Was she corrupt? In Paris on her honeymoon with Richard, her shock at the mirrors in their room had subsided to a level interest. This was what people did; this was what they were. She was proud, a little, of having taught Jerry how simple it was. Somehow Ruth had not taught him that. But the sadness of his eyes had penetrated her and for the rest of the day that unfolded Sally was laid open to a vivid and frightening sense of her existence in other people's eyes. The puffy-lidded news vendor in the perfumed lobby saw her as a spoiled young matron. The waitress who served them breakfast at the counter cheerfully took her for a fucked secretary. When Sally relinquished Jerry to a taxi and became alone, she felt herself reflected in every glance and glass entryway. To the Japanese souvenir-store attendants she was big. To the Negro doorman she was white. To everybody she was nobody.

Who was she? What was this burden she carried within her, this ache that like an unborn child was so unquestionably worth bearing? Was she unique? That young black girl like a chocolate swan, that dowager in rouge and wool — was each of these also prey to a clawing love that could literally lift her into the sky? Sally could not believe so; yet she did not like to believe either that she was totally unique, eccentric, mad. She remembered her mother. When her father had died on that last trip, a quiet calm man finally too quiet in a room of the St. Francis (there were no pills, no bottle, all the authorities had agreed), they had moved to Chicago, to be near her mother's people, and her mother though a Catholic had taken not to religion or drink but to gambling. The strangest happiest islands of that time were those days when together they would go by train and bus to Arlington Park, or to the Hawthorne track in Cicero, or to see the trotters at Maywood; at these places everything was thin and nervous and obliquely illuminated by chance — the legs of the horses white with tape, the whips of the jockeys, the slats of the fences, the rods of the turnstiles polished by pushing hands, the sideways glances of the men who might be gangsters, the fluttering scraps of losing tickets torn in half, the oblique rays of the sun like the spokes of a slowly turning wheel. Her mother's fattening hands fiddled again and again at her pocketbook. Horses or men, is the instinct any different? Oh God, when he came he bucked as if he were dying, and now he was gone, lost among these marble buildings. One minute all over her, filling her, whimpering; the next minute meeting an appointment with the Undersecretary of Animation. What sense did it make? Who had made these arrangements? He had gotten her so confused, her husbandly lover, she didn't even know if she believed in God or not. Once she had had a clear opinion, yes or no, she had forgotten which.

As the sun passed noon, her shadow pinched in; her hot feet hurt. Idly Sally wandered north from the hotel, through stagnant blocks of airline offices, past verdant circles where pistachio-colored military men on horses were waving to catch her attention. Jerry was to meet her at the National Gallery at one. The time until then moved forward or backward, depending on the clock she glimpsed; in the haste of her departure she had forgotten her watch. There was a gap in the tan of her arm where the watchband had been.

The iron braziers and stone vases and Asiatic paper knives in the windows of antique shops glinted back at her stupidly as she sought to find herself in them. Once she had cared about these things; once, being in a city alone had fulfilled her and coveting objects and fabrics had been a way of possessing them. Now she sought herself in bronze and silk and porcelain and was not there. When she walked with Jerry, there was something there, but it was no longer her, it was them: her explaining to him, him to her, exchanging their lives, absorbing fractions of the immense lesson that had accumulated in the years before they had loved. She saw each thing only as something to tell him about, and without him there was nothing to tell; he had robbed her of the world. Abruptly, she became angry with him. How dare he tell her not to come and then make love to her when she did come! And then with such sad eyes beg her to feel guilty! How dare he take her free when she could sell herself for hundreds to any honest man on this avenue — to that one. A foreign official with snowy cuffs and an extravagantly controlled haircut preened, gray-horned on the burning sidewalk beside the Department of Justice. He was eyeing her. She was beautiful. This knowledge had been drawing near to her all morning and now it was hers. She was beautiful. Where she walked, people glanced. She was tall and blond and big inside with love given and taken, and when, at last, she mounted the steps of the museum, the gigantic scale of the rotunda did not seem inhuman but right: our inner spaces warrant palaces. She studied Charles V, sculpted by Leone Leoni, and existed as a queen in his hyperthyroid gaze.

"Stop," Jerry said, taking her elbow from behind. "Stop looking so beautiful and proud. You'll kill me. I'll drop dead at your feet, and how will you get the body back to Ruth?"

Ruth, Ruth: she was never out of his mind. "I was feeling very indignant about you."

"I know. It showed."

"You think you know everything about me, don't you? You think you own me."

"Not at all. You're very much your own woman."

"No, Jerry. I'm your woman. I'm sorry. I'm a burden to you."

"Don't be sorry," he said. "It's a burden I need." His eyes were watching her face for a warning, a change. "Shall we look," he asked timidly, "or eat?"

"Let's look. My stomach is funny."

And in the galleries, she was conscious of existing among paintings, of shining in portraits' eyes, of glancing, bending closer, backing off, of posing in a rapt and colorful theatre. Jerry was manic in museums; all the old art school came out in him. His enthusiasm tugged her from room to room. His hands demonstrated, slid hungrily through the motions of tranquil masterpieces. People obedient to lecturing boxes plugged into their ears glared. She must seem his dumb student. He had found what he wanted — the wall bearing three Vermeers. "Oh, God," he moaned, "the drawing; people never realize how much *drawing* there is in a Vermeer. The wetness of this woman's lips. These marvellous hats. And this one, the light on her hands and the gold and the pearls. That *touch*, you know; it's a double touch — the exact color, in the exact place." He looked at her and smiled. "Now you and me," he said, "are the exact color, but we seem to be in the wrong place."

"Let's not talk about us," Sally said. "I'm too tired to be depressed. My feet hurt. I must have walked miles this morning. Couldn't we sit down and eat?"

The cafeteria walls were hung with beady-eyed Audubon prints. Sally's stomach sank under the weight of unwelcome food. She had no appetite, which was unlike her; perhaps it was sleeplessness, perhaps the pinch of dwindling time. Whereas Jerry ate briskly, to keep from talking, or in relish that another adulterous escapade was all but safely completed. They were silent together. The immense lesson she thought they had for each other felt to be fully learned.

She sighed. "I don't know. I guess we're just terribly selfish and greedy."

Though she had said it to please him, he disagreed. "Do you think? After all, Richard and Ruth weren't giving us much. Why should we die just to keep their lives smooth? Quench not the spirit, didn't St. Paul say?"

"Maybe it's just the newness that makes it seem so wonderful. We'd get tired. I'm tired now."

"Of me?"

"No. Of it."

"I know, I know. Don't be frightened. We'll get you back safely."

"I'm not worried about that. Richard doesn't really care."

"He must."

"No."

"I don't think Ruth really cares either, if she just knew it."

And though she knew Jerry said this just to match her, she heard herself pressing him with, "Do you want to not go back? Shall we just run off?"

"You'd lose your children."

"I'm willing."

"You say that now, but a week with me and you'd miss them and hate me because they weren't there."

"You're so wise, Jerry."

"But it doesn't help, does it? My poor lady. You need a good man for a husband and a bad man for a lover, and you have just the opposite."

"Richard's not such a bad man."

"O.K. Pardon me. He's a prince."

"I love it when you get mad at me."

"I know you do. But I don't. I won't. I love you. If you want to fight, go home."

She looked around at the tables — the art students, the professors with taped spectacles, the plump women escaping the heat, the ever-so-dead-looking birds on the walls. "That's where I'm going," she said.

"Yes. It's time. We'll have to stop somewhere and buy my damned kids something."

"You *spoil* them, Jerry. You'll have hardly been gone a day."

"They expect it." He stood up and they left, by the ground level exit. His anxious long stride hurried her past the Popsicle vendors and the tourist buses, and she had no breath for words. Pitying, he took her hand, but the contact was damp and made them self-conscious; they were too old to hold hands. At the door of the drugstore displaying the usual cheap souvenirs — piggy-bank monuments, flags, sickly Kennediana — she panicked and refused to go in.

"Why not?" he asked. "Help me choose."

"No. I can't."

"Sally."

"Do it yourself. They're your children — yours and Ruth's."

His face went pale; he had never seen her like this.

She tried to make it better. "I'll walk to the hotel and pack your suitcase. Don't worry. Please don't make me buy the toys with you."

"Listen. I love —" He tried to take her arm.

"Don't embarrass me, Jerry. People are trying to get by."

In walking down Fourteenth Street alone, the pavement pricking her eyes with mica, she began to cry, and realized it didn't matter, for no one was looking at her, no one at all in these multitudes.

CONTRIBUTORS

Ann Beattie

A native of Washington, D.C., Ann Beattie was educated at American University and the University of Connecticut. She has taught at the University of Virginia and at Harvard. Her first novel, *Chilly Scenes of Winter* was made into a motion picture, first entitled *Head Over Heels* and later re-released wih the novel's title. She has published two other novels—*Falling in Place* and *Love Always*—and four collections of short stories, *Distortions, Secrets and Surprises, The Burning House,* and *Where You'll Find Me.* She has received a fellowship from the Guggenheim Foundation and in 1980 was presented an award in literature from the American Academy and Institute of Arts and Letters.

Raymond Carver

Born in Clatskanie, Oregon, Raymond Carver is the author of three collections of short stories. The first collection, *Will You Please Be Quiet, Please?*, was nominated for the National Book Award. That book was followed by *What We Talk About When We Talk About Love* and *Cathedral,* which was nominated for the National Book Critics Circle Award. He has also published *Fires: Essays, Poems, Stories* and three collections of poetry. Carver was a Guggenheim Fellow in 1979, and he has twice been awarded grants from the National Endowment for the Arts. In 1983 he received the Mildred and Harold Strauss Living Award, and in 1986 he was awarded the Levinson Prize for poetry.

Robb Forman Dew

Robb Forman Dew was born in Mount Vernon, Ohio, and grew up in Baton Rouge, Louisiana. She is a member of a distinguished literary family: her grandfather was the poet and critic John Crowe Ransom; her godfather is Robert Penn Warren. *Dale Loves Sophie to Death*, her first novel, was published in 1981 and won the American Book Award. She is also the recipient of a Guggenheim Fellowship. Her second novel, *The Time of Her Life*, was published in 1984. First chapters from both novels appeared in somewhat different form in the *New Yorker*, and Dew's short stories have appeared in the *Southern Review* and *Virginia Quarterly*.

Michael Dorris
Author of two nonfiction books on American Indians, Michael Dorris is of Modoc, Irish, and French descent and was awarded the 1985 Indian Achievement Award. He established the Native American Studies department at Dartmouth College, where he teaches, and he is a graduate of Georgetown and Yale Universities. He has received grants from the Guggenheim, Rockefeller, Woodrow Wilson, and Danforth foundations. His first novel, *A Yellow Raft in Blue Water*, was published in 1987.

Clyde Edgerton
A native North Carolinian, Clyde Edgerton attended the University of North Carolina, where he received undergraduate and graduate degrees in English Education. His first novel, *Raney*, a first-person account by young Raney Bell, a newlywed living in a small town in the South, was published in 1985. *Walking Across Egypt*, his second novel, was published in 1987.

Emily Ellison
Born in Dalton, Georgia, and reared in Fort Lauderdale, Florida, Emily Ellison has worked as a journalist, editor, and fiction writer. She is the author of two novels, *Alabaster Chambers* and *First Light*, and she has published articles and essays on numerous contemporary American writers. In 1987 she received the Mayor's Fellowship in the Arts for literature in Atlanta.

Louise Erdrich
Of German and Chippewa descent, Louise Erdrich is a member of the Turtle Mountain Band of Chippewa. In 1976 she graduated from

Dartmouth College, where she received several writing awards, including the American Academy of Poets Prize; she received her M.A. in Creative Writing from Johns Hopkins University in 1979. A collection of her poetry, *Jacklight,* was published in 1984 and named one of the best books of poetry of that year by the *San Francisco Chronicle. Love Medicine,* Erdrich's first novel, was also published in 1984 and won the National Book Critics Circle Award, the *Los Angeles Times* Award for best novel of 1985, and the Sue Kaufman Prize for best first novel. A second novel, *The Beet Queen,* was published in 1986. She is the recipient of a National Endowment for the Arts Fellowship, two PEN newspaper awards, and a Guggenheim Fellowship.

Perry Glasser

For ten years Perry Glasser taught English in public schools in Brooklyn, New York, before attending the University of Arizona's graduate creative writing program. He received his M.F.A. in Fiction Writing there in 1982. His first collection of short fiction, *Suspicious Origins,* was a winner of the Minnesota Voices Project Competition in 1983. His fiction has been awarded PEN Syndicated Fiction Prizes twice and has appeared in such journals as *TriQuarterly, Ms., North American Review,* and *The Twilight Zone Magazine. Singing on the Titanic,* the collection in which the novella *Mexico* appears, was published in 1987. Glasser teaches writing at Bradford College in Massachusetts.

Gail Godwin

Gail Godwin was born in Alabama and spent her childhood in the South. She graduated from the University of North Carolina and received the M.A. and Ph.D. from the University of Iowa, where she taught English and creative writing. The first of her six novels, *The Perfectionists,* was published in 1970. Since that time she has written *The Glass People, The Odd Woman, Violet Clay, A Mother and Two Daughters,* and *The Finishing School,* along with two collections of stories, *Dream Children* and *Mr. Bedford and the Muses.* Her awards include grants from the National Endowment for the Arts, a Guggenheim fellowship, and an O. Henry Award.

Judith Guest

Born in Detroit, Judith Guest graduated from the University of Michigan. She has taught grade school, high school, and creative-writing seminars for adults. In 1976 her first novel, *Ordinary People,* received both critical acclaim and popular success and was published in thirteen foreign languages; it was also made into a motion picture that won the Oscar for Best Picture in 1980. Her second novel, *Second Heaven,* was published in 1982.

Jane Hill

Jane Hill was born in Seneca, South Carolina, and grew up in Clemson, South Carolina. She received the B.A. and the M.A. in English from Clemson University and the Ph.D. from the University of Illinois in 1985. She has taught high-school and college English in South Carolina, Illinois, and Georgia. The anthology *An American Christmas/A Sampler of Contemporary Stories and Poems,* which she edited, was published in 1986. She has published numerous articles on contemporary authors, including Ann Beattie, John Irving, Gail Godwin, and Gloria Naylor.

Josephine Humphreys

A native of Charleston, South Carolina, Josephine Humphreys in 1967 was graduated from Duke University, where she studied writing with Reynolds Price and William Blackburn. She earned a master's degree from Yale University in 1968 and taught English at the college level for several years before turning to writing full time. Her first novel, *Dreams of Sleep,* was published in 1984 and received the Hemingway Award for best American first novel of that year. She was awarded a Guggenheim Fellowship in 1986, and her second novel, *Rich in Love,* was published in 1987.

John Irving

John Irving was born in Exeter, New Hampshire, a setting not unlike the fictional one where T. S. Garp grows up in *The World According to Garp,* his fourth novel. He is the author of five other novels: *Setting Free the Bears, The 158-Pound Marriage, The Water-Method Man, The Hotel New Hampshire,* and *The Cider House Rules.* He has received awards from the National Endowment for the Arts, the Rockefeller Foundation, and the Guggenheim Foundation, and his fiction has been translated into fifteen foreign languages. Both *The World According to Garp* and *The Hotel New Hampshire* have been made into motion pictures.

David Leavitt
Reared in Palo Alto, California, David Leavitt graduated from Yale in 1983. His stories have appeared in *The New Yorker, Harper's, Prism,* and *The O. Henry Awards: Prize Stories of 1984. Family Dancing,* his first collection of short fiction, was published in 1984.

Alison Lurie
Born in Chicago, Alison Lurie received her A.B. from Radcliffe College. *Love and Friendship,* her first novel, was published in 1962. She has since published a nonfiction book, *The Language of Clothes,* and six other novels: *The Nowhere City, Imaginary Friends, Real People, The War Between the Tates, Only Children,* and *Foreign Affairs,* which won the Pulitzer Prize. She is Professor of English at Cornell University in Ithaca, New York. Her work is known for its acerbic wit and, as novelist Mary Gordon has said, its "insight and the kind of bracing yet merciful vision all too rare in American fiction."

Gloria Naylor
Born and reared in New York City, Gloria Naylor received her B.A. in English from Brooklyn College and her M.A. in Afro-American Studies from Yale University. Her first novel, *The Women of Brewster Place,* won the American Book Award for First Fiction in 1983, and was produced in 1985 as a segment of public television's "American Playhouse" series. *Linden Hills,* her second novel, was published in 1985.

Reynolds Price
A native of North Carolina, Reynolds Price graduated from Duke University in 1955 and studied for three years at Merton College, Oxford, as a Rhodes Scholar. In 1958 he returned to Duke, where presently he is James B. Duke Professor of English. His first novel, *A Long and Happy Life,* was published in 1962 and received the William

Faulkner Award for the most notable first novel of that year. The following year he published a collection of stories, *The Names and Faces of Heroes*. Price has written essays, stories, translations, poems, plays, and a total of six novels, including *A Generous Man*, *The Surface of the Earth*, *The Source of Light*, and *Kate Vaiden*, which won the National Book Critics Circle Award for the best work of fiction of 1986.

Anne Tyler

Born in Minneapolis, Minnesota, Anne Tyler grew up in Raleigh, North Carolina, studied at Duke University and did graduate work at Columbia University. Her first novel, *If Morning Ever Comes*, was published in 1964 when she was twenty-two years old. Over the past two decades she has proved to be one of America's most prolific writers and has to date published ten novels, including *Celestial Navigation*, *Morgan's Passing*, *Dinner at the Homesick Restaurant*, and, most recently, *The Accidental Tourist*. Her short stories have appeared in such magazines as *The New Yorker*, the *Saturday Evening Post*, the *Southern Review*, and *Quest*, and she has received numerous awards and honors.

John Updike

Since 1958 and the appearance of John Updike's collection of light verse, *The Carpentered Hen*, he has published at least one book a year. That impressive body of work includes poems; short stories; a play; children's books; essays, criticism, and other nonfiction prose; and nearly a dozen novels. Born in Shillington, Pennsylvania, Updike graduated from Harvard in 1954 and spent a year as a Knox Fellow at the Ruskin School of Drawing and Fine Art in Oxford, England. From 1955 to 1957 he was a staff member of *The New Yorker*, where he continues to be a frequent contributor of stories, poems, and book reviews. He has been honored with many literary prizes and awards, including the American Book Award, the National Book Critics Circle Award, and the Pulitzer Prize. His most recent work, a collection of stories titled *Trust Me*, was published in 1987.